The Political Economy of Competitiveness

The Political Economy of Competitiveness presents the latest thinking on a range of political and economic issues, challenging conventional wisdom on the state of the British Economy. The book discusses the lessons of economic theory and policy within a broad framework, recognising that history matters, as do political institutions. The authors incorporate lessons from other social sciences while bringing economic analysis to bear on real world problems.

Policy issues include:

- The sustainability of fixed-rate exchange rate systems
- Public policy regarding growth and employment/unemployment
- Corporate performance and what makes firms competitive

The Political Economy of Competitiveness is a clearly written, accessible, interdisciplinary text which avoids jargon. It will prove to be indispensable to students of economics, politics and business and management, with great appeal to all those with an interest in economic policy issues.

Michael Kitson is a Fellow and Lecturer at St Catharine's College, Cambridge and Newton Trust Lecturer in the Faculty of Economics and Politics, University of Cambridge. **Jonathan Michie** is Sainsbury Professor of Management at Birkbeck College, University of London.

Contemporary political economy series
Edited by Jonathan Michie
Birkbeck College, University of London, UK

This series presents a fresh, broad perspective on the key issues in the modern world economy, drawing in perspectives from management and business, politics and sociology, economic history and law.

Written in a lively and accessible style, it will present focused and comprehensive introductions to key topics, demonstrating the relevance of political economy to the major debates in economics and to an understanding of the contemporary world.

Reconstructing Political Economy
The great divide in economic thought
William K. Tabb

The Political Economy of Competitiveness
Essays on employment, public policy and corporate performance
Michael Kitson and Jonathan Michie

Global Economy, Global Justice
Theoretical and policy alternatives to neoliberalism
George De Martino

Global Instability
The political economy of world economic governance
Edited by Jonathan Michie and John Grieve Smith

The Political Economy of Competitiveness

Essays on employment, public policy and corporate performance

Michael Kitson and Jonathan Michie

London and New York

First published 2000
by Routledge
11 New Fetter Lane, London EC4P 4EE

Simultaneously published in the USA and Canada
by Routledge
29 West 35th Street, New York, NY 10001

Routledge is an imprint of the Taylor & Francis Group

Typeset in Garamond by
RefineCatch Ltd, Bungay, Suffolk
Printed and bound in Great Britain by
Biddles Ltd, Guildford and King's Lynn

British Library Cataloguing in Publication Data
A catalogue record for this book is available from the British Library

Library of Congress Cataloging in Publication Data
Kitson, Michael and Jonathan Michie
The political economy of competitiveness: essays on
employment, public policy and corporate performance / Michael
Kitson and Jonathan Michie
p. cm. — (Contemporary political economy series)
Includes bibliographical references and indexes
1. Great Britain—Economic conditions. 2. Great Britain—
Social conditions. 3. Competition—Government policy—Great
Britain. 4. Economics. 5. Competition. I. Kitson, Michael.
II. Title. III. Series.
HC256.M5 1999
338.6′048′0941—dc21   99–057353

ISBN 0–415–20495–X (hbk)
ISBN 0–415–20496–8 (pbk)

This book is dedicated to our wives,
Jane Denney and Carolyn Downs

'Anyone seeking a clear and stimulating account of a range of major economic issues will find this book an invaluable help.'

Malcolm Sawyer, Professor of Economics, *University of Leeds*

'If you think economics is all about complex algebra, this book is not for you. If, on the other hand, you are looking for a clear explanation of what is going wrong in the economy and how to put it right, I could hardly recommend it more highly.'

Larry Elliott, Economics Editor, *Guardian*

'This book brings theory and evidence to bear on key policy issues. An important and accessible contribution, it will be useful to students and all those interested in economic policy.'

Mario Pianta, Professor of Economic Policy, *University of Urbino,* Italy

'If you are interested in contemporary economic policy issues, this is a book you should read – particularly if you are searching for alternatives to current orthodoxies.'

Roger Berry MP, Chair, *Full Employment Forum*

'This collection covers important issues and represents a serious and yet accessible economic analysis of real world problems.'

Paul Hirst, Professor of Politics and Sociology, *University of London*

'At last, the political economy of trade is a front-and-center worldwide concern, not just a matter for international bureaucrats, corporate lawyers, and academics. Kitson and Michie are outstanding progressive thinkers in this area. This new book is an important and timely contribution.'

Robert Pollin, Professor of Economics and Co-Director,
Political Economy Research Institute, *University of Massachusetts-Amherst*

Contents

Figures

Tables

Foreword

Once a 'workshop of the world' the UK economy today hardly accounts for 5 per cent of the OECD's manufacturing production. It has suffered massive deindustrialisation in the last two decades in the sense that the number of people working in industry has literally been halved. Between 1970 and 1993, the UK's manufacturing labour force fell from 7.5 million workers to 4.3 million, a drop of 45 per cent. Other industrial countries also suffered declines in their manufacturing labour force during this period but none of anything like the same magnitude. The average loss of manufacturing employment for the G7 countries in the period was 15 per cent. There is however an apparent bright side to this story which cannot be ignored. Notwithstanding this poor comparative record of UK manufacturing in terms of production and employment during the last quarter century, its productivity growth relative to other European countries has greatly improved.

Kitson and Michie provide a stimulating and incisive analysis of these paradoxes of the UK economy. They adopt a political economy perspective which takes full account of the historical and institutional specificities of the UK situation. Combining economic analysis with this historical and institutional approach, this book examines important developments in a clear and realistic fashion. The authors' analysis of the performance of and prospects for the UK economy confirms the key role played in industrialised economies by the manufacturing sector, however much the differential productivity growth between the manufacturing and service sectors may lead to a declining share for industrial employment. The phenomenon of deindustrialisation is a complex one, which I raised myself back in the 1970s, with many of the issues having already been realised by Lord Kaldor in the 1960s. Kitson and Michie's discussion of globalisation is also significant, demonstrating as it does the importance of creating new institutional arrangements at the global as well as regional and national levels, if we are to introduce a degree of stability and equity into international financial and economic relations.

Routledge are to be congratulated on launching this contemporary political economy series analysing the key issues in the modern world economy.

Kitson and Michie's book is in the best traditions of political economy and will be an important contribution to the series. However, the authors' work is distinguished not only by its political economy perspective but also by the fact that its conceptual framework is rooted in the work of Cambridge economists – John Maynard Keynes, Pierro Sraffa, Joan Robinson, Richard Kahn and above all Lord Kaldor. It also draws on the work of more mainstream Cambridge economists such as Alfred Marshall and Austin Robinson. The difference between the Cambridge and the mainstream approaches is epitomised in Joan Robinson's assessment of Alfred Marshall as the greatest of all neo-classical economists and that of Paul Samuelson who regarded Marshall as the worst of all neo-classical greats. Based on an impressive understanding of the actual workings of firms and industries, Marshall's writings on industrial districts continue to inform applied economic research into such clustering effects – an issue Kitson and Michie discuss in their analysis of the complex interaction of competition and cooperation between firms.

This collection will be of interest to anyone wanting to understand current economic issues. Real world economies are extremely complex and continually changing. To understand such developments requires a proper appreciation of the role of history and of institutions. Abstract models, general equilibrium analysis, and equilibrium economics provide only limited insights into these issues. Less formal analysis, when it is skilfully integrated with historical and institutional approaches, as in this book, is often a great deal more illuminating.

Ajit Singh
Queens' College, Cambridge

Preface

There is a widespread interest in economic theory and policy. Yet many are put off from pursuing the subject because it is so often presented in a needlessly narrow and inaccessible style. The two co-authors encounter this demand for economic issues to be discussed in a broad, interdisciplinary and policy relevant way from students and colleagues alike through the courses in which we are involved – one in a Faculty of Economics and Politics, the other in a School of Management and Organisational Psychology. We also encounter it more widely, from all interested in economics and economic policy. One particular request that this demand often takes is for a book on economics that someone with an interest in the topic could read who would not want to have to plough through a textbook. The current book attempts to meet this demand by focusing on important policy issues.

We have also approached the topics in an explicitly interdisciplinary fashion. There has been a growing – and we would say welcome – recognition in both academic and policy circles of the value of interdisciplinary work. Yet much of mainstream economics has moved in the opposite direction, attempting to extend very narrow economic methods to other areas of enquiry, rather than attempting to incorporate lessons from other social sciences when bringing economic analysis to bear on real world problems. This book deliberately sets out to discuss the lessons of economic theory and policy within a broad political economy approach, recognising that history matters, as do political institutions.

The book brings together and updates some of our previous published work, along with related material on which we are currently working. The book aims to be of use to economics students, particularly for political economy papers, or conversely for management students for their economics papers. It should also appeal to all those with an interest in economic policy issues.

Michael Kitson
Jonathan Michie
February 2000

Acknowledgements

We are grateful to a large number of colleagues and friends for their comments on and suggestions for the contents of this book, as well as for more general support and collaboration over the past few years. From Cambridge we are particularly indebted to our colleague Jane Humphries, with whom we both worked, at different times, at Newnham College. We would also like to acknowledge our productive collaboration with various colleagues on the Editorial Board of the *Cambridge Journal of Economics*. We enjoyed particular support in various projects from Geoff Harcourt and Frank Wilkinson.

On the individual chapters, we would like to thank Daniele Archibugi and Roger Berry for collaborative work and helpful comments on Chapter 2, 'Globalisation, unemployment and Government policy'. We are grateful to the late John Wells for providing us with unpublished data for use in Chapter 3, 'Trade theory and policy', on which we are also grateful for comments from Jonathan Perraton. We are similarly grateful to John Wells and Jonathan Perraton for data provision and comments on an earlier version of Chapter 4, 'Trade and growth: a historical perspective', on which helpful comments were also received from John Grieve Smith and Solomos Solomou. Chapter 5, 'Recession and economic revival in Britain: the role of policy in the 1930s and 1980s', benefited from comments from Solomos and also from Frank Wilkinson. On Chapter 6, 'A tale of two recessions: 1929 and the Gold Standard, 1992 and the ERM', we are grateful for comments from Andrew Glyn, Wynne Godley, Brian Gould, Bill Keegan, Brian Reddaway and Solomos Solomou. Chapter 7 on 'Britain's industrial performance since 1960: underinvestment and relative decline' benefited from comments from Nick Crafts, Rick Delbridge, Huw Dixon, Walter Eltis, Laurence Harris, Jane Humphries, and the late Jim Lowe. Chapter 8, on 'From welfare to work?' was written jointly with Holly Sutherland, and we are grateful to her for allowing this to be included in the current volume. This draws on joint work with Roger Berry, to whom we are also grateful. Chapter 9 on 'Markets, competition and innovation' came from work we did using data from the ESRC Centre for Business Research, to which we are both attached, and we are therefore grateful to the Centre, and in particular to Alan Hughes and

Frank Wilkinson; we are also grateful for comments from Keith Cowling and Lawrence Harris.

A number of the chapters originated from the annual conferences organised at Robinson College by John Grieve Smith and Jonathan Michie, and we are therefore particularly grateful to John Grieve Smith, as well as to Robinson College.

We are grateful to Alison Kirk, Rob Langham, Andreja Zivkovic, Emma Davis, Lesley Felce and Goober Fox of Routledge for encouraging this project and for their speedy and efficient handling of the manuscript, and likewise to the copy-editor, Michael Doughty.

Finally, our greatest debt and gratitude is to our wives, Jane and Carolyn, to whom this book is dedicated, and our children Beth and Harry, and Alex and Duncan.

Copyright acknowledgements

We are grateful to the publishers for permission to reproduce, or use material from, the following published works:

Berry, R., Kitson, M. and Michie, J. (1995), *Towards Full Employment: The First Million Jobs*, Full Employment Forum.

Berry, R., Kitson, M. and Michie, J. (1996), 'Creating jobs fast', *New Economy*, 11: 133–137.

Kitson, M . (1999), 'Recession and economic revival: the role of policy in the 1930s and 1980s', *Contemporary European History*, 8 (1): 1–27.

Kitson, M. and Michie, J. (1993), *Coordinated Deflation – The Tale of Two Recessions*, Full Employment Forum.

Kitson, M. and Michie, J. (1994), 'Depression and recovery: lessons from the interwar period', in J. Michie and J. Grieve Smith (eds), *Unemployment in Europe*, London: Academic Press.

Kitson, M. and Michie, J. (1994), 'Fixed exchange rates and deflation: the Gold Standard and the ERM', *Economics and Business Education*, II (5), reprinted in N. Healey (ed.), *The Economics of the New Europe*, London: Routledge.

Kitson, M. and Michie, J. (1995), 'Trade and growth: a historical perspective', in J. Michie, and J. Grieve Smith (eds), *Managing the Global Economy*, Oxford: Oxford University Press.

Kitson, M. and Michie, J. (1995), 'Conflict, cooperation and change: the political economy of trade and trade policy', *Review of International Political Economy*, 2 (4): 632–657.

Kitson, M. and Michie, J. (1996), 'Britain's industrial performance since 1960: underinvestment and relative decline', *Economic Journal*, 106 (434): 196–212.

Kitson, M. and Michie, J. (1996), 'Manufacturing capacity, investment, and employment', in J. Michie and J. Grieve Smith (eds), *Creating Industrial Capacity: Towards Full Employment*, Oxford: Oxford University Press.

Kitson, M. and Michie, J. (1997), 'Does manufacturing matter?', *International Journal of the Economics of Business*, 4 (1): 71–95.

Kitson, M. and Michie, J. (1997), 'Are we all Thatcherites?', *Prospect*, April: 16–18.

Kitson, M. and Michie, J. (1998), 'Markets, competition and innovation', in J. Michie and J. Grieve Smith (eds), *Globalisation, Growth and Governance: Towards an Innovative Economy*, Oxford: Oxford University Press.

Kitson, M. and Michie, J. (1998), *Globalisation, Unemployment and Government Policy*, Full Employment Forum.

Kitson, M., Michie, J. and Sutherland, H. (1996), '"A Price Well Worth Paying"? The benefits of a full-employment strategy', in J. Michie and J. Grieve Smith (eds), *Employment and Economic Performance: Jobs, Inflation, and Growth*, Oxford: Oxford University Press.

Kitson, M., Michie, J. and Sutherland, H. (1997), 'The fiscal and distributional implications of job generation', *Cambridge Journal of Economics*, 21 (1): 103–120.

1 Introduction and overview

On my first day as a graduate student in economics at the Massachusetts Institute of Technology, the professor introduced the discipline by intoning, 'All of economics is a subset of the theory of separating hyperplanes.' (You don't want to know what that mathematical term means.) I started to giggle. But then I looked around. Everyone else was scribbling notes. So I wiped the smirk off my face and muttered, only to myself, that I had thought economics was about the plight of people living in sub-Saharan Africa, of the impact of technological change on living standards. Apparently I thought wrong – and wondered whether I had made a terrible career choice.

(Michael M. Weinstein, former *New York Times* economic columnist, 2000)

Economics is a strange subject. Most people think it's important. It certainly is – it concerns how well off we are, or aren't; how goods and services – public and private – are produced and paid for; how these are distributed; and so on. Yet most people are put off it as a subject, and economists are generally regarded with, at best, some scepticism – and more usually with contempt.

This book aims to make economics intelligible and interesting. The following pages explain:

why understanding economics is important;
why people are so often put off the subject – and why they shouldn't be;
how this book approaches the basic principles of economics.

This introductory chapter is written for undergraduate students – any other readers should skip straight to Chapter 2. We hope that the students who do read this chapter will be encouraged to go on and read the whole book, or to at least dip into those chapters that deal with whichever policy issues are of most interest.

Why understanding economics is important

The shooting of Archduke Ferdinand caused the First World War. That, at least, was more or less the version taught over the years to British schoolchildren. In reality, the rival economic interests of Germany and those it had lost out to in the 'scramble for Africa' – the British and French empires – also had a part to play. Germany's relatively late industrialisation had left it at a competitive disadvantage regarding overseas markets, sources of raw materials, and profitable outlets for overseas investment and expansion. Such economic factors were undoubtedly important. (We deal with the issues of comparative and competitive advantage in Chapter 3, and the processes of cumulative causation whereby a country's economy can be caught in a virtuous circle of success breeding success, or else a vicious cycle of relative decline in Chapters 4 and 6.)

The peace treaty ending the First World War provides a second example of the importance of understanding economics. To understand the role that this treaty played in subsequent world history, it is not enough to study politics or international relations. The key was the *economics* of the treaty. It was this – along with other factors of course – that led to the German hyperinflation and the subsequent mass unemployment which in turn laid the ground for Adolf Hitler's rise to power. John Maynard Keynes is best known today for his *General Theory*, published in 1936, advocating government economic policies to tackle unemployment. But already in 1919 he had published *The Economic Consequences of the Peace*, warning of its economic folly. He pointed out that to imagine that reparations were payable was only possible if one was unaware of Germany's currency depreciation, balance-of-payments position, and so on. Such factors are clearly worth understanding, and we return to them later in the book – inflation (Chapter 5), unemployment (Chapter 8), currency depreciation (Chapter 6) and the balance of payments (Chapter 7).

There are countless other examples that could be given, illustrating the importance of understanding how the economy works and what role economic factors play in events, even if they are not always immediately apparent. Perhaps we can conclude by quoting someone else who was trying to stress to his colleagues the importance of economic issues – Bill Clinton, who allegedly had the sign 'It's the economy, stupid' hanging in his Presidential election campaign headquarters.

Why people are so often put off the subject – and why they shouldn't be

The point here is not to imply that only economists can understand the world. Indeed, one of the examples we thought of giving above, of how a study of economics might be helpful, was that of the 'sun-spot' theory of recession. This used to be given as the explanation for recessions – that they were caused by explosions of gas on the surface of the sun, known as sunspots. (The argument was that these affected the weather, which in turn affected agricultural crop yields, which in turn affected other parts of the economy.) Now one might think it obvious that to try to explain why an economy was in recession, it would be more appropriate to investigate factors such as consumer confidence, investment levels, interest and exchange rate movements, and so forth. We certainly think like this. However, there are, still, some few economists who persist in the study of sunspots as an explanation for economic fluctuations. Economics is a very broad church, and even more so under the name 'Political Economy'.

Why do economists always disagree?

One reason that there is scepticism about economists is that they frequently seem to disagree. One will say that interest rates should go up, another that they should come down, a third that it doesn't matter. One will say that Britain's relative economic decline this century was caused by the financial interests of the City of London engendering 'short termism', another that it was too-powerful trade unions, a third that it was the result of industry being managed by public school boys.[1] Winston Churchill once said that if you put two economists in the same room you would get two opinions, unless one of them was John Maynard Keynes in which case you would get three.

There is a serious point here, which it is important for students of economics to understand early on. The economy is not a machine that can be analysed with the certainties of engineering or physics. (This is not to suggest that there are no uncertainties in either of these latter two subjects. But the degree of uncertainty in economics is orders of magnitude greater.) It is not the case that there are levers to be pulled which will provide the same – calculable – effect each time. The British economist Paul Ormerod put this rather well when he described the economy as more like an animal. Prod it once and it might jump one way; prod it again and it could well jump some other way.

The point, therefore, is that there are bound to be disagreements on economic issues, even by those who understand the subject well. In part these disagreements will reflect political and social views (for example, how highly – if at all – the protagonist values equality) but in part they will reflect the nature of the subject.

'Economics is completely unrealistic'

There are several reasons why the economy is not amenable to simple modelling. Or rather why, when it *is* subjected to simple modelling – by economists – the results should be treated with a judicious degree of caution. To be specific, the results should be interpreted as applying to the particular model, not necessarily to the economy.

First, there are a huge number of economic – and non-economic – factors continually interacting. Many of these interactions are two-way – where one factor will change, causing other things to change, and then these changes themselves affect the initial factor – causing a new cycle of interaction, and so on.

Second, the nature of the causal mechanisms themselves alters over time.

Third, one may sometimes find a causal mechanism from one variable to another that appears absolutely stable, so one can predict that if a certain event happens it will always be followed by the same consequence. But if something new is introduced – for example a policy intervention suggested by the economist who has discovered this stable relation – then that may well cause the previously stable correlation to break down. This may sound rather esoteric, but it became crucially important when, for example, policy makers accepted the claim that there was a stable relationship between money and prices, so that if the money supply was controlled, inflation could be eliminated painlessly. In the event, as governments clamped down on the money supply, people just used the existing money stock more intensively. This hadn't happened before, but it did now. This phenomenon – that intervening on the basis of past behaviour can actually change that behaviour in the future, thus undermining the intervention – came to be known as 'Goodhart's Law'. (After Charles Goodhart, an economics professor at the London School of Economics and a member of the Bank of England's Monetary Policy Committee, who had pointed out that this was indeed likely to be the result of the Conservative Government's monetarist policies in the 1980s.)

Fourth, many of these 'laws', causal mechanisms, call them what you will, depend on what decisions actually come to be taken by various people in the economy (and, indeed, in other economies). So an economist might predict that since a fall in interest rates will reduce the cost of borrowing to make an investment, investment will therefore increase if the interest rate is reduced. And so, often, it does. But if, on the other hand, investors decide not to invest after all, say because of their uncertainty about the future, then that's that. And if the decision is a general one, then our economist will be proved wrong. End of story. This is why Keynes described 'animal spirits' as playing a part in investors' decisions (meaning their business and financial instincts). Indeed, the terms 'bear' and 'bull' market are used to describe the stock exchange when it's on the way down or up, respectively.

And fifth, many of the things which economists are analysing – what the effect of changing interest rates will be, or which will be the richest ten countries in five, ten or twenty years time – are simply unknowable. The answer will depend on what happens to a whole range of other factors, about which we can't be sure.

These difficulties are not, in our view, what put people off the subject. But they do lie behind one of the off-putting factors, which is, rather, that too many economists are either unaware of, or else forget, the above. They talk as if the results of simple models can be translated directly into policy for the real world. Students often object to this – rightly – saying that 'economics is completely unrealistic'. The problem, though, is not economics – it is the misuse of economics.

Neither should the above points be taken to mean that we shouldn't build simple economic models. On the contrary, in most subjects you have to simplify. It's no good going on a hike carrying a one-to-one map. You need some degree of simplification – or 'stylised facts' about the way economies tend to behave.

In economics this means that much of our discussion has to be on the basis of 'other things being equal'. This allows us to focus in on the key question we want to consider. What is important, though, is that we remember that 'other things' most likely will not be equal, so we should be cautious about the applicability of any of the results which were derived on the basis of assuming other things equal.

'I've got a block against economics'

A third thing that appears to put students off economics is that everyone else appears to know much more than they know; so they think they must have no aptitude for it. Or at least they think there will be too much work to try to catch up with everyone else – and here we're not referring to everyone else in the class, but to people on TV, in the newspapers, politicians and so on. What is not generally appreciated is that most of the people we see talking knowingly about economic issues would probably admit in private – if they were honest – that they don't feel they really *understand* the issues. This is one of the ways in which economics is a strange subject. Someone can learn the jargon and get a grasp of the basics and then sound as profound as someone who has been pursuing economics research for 50 years. Although the news always reports the FTSE, the Dow Jones, the sort of day the pound has had, and so on, most people watching will not have a clue what the point of it is. And the City commentators who then give a sound bite will no doubt understand the basics, but their opinion of whether interest rates should go up or down is unlikely to be grounded in a particularly deep appreciation of economic theory.

If this all sounds a bit extreme then watch next time the newscaster announces the day's movements on the foreign exchange markets. Sometimes they simply report that the pound rose or fell. But sometimes they prefix it with, 'it was a good day for the pound on the foreign exchange markets'. What does this mean? Did the value of sterling rise or fall? Invariably the newscaster will announce that 'it was a good day' because it rose. Why is that good? Was the currency undervalued? If not, then perhaps it was overvalued? In which case a rise in the domestic currency's value will cause domestically produced goods to become even more uncompetitive. Domestic firms may lose orders and have to lay off workers. The newscaster of course is only doing his or her job. But it gives the impression that everyone understands that a rise in the currency's value must be a 'good thing'. When most people will not understand the statement, it is at best rather meaningless and at worst positively perverse.

Another example – that those who appear to understand economics, may not – comes from Margaret Thatcher. Now she was, apparently, excellent at being briefed, and she was certainly briefed intensively on economic issues. The first of her General Election victories came after a campaign in which economic issues played a dominant role, including her advocacy of the doctrine of monetarism, whereby the controlling of the money supply by the Bank of England would eliminate inflation from the system, for ever. Here is her description of the economic doctrine on which she fought the election, and which she then imposed on the country for a number of years:

> *Mr James Callaghan, Leader of the Opposition* – . . . will she tell us clearly whether increases in wages are a cause of inflation or not?
> *Mrs Thatcher* – Over a period the cause of increased inflation is increases in the money supply. Within money supply, there will be a different distribution both between the public sector and the private sector and within those sectors there will be increases in pay within the general money supply well beyond what are warranted, and they may come through in increases in particular products which will not necessarily affect the general price level.
> *Mr James Callaghan* – May I thank her for that reply and say that I did not understand a word of it.
>
> (Hansard, 3 July 1980)

As mentioned above, Margaret Thatcher usually mastered her brief rather better than this. But the point is that the level of actual understanding of economics of most politicians and commentators is likely to be less than that of the average economics graduate. You should not be put off economics on the false assumption that as everyone else seems to understand it, you must lack the natural aptitude for it.

'*I can't do the maths*'

A fourth and final reason that people often give for being put off economics – in addition to the fact that economists can't even agree amongst themselves, that the subject is unrealistic, and that everyone else appears to understand it already – is the mathematics.

It is true that the discipline has become increasingly formalised over the years, with an increasing reliance on high-level mathematics. But this is certainly not necessary for an understanding of how the economy works. First, though, a distinction should be made between statistics, econometrics, and mathematics. Some degree of statistical competence is important – it's no good trying to discuss inequality, say, if you don't know what an 'average' income means (although this example is not as trivial as it appears, since it will be important to understand the difference between the 'mean' and 'median'). However, there are very few people who really cannot grasp statistics. Likewise with econometrics, which is basically the application of statistical techniques to economic data in order to investigate whether various factors are related or not.

Leaving aside the statistics and econometrics, not much maths is actually required just to get a basic understanding of the principles of economics. It is true that the subject has become increasingly mathematical, but most of the highly mathematical economics articles are some way from discussing how the economy actually works. For those who want to avoid the mathematical aspects then the bottom line is simply how much maths will be required in the exam. Of course, the more maths you can master then the greater range of economic articles you will be able to read and make sense of. But if you really can't do maths, it is still possible to understand the principles of economics.

Indeed, there is a widespread view that economics has become over-formalised. This relates to the objection discussed above about economics being unrealistic. There is an increasing premium being put on the use of maths in economics articles – sometimes put down to physics envy. This often results in contributions which are needlessly unrealistic, in the sense that simplifying assumptions are made for no other reason than that it makes the maths easier to do. The Cambridge economist Joan Robinson once said that her great advantage was in not knowing mathematics, so she was forced to think instead.

This book's approach to the principles of economics

This book sets out to discuss principles of economics by analysing how the economy functions, and what role economic policy plays. An important feature of the text is its grounding in real world issues. The theory is of course explained and, as indicated above, unrealistic assumptions are made where this helps to focus on the issues at hand. But the fact that such assumptions are made for a purpose – to help think through real world issues – is not forgotten. This should avoid the feeling that 'economics is completely unrealistic'.

The book is international in scope. Most textbooks[2] have a chapter on 'trade' added near the end of the book, most of which has up to that point assumed a closed economy (whether explicitly or implicitly). This book opens with a discussion of global economic issues. In our view we should most definitely care about events in some far off country or countries of which we know little. For example, the 1997–98 problems in Asia led to currency depreciations which make their goods relatively cheaper than UK produced ones, and could lead to a cut-back or even reversal of foreign direct investment in the UK. This shows first why such economic events should be of interest to us, and second the way in which an understanding of economic theory can help us to understand what the likely effects of such events might be.

Structure of the book

Part I, on 'Globalisation', opens with Chapter 2, 'Globalisation, unemployment and Government policy'. The globalisation of the economy appears from daily news bulletins to be wreaking havoc. Yet we are told that this same globalisation precludes national governments from doing much about it. This was nicely illustrated in 1998 when the *Guardian* newspaper reported Tony Blair as arguing that globalisation had constrained the ability of any Government, such as his, from doing much about the economy, alongside a report that the arch global speculator, George Soros, was warning that global capitalism faced collapse and that Governments must intervene to stabilise and regulate the system.

Domestic and international economic policy is still dominated by *laissez faire* economics, despite the failure of such policy in the 1980s and 1990s to have brought about the sort of economic growth and high employment witnessed through the 1950s and 1960s. The dominant feature of international trade theory is the assumed superiority of free trade and non-intervention. In Chapter 3, 'Trade theory and policy', we argue that the neoclassical case for free trade is based on inappropriate assumptions; relax these assumptions and the case for non-intervention goes with them.

In Chapter 4, 'Trade and growth: a historical perspective', we argue that to return to a situation of reasonable stability and balanced growth for individual countries, and for the world economy as a whole, increased management of the international trading and monetary systems will be required.

Part II, 'History versus equilibrium', opens with Chapter 5 on 'Recession and economic revival in Britain: the role of policy in the 1930s and 1980s', which argues that contrary to accepted opinion, the extent of unemployment was greater in the 1980s than during the Great Depression. Measuring on a consistent basis shows that UK unemployment reached 11.1 per cent in 1986 compared with 10.6 per cent in 1932. In both periods, unemployment has been a major cause of poverty driving families below the most basic of subsistence levels and leading to deteriorating health.

From the mid-1920s the cornerstone of international economic management was the Gold Standard. Its effect was to depress output and employment and undermine the capacity of individual governments to deal with domestic economic problems. This not only lowered growth and raised unemployment but hampered long-run competitiveness. The dampening of domestic demand reduced the benefits of mass production and the exploitation of scale economies. Deflation to maintain external equilibrium raised unit costs and generated a further loss of competitiveness and declining shares of world markets. Such a process of cumulative causation led to a vicious cycle of stagnation. Locked into a fixed exchange rate system there were few policy options to reverse the process.

The system combined together countries with different economic conditions and problems. These problems were not eradicated by the regime; rather they were accentuated. Discretion over the use of monetary, fiscal and exchange rate policy was removed. And the regime was not able to accommodate adverse economic shocks to the system; on the contrary, the operation of the international monetary system magnified the impact of any such recessionary forces. The regime was inappropriate for members with different economic structures and a recession phased differently amongst the international community.

The extent and magnitude of the Great Depression put the Gold Standard under severe strain. A series of financial and balance-of-payments crises ultimately undermined the system, culminating in Britain's decision to abandon the Gold Standard and devalue in September 1931. Growth and improved economic performance during the 1930s was dependent on countries untying themselves from the strictures of the Gold Standard and adopting independent policies, with different exchange rate regimes created and with some countries also reaping the advantages of increased protectionism and fiscal expansion. What is apparent is that the cooperative regime failed and uncoordinated policies were a vast improvement.

Chapter 6, 'A tale of two recessions: 1929 and the Gold Standard, 1992 and the ERM' draws the lessons from history of the ill-fated ERM and the current step into the EU's single currency abyss. Unless current European economic policy is reorientated towards the objective of full employment, embracing an active industrial and regional policy, rather than being stuck on the myopic concern with zero inflation, the route forward must once again be based on independent national growth strategies which would not only allow countries to help themselves, but by doing so would help each other. Competitive deflation was the real 'beggar my neighbour' policy of the 1920s, as it proved again in the 1990s. To push ahead with the single currency on the current basis threatens to repeat these historical mistakes.

Chapter 7, 'Britain's industrial performance since 1960: underinvestment and relative decline' argues, as the title suggests, that Britain's relative economic performance remains unimpressive. Many of the reasons go back well before 1960, as illustrated by the previous chapters.

Finally, Part III on 'Public policy and corporate performance' focuses on policy action. Chapter 8, 'From Welfare to Work?', advocates a far more active approach than that being pursued by the New Labour Government elected in Britain in 1997. Chapter 9, 'Markets, competition and innovation' suggests that to turn around the poor industrial performance documented in Chapter 7, and to lay the economic foundations for successful labour market policies as advocated in Chapter 8, requires an active industrial policy which appreciates the importance of productive cooperation between private firms as well as between private firms and public bodies.

Part I
Globalisation

2 Globalisation, unemployment and government policy

> What is called globalisation is changing the notion of the nation state as power becomes more diffuse and borders more porous. Technological change is reducing the power and capacity of government to control its domestic economy free from external influence.
>
> (Tony Blair, speaking to executives of Rupert Murdoch's News Corporation, quoted in the *Financial Times*, 20 March 1996.)

1 Introduction

The process of globalisation clearly has important implications for the conduct of economic policy. But what are these implications? Are they – as the above quotation would suggest – the reduction of the power and capacity of government? If so, what should be the response of governments? And their electorates? Most important from the point of view of this chapter – and indeed for much of this book – does it mean that national governments are now powerless to pursue policies for full employment?

Once we start asking these questions it soon becomes clear that in the academic literature, just as in the policy debates, there is little clarity over what the term 'globalisation' signifies. Likewise, there is certainly no consensus over what the implications of any of this should be for government economic policy.

The 'powerless state' perspective sees the world economy as a truly global system that has undermined the ability of national governments to implement independent policies. Hirst and Thompson (1996) have challenged this view. However, most such critiques accept the basic claim, that to the extent that the degree of globalisation has increased, the scope for government action is thereby diminished. It is only the degree to which government policy has become less effective which is disputed.[1]

We agree with the sceptics that there is much exaggeration regarding 'globaloney'. But we would take the criticism further. We have argued elsewhere that, first, while there has been an increase in globalisation, most commentators have exaggerated the phenomenon; and second, most commentators have misinterpreted the implications in a number of important ways. It is *not* the case that some natural or technologically driven phenomena of globalisation have taken power away from national governments. On the contrary, it has in many cases been governments themselves that have transferred power to multinational corporations and global financial markets. The latest and most dangerous example is the proposed 'Multilateral Agreement on Investment' which has been pursued through the Organisation of Economic Cooperation and Development. While these negotiations have, at the time of writing (October 1999), stalled, there are active attempts to pursue the deregulatory aims through other avenues.[2] The aim is to prevent national governments having any control over the actions of multinational corporations.

So while governments may claim that they would like to pursue progressive policies if only they had the means, in most cases any loss of means has been a deliberate act of governments themselves. (This is documented further in Chapters 3 and 4, below.)

A second important point is that the degree of *difficulty* in pursuing policy at the national level is different from the question of its *desirability*; even if the implementation of policy has become more difficult, this does not necessarily make it any less desirable or important.

And there are certainly aspects of policy – such as the creation of international institutional arrangements (on which, see Robinson College Working Group, 1999) or the pursuit of competitive advantage – where policy at the national level has actually become *more* important. If the pursuit of such policy has become more difficult then the appropriate conclusion might be the precise opposite of the one normally asserted or accepted in such discussion. Rather than government intervention having become outdated, it may be that to see through the necessary policy will require more far-reaching and radical intervention on the part of national governments than would have been the case in the previous, easier circumstances.

This chapter thus argues that there are indeed trends towards increased globalisation, and that there are 'winners and losers' between as well as within nations. Globalisation is playing a role in the increased inequality and unemployment witnessed in the industrialised countries (see Wood 1994). But again this process has been exaggerated – we would agree with the more sceptical views of Eatwell (1995) and Singh and Zammit (1995). The main cause of these problems has been the pursuit of orthodox economic policies.

There is thus a need for increased government intervention to maintain and improve economic performance in an increasingly integrated world economy, as well as to combat inequality domestically. Although the analysis in this chapter is primarily concerned with the performance of industrialised countries in general and Britain in particular, many of the arguments also apply to developing countries.

The chapter is organised as follows. Section 2 considers the evidence regarding trends and patterns of globalisation. Section 3 then considers the link between increased openness – in terms of the growth in international trade – and economic performance. Section 4 considers the implications of all this for national economic policy, and Section 5 concludes.

2 Trends and patterns in globalisation

The concept of globalisation has been applied to a wide variety of variables – including social, political and cultural. Here we adopt a narrower focus, looking at the globalisation of economic and technological activities with a view to the implications for unemployment, and for government policy to combat unemployment.

Economic globalisation

Looking back over the past century and more, the process of increased global integration has been erratic. It has been punctured by periodic crises, the formation of regional trading blocs, and shifting world economic leadership.

During the 1870 to 1913 period there was an almost continual increase in world trade and world output. As shown in Figure 2.1 world trade increased by an average of 3.5 per cent a year whereas world output increased by an average of 2.7 per cent a year. There were cyclical variations in trade and output and significant differences in national growth rates but only in four years did world trade decline (1885, 1892, 1900 and 1908) and only in three years did world output decline (1876, 1893 and 1908).

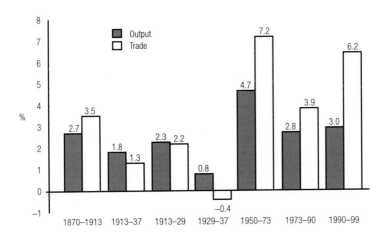

Figure 2.1 Growth of world output and world trade, 1870–1999

Sources: Authors' calculations from IMF (1998); Lewis (1981); Maddison (1962); and Wells (1993a).

Note
The figures for 1990–99 include IMF projections for 1998 and 1999.

The period between the First and Second World Wars saw major discontinuities in growth and trade. The relative stability of the 1920s was followed by the turbulence of the 1930s. As shown in Figure 2.1, during the 1913–29 period world trade grew at an average annual rate of 2.2 per cent, whereas output grew at an average annual rate of 2.3 per cent. The disruptions and dislocations of the First World War can explain much of this relatively slow growth. The international trading system was in considerable disarray and only recovered slowly; by 1924 the volume of world trade was only 7 per cent above the 1913 level.

During the 1930s, or more precisely from 1929, the world economy suffered severe disruptions. The Great Depression of 1929–32 was the most severe depression in the world economy since the Industrial Revolution. During these three years world trade collapsed at an average annual rate of 9.9 per cent and world output declined at an average annual rate of 6.2 per cent. The disintegration of the world trading system was reflected in a movement towards a more closed world economy – a reversal of the 1920s trend towards increased openness. From 1932 there was a world recovery, albeit one with large inter-country variations. During the period 1932–37, world output grew at an average annual rate of 5.2 per cent and world trade at 5.8 per cent, although this failed to return trade to its 1929 level.

During the post-Second World War period world output and trade grew at a faster rate than in any previous period. Only in one year (1982) did world output fall; and only in four years did world trade fall (1952, 1958, 1975, 1982).

The post-Second World War period can be divided into a number of sub-periods. The Bretton Woods period, from 1950 to 1973, witnessed a rapid growth of trade (average annual growth of 7.2 per cent) and output (average annual growth of 4.7 per cent). There was a significant rise in the openness of the world economy: in part this can be explained by a catching-up process as the world economy adjusted from the dislocations of the Second World War. It was not until 1968 that openness got back to the level of 1913. It also reflects, however, the increasing integration of the world economy based on an effective and stable international trading system.

The design of the international trading regime established after the Second World War was formulated in the context of the perceived failings of the interwar system: the disintegration of world trade in the early 1930s and the subsequent development of uncoordinated trade policies. The system took its name from the conference held in 1944 at Bretton Woods, New Hampshire, which put into place the rules that would regulate the international monetary and trading system in the postwar world.

Within the Bretton Woods system every country had to peg its currency to gold or the US dollar (which, in turn, was pegged to gold). Before it could change its exchange rate a country would have to show that it faced 'fundamental disequilibrium'. This term lacked adequate definition although in effect it was interpreted as that condition where the exchange rate parity was inconsistent with acceptable levels of unemployment or inflation. There was a resistance to make general exchange rate realignments (one notable exception was the realignments made in 1949 following the sterling devaluation of that year). Furthermore, the exchange rate adjustments that were made tended to be devaluations by deficit countries rather than revaluations by surplus countries. The Bretton Woods system did not function symmetrically; the burden of adjustment was borne by the weaker deficit countries, with the stronger countries accumulating increased reserves.

Despite its asymmetry, the Bretton Woods system was relatively successful because it accommodated a number of adjustment mechanisms and was anchored by US monetary hegemony. Two of the adjustment mechanisms, which complemented each other, were first, the discretionary use of domestic monetary and fiscal policy and second, the use of capital controls. These mechanisms provided some flexibility.

The stability of Bretton Woods was undermined, though, by the relative decline of the US economy and the increasing inconsistency between US domestic policies and the needs of the world economy. For most of the life of the Bretton Woods system, US monetary and fiscal policies were directed at domestic targets. There are parallels here with the problems faced within the European Exchange Rate Mechanism (ERM), with German monetary policy dictated by domestic rather than European needs. Furthermore, the need for the US to run balance of payments deficits to supply reserves to the rest of world, such that its dollar liabilities exceeded its gold stock, undermined the viability of the system. A series of exchange rate crises in the early 1970s signalled the demise of the system, the end coming in early 1973 with the floating of the Yen and the currencies of the six members of the European Community.

The collapse of the Bretton Woods system ushered in a period of slower growth of world trade and output. From 1973 to 1990, world trade grew at an average annual rate of 3.9 per cent, around half that achieved in the Bretton Woods period, and output increased at an average annual rate of 2.8 per cent. Within this period there were major setbacks in the mid-1970s and the early 1980s; the former caused by the first OPEC (Organisation of Petroleum Exporting Countries) shock and the latter by 'OPEC 2' and the 'monetarist' shock of deflationary policies being adopted in a number of the leading industrialised countries.[3] In the 1990s the annual growth of world trade increased to 6.2 per cent but the annual growth of world output increased only marginally – averaging 3.0 per cent for the decade.

There were several reasons for the 1945–73 era of relatively rapid growth coming to an end. The 1973 oil crisis is often cited. But this was more a symptom than a cause – there was a general rise in fuel and raw material prices caused on the one hand by the relatively rapid growth itself, combined on the other with no global system to manage the production of fuel and raw materials. The original ideas following the Second World War for developing some such international arrangements were quietly dropped when the leading capitalist countries found that they had ready access to such supplies at very low prices. This attitude was to prove shortsighted. On a global scale the balance of forces shifted gradually away from the industrialised countries towards the producers of energy and raw materials. And a similar shift in the balance of forces occurred domestically in the advanced economies as the era of full employment led to a strengthening of labour's bargaining power at the negotiating table and in the workplace. This had been predicted by one of the architects, along with Keynes, of demand-management policies for tackling unemployment. Thus Michal Kalecki had warned in 1943 that if the sort of policies which both he and Keynes had developed for the maintenance of full employment were implemented:

> a strong opposition of 'business leaders' is likely to be encountered. Lasting full employment is not at all to their liking. The workers would 'get out of hand' and the 'captains of industry' would be anxious to 'teach them a lesson'. In this situation a powerful bloc is likely to be formed between big business and the *rentier* interests, and they would probably find more than one economist to declare that the situation was manifestly unsound. The pressure of all these forces, and in particular of big business would most probably induce the Government to return to the orthodox policy of cutting down the budget deficit. A slump would follow.[4]

Thus the inflationary pressures brought about by the long period of unplanned and uncoordinated global economic expansion through the 1950s and 1960s were met with deflationary policies. The impact of this was to impede the openness of the world economy. The post-Second World War trend towards a more open world economy was thus halted from the mid-1970s and only resumed from the mid-1980s. But as indicated above, this move to a more open world economy is far from being a simple shift from the nation state to the world arena. As in the past, these processes are largely driven by nation states, and by individual firms that, while multinational, have clear national bases. And much of what is described as 'globalisation' is actually 'regionalism'.

Regionalism emerged in the world economy in a significant way in two periods: first in the 1930s, and then again in the 1980s (on which, see Chapter 3 below). Much of the increase in international integration in the latter period has not been on a global scale but has been between countries in the same geographic region or between countries who have established regional trade agreements. Thus, much of the rapid growth of the Asian share of world trade has been internal to that part of the world. Regionalism has been both a defensive and an aggressive response to intensified international competition.

Another development in the history of the world trading system has been changes in the leading nation (on which see Chapter 3). The leading nation in the world economy has shifted during different epochs of international economic development. The Pre-First World War era saw Britain, the first industrialised economy, as the dominant economic power but its relative position declined with the rising economic might of the US, Germany and others. During the interwar period Britain attempted to re-impose its hegemony, but its long-run relative decline continued. By 1929 the US share of the capitalist world's GDP was four times that of Britain and it had overtaken Britain as the world's leading exporter.[5] The post-Second World War 'Golden Age of Capitalism' was underpinned by this strength of the US economy, with the dollar thereby being able to act as the anchor to the international monetary system. However, the growth of the world economy and the emergence of other economies, in particular Germany and Japan, was to undermine the US's relative position to a significant degree.

The US share of world exports has been declining since the early 1970s whereas the Japanese share has been increasing significantly. While the global instability and crises since 1997–98, which have particularly affected the Far East, will lead to further changes in the relative economic position of the leading powers, the nature of these changes cannot be predicted in a simple fashion. One of the ironies is that the economies worst hit will tend to see their currencies devalued the most. This can then put them at a competitive advantage over the subsequent period.

In terms of shares of world manufactured exports, as shown in Table 2.1, Japan had by the early 1990s certainly caught up with, if not overtaken, the US. And while the European Union (EU) had, as recently as 1980, a share almost double that of Japan, this had fallen significantly by the early 1990s. On these measures, the balance of forces appears now to be very much a three-way one. The East Asian crises of 1997 and 1998, and Japan's recent economic difficulties are unlikely to significantly alter this global balance, or perhaps more accurately, imbalance.

Furthermore, not only has Japan been capturing a growing proportion of OECD trade it has also been rapidly increasing its share in high-tech trade. These changes in relative shares were accompanied over the 20 years up to the early 1990s by a fall in OECD manufacturing employment of 8 per cent. Yet manufacturing employment actually rose in Japan over the same period by 2 per cent and was barely unchanged in the US. It was the European Union (EU) which had the big manufacturing job losses, amounting to 20 per cent

Table 2.1 Shares of world exports of manufactures (%)

	1980	*1986*	*1992*
Japan	11.2	14.1	12.3
US	13.3	10.8	12.8
EU	21.9	19.4	17.6
Intra-EU	24.1	22.9	26.1
Rest of world	29.4	32.8	31.2

Source: Kitson and Michie (1995).

over those 20 years up to the early 1990s, with the worst case being the UK, suffering a 35 per cent fall. This in turn was reflected in the relatively poor EU employment rates and correspondingly high unemployment.

Technological globalisation

According to the quotation from Tony Blair with which this chapter opens, it is 'technological change' that's guilty of 'reducing the power and capacity of government to control its domestic economy free from external influence'. This section considers and discusses this claim.

To start with, a distinction can be made between three separate processes that are often subsumed within the catchall general term technological globalisation (on which, see Archibugi and Michie, 1995b, 1997, and Iammarino and Michie, 1998). First, the international *exploitation* of national technological capabilities: firms try to exploit their innovations on global markets either by exporting products or by licensing the know-how. Second, *collaboration* across borders among both public and business institutions to exchange and develop know-how. Firms are expanding their non-equity agreements to share the costs and risks of industrial research. Of course, the scientific community has always been international in scope, but public research centres and academia have recently increased their proportion of cross-border linkages substantially. Third, the *generation* of innovations across more than one country, which refers particularly to the activities of multinational corporations.

The first two of these dimensions to the globalisation of technology have increased in importance. Trade and patent flows and international technical agreements, have increased dramatically over the past two decades or so. On the third category of the extent to which multinational corporations have increased their technological operations in host countries, the evidence is less clear. Patel (1995), taking into account the patented inventions of more than 500 of the world's largest enterprises, shows that the vast majority of inventions are developed in the firms' home nation. Multinational corporations tend to be loyal to their own home-based country when they have to locate a strategic asset such as technology.

These issues are important not only because of the implications for the future industrial development of the countries concerned but also because of the immediate employment implications of where economic activities take place. Less developed countries may offer an adequately trained workforce but at salaries which are much lower than in the developed countries while information technologies make the geographical location of high-tech jobs less relevant. This leads to the concern that industrial countries could lose skill-intensive jobs.

The key point is that the competitive advantage of firms and of the economies from which they operate is built up by conscious policy action by firms, governments and others. Competitive advantage does not drop from the sky.

And as the economy becomes more globalised, any competitive advantage gained (or lost) will have that much greater effect on market shares, output and employment levels and living standards. Thus, far from being swept aside by the forces of technological globalisation, economic and industrial policy is becoming more, not less important. And central to this need for active government – nationally, locally and globally – lies technology and innovation policy.

3 Trade and economic performance

From the above it should be clear that while the world economy is indeed becoming more integrated, the notion that we have a fully globalised economy is a misleading simplification. Historically, the pace and extent of globalisation have varied during different international policy regimes and have been interrupted by intermediate developments, such as the formation of regional trading blocs.

Conventionally, it has been argued that 'globalisation' makes it no longer feasible for individual countries to pursue independent economic policies in the face of globalised financial markets. National economic policy objectives should be limited, it is argued, to seeking 'stability' and 'convergence'. Stability is interpreted, perversely, as stability of policy instruments – interest rates, exchange rates, fiscal balances, and so on – despite the fact that stability in these may cause instability in real economic variables. Thus Britain's membership of the Exchange Rate Mechanism (ERM) promised wonderful stability for the exchange rate, but at the cost of instability for growth and employment – and hence ultimately instability for the exchange rate itself. Convergence is interpreted, again perversely, as the convergence of policy instruments – interest rates, tax rates, and government expenditure – to the lowest level, despite the fact that such convergence may generate divergences in real economic variables.

Contrary to the developing orthodoxy, we would argue that increased economic integration increases the need for the active use of economic instruments to target real variables such as output and employment.

Variations in trade performance in an increasingly integrated world economy may lead to persistent divergences in growth rates. Success in international trade becomes cumulative as increasing demand for net exports allows countries (or more specifically, the firms and industries within them) to exploit economies of scale and scope, improving their competitiveness and leading to further improvements in their trade performance. This was the case, for example, for the German economy in the post-Second World War era. Conversely, weaker trading nations may fail to maintain balance of payments equilibrium at a high level of economic activity, with deflationary policies then pursued in an attempt to maintain external balance. This was very much the story for Britain prior to the discovery of North Sea oil. The combined impact of poor trade performance and domestic deflation is likely to lead to a cumulative deterioration in relative economic growth as countries fail to exploit the increasing returns associated with a high level of economic activity. These twin processes of virtuous circles of growth and vicious cycles of decline illustrate that the benefits of trade integration may not be evenly spread.[6]

With trade integration increasing the potential costs and benefits which will result from one nation's competitive advantage or disadvantage, increasing globalisation makes national institutions and policies more important rather than less. The costs of falling behind are exacerbated.

4　Implications for economic policy

Thus we would argue that globalisation increases the need for active government economic, trade, industrial and technology policies. A failure to formulate a cohesive policy framework can lead to an individual country being locked into slow growth due to an inability to effectively compete in an increasingly integrated world economy.

The recent financial crises in Asia and elsewhere illustrate the need for international initiatives to ensure global economic stability and growth. The inherent instability of global financial markets is depressing output and employment throughout the world economy. Furthermore, the volatility of capital flows and exchange rate instability have been associated with widespread financial crises. A global initiative would require policies to stabilise capital flows and exchange rates; more effective regulation of financial institutions; and a more effective means of managing financial crises (on the detail of such a global strategy see Robinson College Working Group, 1999).

A global initiative will not obviate, but will reinforce, the need for action at the national level. A first requirement is stable growth of real variables, such as output and employment, rather than stability of nominal variables such as prices. Fiscal, monetary and exchange rate policies should aim to ensure a continuous and sustainable expansion of aggregate demand, with flexibility to counteract external shocks. The damaging impact of temporary shocks on output and employment will be particularly severe in economies highly dependent on skills and sophisticated capital equipment. Hence the importance of governments pursuing active counter-cyclical policies in the face of any such shocks. In addition it shows the danger of resorting to deflationary policies to counter inflation. These may harm long-run growth potential, thus making the economy less able to absorb increased world raw material and fuel costs in the future. The short-term pain brings long-term damage.

British economic prospects have thus been put at real risk by the New Labour Government's abandonment of interest rate policy, and hence also of monetary and exchange rate policy. The monetary policy pursued by the independent Bank of England is unlikely to properly target this broad policy agenda of investment, growth and employment. Certainly its behaviour to date reinforces such concerns. Part of the problem, to be fair to the Bank, is that the New Labour Government has instructed it, in effect, not to be concerned with such issues. To focus only on inflation has actually been their remit, even if the Chancellor Gordon Brown has since contradicted himself by implying that they should after all be concerned with the threat of global economic recession. But in addition to this inadequate – and contradictory – remit from Gordon Brown, there is a further problem. This is that the Bank's outlook and policy is based on an economic model that *assumes* an equilibrium rate of unemployment at which inflation will be stable. This is why, in October 1998, the Governor Eddie George proffered the view that inflation is best tackled by interest rate rises which, he admitted, would have the effect of making people in the North of England unemployed. Underlying such statements is the Bank's orthodox economic modelling, based as it is on unrealistic assumptions and refuted by the empirical evidence.[7]

Macroeconomic management requires the integrated use of both monetary and fiscal policy, which is made more difficult by the Government's surrender of monetary policy.

A second requirement is an effective industrial and technology policy. Nation-specific factors play a key role in the development of technological innovation. The concept of a national system of innovation is defined and applied differently, although it usually embodies education, innovation and R&D policies, as well as historical and cultural factors. Thus the ability to utilise increasingly globalised technology will depend on national systems, or 'social capability' (for further discussion of these issues, see Archibugi and Michie, 1997a, and Archibugi, Howells and Michie, 1999).

Recent research suggests that an essential element in the creation of a competitive and successful economy is effective collaboration by firms with others – customers, suppliers, higher education establishments and so on (see Kitson and Michie, 1998, and Kitson and Wilkinson, 1998b). Such collaboration allows firms to expand their range of expertise, develop specialist products, and achieve other corporate objectives. Collaboration is also one of the most important means of fostering innovation and effective competition in international markets. Instead of the 'freeing up' of labour and product markets through policies of deregulation and casualisation we need active industrial innovation, and macroeconomic policies. New forms of corporate finance need to be developed and effective mechanisms of corporate governance created. A modern productive infrastructure needs to be put in place for firms to utilise, in many cases in a cooperative fashion.

Two broad categories of government action can be identified: first, financial incentives to companies to attract companies' innovative activities; and, second, public supply of infrastructures to make a country attractive for the deployment of such activities. The latter approach, which includes investment in education, communications and university–industry partnerships, has increased in importance and is likely to be more effective than the financial incentive approach. The effectiveness of financial incentives may be greater in attracting lower-tech activities, which are more cost sensitive and more internationally mobile. Additionally, the positive externalities from a public investment strategy are likely to be greater, as private firms benefit from the cost and quality advantages of a modern, efficient, productive infrastructure, from a well-trained workforce, from the results of research into innovative products and processes, and so on.

While globalisation may result in national action having greater payoffs – and national inaction greater costs – it could still be the case that although globalisation makes national action more rather than less important, at the same time it makes it more difficult, or less feasible. Has the process of globalisation removed discretion over domestic economic management? Our answer would be no. The state's involvement in domestic economic activity varies widely – with significant differences in government expenditure, taxation, size of the welfare state, the extent of income distribution, and industrial and labour market policies. Furthermore, there is little evidence that there is any trend towards economic policies converging. Among the larger economies, the gap between the lowest and highest shares of government expenditure has increased since 1980. And this was during a period when the *average* public spending/GDP ratio increased: from around 35 per cent of GDP in 1979 to around 40 per cent for the OECD countries taken together, or from around 45 per cent to 50 per cent over the same time period for the EU countries on average. Only Britain did not increase the ratio of public spending to GDP over this 20-year period.[8]

The aspect of globalisation that has had the greatest impact on domestic policy has been the internationalisation of capital markets. Yet, even here the impact has been mixed. Glyn (1995) has argued that the free movement of capital is likely to constrain an expansionary domestic programme as the reaction of foreign-exchange markets will lead to large initial depreciation which will 'front-load' the impact on real wages. But a depreciation will increase the demand for tradables (exports and import substitutes) which will increase output and employment and may allow real wages to increase in the medium term. Nevertheless, there is no doubt that the current free-for-all in global financial markets is destabilising. Even Soros, the speculator, admits that regulation is required.

5 Conclusions

The postwar era of full employment has been dubbed the 'Golden Age of Capitalism'; it is a description which appears increasingly appropriate with the continued failure of the advanced capitalist economies to return to the levels of economic growth and employment witnessed from 1948 to 1973, and as inequality grows. The demise of that era around 1973 has now been followed by more than 25 years of global instability and varying degrees of mass unemployment. Far from a concerted effort to construct a new global economic framework for stability and growth – as was the case in 1944 with

Bretton Woods as the end of the Second World War came into sight – regional conflicts have marked the end of the Cold War. The 'freeing of the market' in the former Soviet Union and Eastern Europe destroyed many existing institutions without developing effective alternatives, resulting in massive economic regression there.

Increased global competition from the Newly Industrialising Countries has been blamed by some for aggravating unemployment in Western Europe and North America. It has led to calls for an abandonment of Welfare States and the associated social security and other provisions that are alleged to make Western Europe, in particular, uncompetitive. The Third World Debt crisis may have slipped out of the news but is hardly resolved. And the world economy seems set to enter the twenty-first century with the industrial world divided between the three main trading blocs – the European Union, the North American Free Trade Area, and the Pacific Rim countries.[9] This three-way division could either form the basis for negotiation and cooperation, or else lead to the sort of unstable economic and political developments only before witnessed in the preludes to the two world wars.

The situation demands action from national governments to tackle economic recession and unemployment. This requires cooperation between governments towards these ends, and calls for new international institutions. The global economy can be imagined to be a self-equilibrating mechanism of the textbook variety. Or it can be recognised as being subject to processes of cumulative causation whereby if one or more countries fall behind the pack, they risk falling further behind rather than enjoying an automatic ticket back to the equilibrium solution path. These two alternative, conflicting views of real world economic processes have very different implications regarding institutional needs and arrangements.

There has been a false choice posed in policy discussion between action by individual national governments, on the one hand, and international co-operation on the other. The argument has tended to run something like this: national, 'go it alone' policies were all very well in the past, but in the modern era of global financial markets and transnational corporations, individual governments are powerless; instead, international cooperation is the only way forward. The striking thing about this characterisation is that we had far more international cooperation in the immediate postwar era when apparently it was not needed than we have had since, when supposedly it is the only option. A more honest distinction would be between first, the present era when governments have in practice attempted very little intervention in the operation of the free market, whether national or global, and second, previous eras when they were less inhibited.

A 'new' orthodoxy has been established around the following two propositions. First, that we now live in a globalised world and so the sort of intervention seen over the past decades, including the postwar Golden Age of Capitalism, is no longer feasible. And second, that international cooperation is preferable to countries attempting to 'go it alone'. The first argument, that we now live in a brave new globalised world, might be characterised along the following lines:

> All old-established national industries have been destroyed or are daily being destroyed. They are dislodged by new industries, whose introduction becomes a life and death question for all nations, by industries that no longer work up indigenous raw material but raw material drawn from the remotest zones; industries whose products are consumed not only at home, but in every quarter of the globe. In place of the old wants, satisfied by the productions of the country, we find new wants, requiring for their satisfaction the products of distant lands. We have universal interdependence of nations. And as in material, so also in intellectual production.

True, of course. But new? This characterisation of globalisation was actually published more than 150 years ago.[10] And of course, policies for macro-economic expansion to tackle unemployment would best be pursued internationally. But again this is nothing new. Kalecki's call in 1932 for expansionary policies to tackle unemployment made precisely this 'new realist' point: discussing the possibility of increasing employment by 'major public investment schemes, such as construction of canals or roads', financed by borrowing or increasing the money supply, he stressed the effects on the trade balance of increasing output – 'if it were to be carried out on a large scale, it would have to be co-ordinated by an international agreement of the individual capitalist governments, which, given today's quarrelling imperialisms, is almost out of the question'.[11]

The real question, then, is not whether it is best to act at the national or international level; it is how best to secure international action. For all to remain frozen until such time as everyone else moves is inadequate - however eloquent the calls for movement being made might be. Action at the local, regional, national or bloc level, far from being a utopian alternative to the real international stage, might in reality prove a prerequisite to cooperation.

The other question is what *sort* of action should be pursued. The past 20 years have been dominated by a deregulatory, slash and burn mentality. This has brought global instability, increased the power of international speculators, and reduced the capacity of governments. But it is quite dishonest for politicians to claim that their capacity to act has been reduced by something called 'globalisation'. It is they who have abolished exchange controls, handed power to unaccountable central banks, and now plan to completely tie their own hands with the 'Multilateral Agreement on Investment'.

But why, finally, should the world be stuck in such an impasse when there was by contrast such an active policy agenda pursued in the mid to late 1940s, from Bretton Woods to the Marshall Plan? One clue is to look at what was pushing the ruling powers in that previous era, as compared to the lack of any such push today. When in 1948 the West European countries were struggling to recover from the devastation of war, Marshall Aid was introduced against a background of significant Communist support in many of the countries of Europe and beyond, including Communist Party participation in the governments of France and Italy. It was not thought politically feasible to pursue free market policies that would create mass unemployment. Whether the Bretton Woods system would have been constructed without the Cold War is open to question; certainly the lack of any such political 'threat' or pressure helps to explain today's general failure to act.

The necessary policy action will not be taken, nationally or internationally, until the prevailing fatalistic economic ideology has been discarded and the dissatisfaction of voters puts sufficient pressure on the political establishment. The global financial markets are not God-given: they were created by financial institutions as governments freed financial markets from control over the past decade or so, and they can be remade in a more socially responsible image. Mass unemployment has been created and can be overcome. And there has been no shortage of international cooperation when it has been a matter of freeing markets and limiting the power of democratically elected governments. That priority can be reversed.

The purpose of this chapter has been to consider the implications of economic and technological globalisation for the prospects of such active government policy aimed at promoting economic growth and employment. We find much of the 'globalisation' claim to be exaggerated. And the globalisation that has occurred has not necessarily meant a reduction in national differentiation: on the contrary, it has been accompanied by an increase in technological specialisation (Archibugi and Michie, 1995b) and by global winners and losers in terms of economic growth and development.

Active economic, industrial, and technology policy are made more important rather than less by any increased openness of national economies which means that any loss of competitive advantage is translated all the more rapidly into declining market share, output, employment, and living standards. Policy may be more difficult to implement in face of global pressures. But far from implying a need for less action, such globalisation implies that policy action may need to be more interventionist and far-reaching than was the case in the past, if the necessary goals are to be achieved in these more difficult conditions.

3 Trade theory and policy

1 Introduction

The postwar 'Golden Age of Capitalism' was founded on a stable international monetary system which helped create the conditions for a rapid growth of trade and output. The collapse of the Bretton Woods system of fixed exchange rates in 1973 marked the end of this postwar boom – the 'Golden Age of Capitalism' – and ushered in what is now almost three decades of global economic instability. The series of economic recessions since 1973, and accompanying large scale unemployment on a global scale, demands action from national governments, cooperation between governments, and new international institutions to facilitate such cooperation. The need for increased regulation of the world economy is being resisted by the world's major economic powers, despite rhetorical statements to the contrary.

Although at the time of writing (1999), leaders of the main economic powers have been stressing the need for action around jobs and growth, the policy requirements to achieve these objectives remain sadly lacking. In this chapter we argue that to return to a situation of reasonable stability and balanced growth for individual countries and for the world economy as a whole, following the turbulence of the 1980s and 1990s, will require the increased management of the international trading and monetary systems. The chapter is organised in the following five sections. Section 2 considers conventional trade theory and its limitations. Section 3 presents an alternative Kaldorian analysis based on the stylised facts of trade and growth. Section 4 considers the operation of the sort of active trade policy which, we argue, might follow from such an analysis. Some of the key factors that will shape the future scope and character of any such interventionist trade policies are evaluated in Section 5, and the policy implications of these are discussed in Section 6.

2 The economics of trade and trade policy: the conventional wisdom

The traditional argument in favour of free trade is that it allows countries to specialise in the production of those goods and services in which they have a comparative advantage. Thus, by enlarging consumption possibilities, free trade increases the welfare of individual countries and the world economy as a whole. The imposition of tariffs disturbs the optimal allocation of resources, creates a 'dead-weight' loss on the country imposing tariffs and disrupts the equilibrium of the world economy by creating distortions in the price mechanism. That trade and growth are correlated is not in doubt.[1] However, it is a two-way relation, with growth tending to provoke trade, regardless of the effects of trade on growth. Also, the correlation is a complex one which changes over time, and more particularly over different states of the world. In some situations a relaxation of trade restrictions may boost economic growth. In other situations the same move might undermine expansionary policies already being pursued by governments, which are then forced to deflate in face of trade deficits. Such deficits may themselves represent a deflationary loss of demand from the economy, without necessarily providing a reciprocal reflationary effect in the corresponding surplus country, since this country may react by deliberately avoiding such an effect, via monetary policy.[2]

The standard case for free trade, then, is based on a number of assumptions and simplifications. First, much of the literature ignores the macroeconomic context. Second, each economy is assumed to be small and open and therefore unable to affect relative prices internationally. Third, production is assumed to operate with constant or diminishing returns to scale. And fourth, the economy is assumed to be always at full employment, by definition, and with no other distortions in the economic system. There have been various attempts to revise orthodox trade theory. Mundell (1961) and others have considered the macroeconomic context of tariff policy and exchange rate regimes. The ability to affect world prices has been analysed in the optimum tariff literature. And the role of increasing returns has been incorporated within the so-called 'new trade theory'.[3]

The macroeconomic context

Mundell (1961) concludes that a general tariff will have adverse effects on output and employment under flexible exchange rates but that with a fixed exchange rate, and in the absence of extensive retaliation, a tariff may generate higher output and employment. Under flexible exchange rates the adjustment of the exchange rate, resulting from the imposition of tariffs, will render commercial policy ineffective. Mundell's result relies on the Laursen–Metzler (1950) hypothesis that saving will increase with improved terms of trade, due to an improvement in real disposable income. However, the Laursen–Metzler effect is not a clearly established empirical or theoretical result. The saving function postulated by Laursen–Metzler is an *ad hoc* Keynesian function where consumption expenditure is determined by the level of current disposable income. The final effect of a terms-of-trade shift will depend on direct price effects, wealth effects and intertemporal substitutions which do not, in general, move in the same direction. Thus, it can be shown that a non-retaliatory tariff can have expansionary effects in Mundell's model as long as the restrictiveness of the Laursen–Metzler assumption is dropped (Ford and Sen, 1985).

Much of the recent work on tariff policy has noted the restrictiveness of the Laursen–Metzler assumption and has attempted to see whether the result holds under more generalised assumptions. Boyer (1977) considers the impact of tariffs within a portfolio balance framework, neglecting the Laursen–Metzler effect. His framework is a neoclassical full employment model with two nominal assets. He finds that, under a system of flexible exchange rates, tariffs have no influence on nominal income in the long run when the capital account goes to zero. In the short run the direction of influence on nominal income and the balance of payments depends entirely upon whether the economy is a creditor or debtor in foreign currency denominated assets. Only when a country is a creditor in such assets does commercial policy have an expansionary effect. Chan (1978) shows that, when a money market is added to Mundell's model, a tariff is contractionary even without the Laursen–Metzler assumption. Krugman (1982) argues that Mundell's tariff ineffectiveness result holds for a number of monetary extensions to Mundell's 1961 model. Eichengreen (1981a) looks at a simple dynamic portfolio model and finds that, with rigid money wages and static expectations, tariffs may increase employment and output in the short run while Mundell's result holds in the long run. With rational expectations (a theoretical condition where firms and individuals can predict future events without making systematic errors) Mundell's result also holds in the short run. All these extensions to Mundell's original model have come up with similar results. This is not surprising as they all share similar features; in particular they all share the belief that the quantity theory of money is a valid description of money demand (whereby money demand is determined by income and is not significantly affected by interest rates). In extensions of these models Ford and Sen (1985) have shown that, in a wide number of circumstances, tariffs can have positive effects on output and employment if the money demand function is specified in Keynesian terms, allowing for interest rate effects on money demand.

Such models suggest that tariffs *may* have favourable effects on output and employment for particular industries and for the macroeconomy, with the impact depending on the assumptions employed. However, all the above models neglect the specification of the investment relationship. In Mundell's model investment is not explicitly considered and hence any possible impact from tariffs to investment is ignored. For Krugman (1982), investment is simply an exogenous component of absorption. Eichengreen (1979) has given some consideration to the issue of an endogenous capital stock although his working models and results assume the size of the capital stock is fixed. Eichengreen's flexible capital stock model suggests that under the assumption of no international capital mobility a tariff unambiguously increases the steady state level of the capital stock. Similar results are generated for a model with capital mobility as long as the system is stable. Finally, these simple macroeconomic models assume constant returns to scale; the imposition of a general tariff in a world of increasing returns and a variable capital stock would lead to more favourable effects.

Optimum tariffs

The optimum tariff argument suggests that a country that is large enough to affect world prices may find it advantageous to impose a general tariff. When the tariff is imposed there are two opposing forces at work; first, there is the terms-of-trade effect which is beneficial to the country imposing the tariff and second, there is a volume of imports effect which is harmful. An optimum tariff occurs when the benefit due to the former outweighs the adverse effects of the latter, producing an unambiguous gain in the country's welfare although there will be adverse impacts on the rest of the world (and on the world as a whole).

Increasing returns

Imperfect competition and economies of scale have been introduced into international trade theory to explain the extensive and growing intra-industry trade between industrialised countries, with intra-industry trade flows being due to the existence of differentiated products produced under increasing returns. A diversity of tastes amongst consumers provides an incentive for product differentiation and the presence of economies of scale implies that each country will have to specialise in a limited number of products. The existence of increasing returns and imperfect competition indicates that price is above marginal cost, giving rise to the possibility of welfare-improving interventions. Thus, protectionism may offer a 'second best' instrument for raising welfare.

Within new trade theory the impact of tariffs depends on the specific market structure under consideration – perfect competition, monopoly, monopolistic competition, oligopoly and so on. Within the perfect competition model increasing returns are assumed to be external to the firm. This Marshallian approach therefore creates the case for protecting or supporting those sectors that generate large positive externalities such as technological spillovers. With alternative market structures the case for protection is not simply one of externalities but also the potential to shift rent to domestic producers. Much recent work has focused on cases of oligopoly which are the most difficult to deal with given the diversity of possible features. Under oligopolistic conditions foreign firms are earning pure profits in the domestic market. Tariffs can be used as a method of rent shifting, both through their revenue-raising effect and by switching profits away from foreign to local firms.

Although oligopoly models are dependent on the specific assumptions employed, most models suggest a role for tariffs as a policy instrument to improve welfare (Brander and Spencer, 1984; Dixit, 1984). Krugman (1982) assumes a duopoly (two competing firms) with economies of scale at the margin so that protection, which increases the share of sales of the home firm in the domestic market to the detriment of the foreign firm, lowers the home firm's marginal costs and raises those of the foreign firm. Hence, equilibrium in the foreign market also moves in the home firm's favour, with protection leading to export promotion of intra-industry trade. New trade theory has remained firmly microeconomic in character with protection being considered as an extension of industrial policy; the macroeconomics of tariffs in a world of increasing returns has rarely been considered by mainstream economics.

Unemployment and demand effects

Even when increasing returns are incorporated, as in new trade theory, full employment is still assumed and the competitive process is still reduced to alternative specifications of market structure – monopolistic competition, oligopoly and so on. This is why new trade theory is unable to concern itself with protectionism other than as an industrial policy – evaluating the benefits of protecting 'strategic' sectors or industries – and failing to consider that protection can act as a macroeconomic or development strategy. This has led to a misrepresentation of the impact of protectionism. Although new trade theory can demonstrate welfare gains from protection, this approach argues that first, the benefits are small and, second, there are difficulties in devising and implementing effective trade policies.

The allegedly only small gains arise from considering protectionism solely as an industrial policy within a neoclassical framework. In this context the gains are reduced to rent shifting and externalities. The macroeconomic possibility of domestic demand and output increasing is ignored, as are the dynamic gains from such economic growth. In his advocacy of free trade Romer (1994) suggests that evaluating the gains from trade by measuring consumer and social surplus is inadequate, since this assumes that the set of goods is fixed and complete. Romer argues that protectionism may adversely affect the list of goods available as by reducing demand a tariff may prevent the introduction of some new products. In fact, tariffs may have large positive effects through similar processes that Romer has identified, with tariffs increasing domestic demand, thus stimulating the introduction of new products, and preventing the loss of others, with the gains from protection being much larger than the new trade theorists suggest.

The contention that interventionist trade policies also encounter implementation problems also stems from evaluating protection as an industrial policy. Thus, it is difficult to identify 'strategic sectors'; the (small) gains from protectionism will be lost through retaliation; other industries will be harmed (the general equilibrium problem); the policy framework will be manipulated by interest groups; the rules of the game would be complex. Where protection is devised as a demand management tool, under conditions of unemployment and slow growth, many of these implementation problems are circumvented. First, it is not necessary to identify strategic sectors, just competitive imports versus complementary imports. Second, protection need not lead to retaliation, as the expansion of domestic demand will stimulate the volume of trade (Cripps and Godley, 1978). Third, the general equilibrium problem is not relevant under conditions of underemployed resources. Fourth, the influence of interest groups is reduced when tariffs are used as a general rather than selective instrument.

3 The political economy of trade and trade policy: the case for intervention and regulation

Our intention here is to indicate mechanisms by which tariffs may have favourable effects on economic performance.[4] The perspective we wish to emphasise is Kaldorian, based on the stylised facts of trade and growth.[5] Kaldor's approach (1970, 1982), incorporating the Harrod foreign trade multiplier (Harrod, 1933), emphasises that the trade cycle reflects fluctuations in export demand. Additionally, he argues that investment is best modelled as an induced component of aggregate demand, being determined by the income changes which are in turn induced by the Harrod foreign trade multiplier. Given the importance of increasing returns in manufacturing industry, this relationship may help to explain virtuous circles of growth.

Kaldor argues that the Ricardian rationale for free trade is dependent on the assumption of constant returns to scale. The existence of economies of scale in manufacturing, however, means that a nation that is successfully competing in foreign trade can expect that the advantage of an expanding market will increase its competitiveness. Similarly, a nation with poor performance in international trade can expect a trend of deteriorating competitiveness and declining markets. Thus, while not explaining initial imbalances, the existence of economies of scale indicates why such imbalances may generate virtuous or vicious circles of growth.

In analysing British postwar economic policies Kaldor (1971) argues that the poor economic performance was due to insufficient demand. This was not in the sense of an excessive propensity to save relative to the opportunities to invest but an excessive propensity to import relative to the ability to export – a balance-of-payments constraint. The importance of the idea of export-led growth gave rise to a policy debate on the best means for securing full employment. While exchange rate adjustment seemed the most applicable method, its efficiency was called into question, particularly after the limited impact of the 1967 devaluation. It was argued that any nominal devaluation may have a much lower real impact due to rising import prices, particularly of wage goods. Devaluation is a non-selective policy and raises the prices of all imports, not just competitive ones. Consequently any attempt to generate a substantial and long-term improvement in competitiveness through the exchange rate may require a large reduction in the nominal rate with repercussions for inflation, real income and economic stability.

This led Kaldor and others to argue for some form of protection of competitive manufactures. Against this it has been argued that protection cannot promote export-led growth, since it acts solely on imports (whereas devaluation acts on both sides of the trade account). However, by encouraging import-substitutes, protection can expand the domestic traded goods sector. In terms of the Harrod foreign trade multiplier the means of expansion operate through reducing the propensity to import and thus reducing the leakages from the domestic economy. As Kaldor pointed out in 1951, the objective of protection in an underemployed economy should be to reduce the propensity to import competitive goods, not to reduce the actual volume of imports. If the policy was successful, the rise in domestic incomes should encourage more imports of complementary and subsequently competitive goods.

The key point is not just that a high import propensity may constrain the growth of a domestic economy, but that variations in trade performance in an increasingly integrated world economy may lead to persistent divergences in growth, with success in international trade becoming cumulative as increasing demand for net exports allows countries (or more specifically, the firms and industries within them) to exploit economies of scale and scope, improving their competitiveness and leading to further improvements in their trade performance, while weaker trading nations may fail to maintain balance-of-payments equilibrium at a high level of economic activity, with deflationary policies then pursued in an attempt to maintain external balance.[6] The combined impact of poor trade performance and domestic deflation is likely to lead to a cumulative deterioration in relative economic growth as countries fail to exploit the increasing returns associated with a high level of economic activity.[7] It was these twin processes of virtuous circles of growth and vicious cycles of decline that were clearly identified by, amongst others, Myrdal (1957) and Kaldor (1972). Thus the benefits of trade may not be evenly spread, and the trading system should take account of the initial conditions of its members. What is required is a system with mechanisms that maintain the balanced development of the world economy and allow countries in difficulty some means of adjustment.

Finally on the political economy of trade and trade policy, while the key ideas in what has become the 'new growth theory' were developed by Kaldor in his endogenous growth theory, it is worth reporting Hahn and Matthews' recognition (1994, p. 901)[8] that:

He invented no special functional forms to dress his theory, nor did he think of economies as unfolding along a path determined by a mythical Ramsey maximiser. His inspiration was Allyn Young and, through him, Adam Smith – a different aspect of Smith, needless to say, from that invoked by the vulgar in the 1980s.

The aspect of Adam Smith taken up by Allyn Young (1928) and Kaldor was his analysis of the division of labour being not only determined by, but also itself determining, the size of the market. It is this which allows the development of cumulative causation, with specialisation and learning underpinning increasing returns.[9]

4 Implementing active trade policies

Despite the dominance of the neoclassical paradigm within the economics profession, trading nations have nevertheless tended, historically, to deploy various interventionist trade policies in pursuit of domestic objectives. However, such policies have tended to be *ad hoc*, uncoordinated and dominated by sectional interests. The use of any sort of active trade policy is criticised by Krugman (1994a), although his attack appears rather skewed by his obvious anger at the low esteem in which, in his opinion, the Clinton administration and its economic advisors hold mainstream professional economists.[10] Krugman not only charges this approach with leading to trade frictions, but questions the importance or otherwise of this search for competitiveness:

> The most obvious if least worrisome danger of the growing obsession with competitiveness is that it might lead to a similar misallocation of resources. . . . A much more serious risk is that the obsession with competitiveness will lead to trade conflict, perhaps even to a world war.
> (Krugman, 1994a, p. 41)

Although Krugman cites mainly US authors (and Clinton's pronouncements), it is also true that in Europe the Commission's series of integrationist proposals and measures, from the '1992' process, to the Delors White Paper, through to the Treaty on European Union and the introduction of the single currency, have all been presented as being a necessary response by Europe to the challenge from NAFTA and the Pacific Rim countries in the global battle for competitiveness.[11] The idea that trade flows with the Pacific Rim economies is a significant cause of unemployment in Europe has also been argued in the academic literature, in particular by Wood (1994) although his interpretation has been challenged.[12]

However, Krugman's argument is hardly new and nor, of course, is the alternative view concerning the potential benefits of interventionist trade policy. The problem is that the case for intervention, with perhaps the exception of new trade theory, is less amenable to mathematical economics. Indeed, to illustrate his 1985 BBC Reith Lectures' thesis that there are several key 'common sense' views on economic issues which non-economists tend intuitively to hold but which are in stark contrast to the consensus views of professional economists, David Henderson uses precisely this issue of trade policy as one of his main examples. He argues, for instance, that 'interventionist trade measures, both protectionist and promotional, are largely justified within common sense economics', despite the fact that the 'orthodox economic view', which Henderson takes therefore to be technically correct, 'is that discriminatory trade interventions are generally contrary to the interests of the countries that make use of them'.[13]

In our view, though, it is not enough to see the non-free trade view as being caused by a misunderstanding or ignorance of professional economics. Although neoclassical economics provides internal consistency, it can also distort real world complexities. This is particularly apparent in the analysis of the costs and benefits of interventionist trade policies. Given the dominance of the free trade view, the question has to be posed of why, in face of the conventional wisdom, do nations nevertheless persist in returning to such practices? There are two possible answers, not necessarily mutually exclusive. First, free trade may be in the interests of certain groups within a country, while others may be worse off due to such an arrangement. Second, it is logically possible that free trade is the first-best solution but that it is difficult to enforce in practice because it will always be in the interests of any one country to cheat – a prisoner's dilemma.

Thus, in the context of the orthodox approach, interventionist trade policy reflects sectional interests and uncoordinated policies that are likely to harm the world economy. If we take an alternative Kaldorian view, however, the arguments for intervention are more persuasive and active trade policies may, if suitably constructed and implemented, benefit individual nations and the world economy as a whole.

First, the trade policies appropriate for different countries may differ so that the prisoner's dilemma problem may not arise. As noted above, the expansionary impact of protectionism can increase domestic output and employment. Furthermore, the income-induced increase in imports indicates that such a policy need not be 'beggar thy neighbour'. Thus the result for some countries (and even for the world as a whole) from breaking away (or not moving towards) a world of free trade may be preferable to the free trade position. The UK economy achieved rapid growth from 1932 to 1937 partly due to the stimulus to the economy of protecting domestic manufacturing (Kaldor and Kitson, 1986 and Kitson and Solomou, 1990). As a generalisation, free trade has tended to be favoured by those already in a commanding trade position – a position most usually achieved in the first place with the help of policies to restrict free trade. This last point leads to a further distinction, which is that the degree of interest in free trade may not only differ between countries, but the position held by countries in the league table of free trade supporters will change over time. It used to be said that 'we are all

Keynesians now'. Today it is safely asserted (in this case by John Sutton, the Professor of Economics at the London School of Economics): 'That "history matters" is now obvious to all.'[14]

Second, the effects of free trade versus alternative regimes may well differ between different states of the world economy, for example between periods of economic development on the one hand (Panić, 1990) and, on the other, conditions of recession. Thus, as emphasised by the infant industry argument, protectionism can be an essential tool for promoting the early stages of economic development. Additionally, economies are continuously faced with shocks of an international and national nature that generate unemployment with large social and economic costs, and even a temporary shock may have lasting effects. If policy makers are concerned with minimising such costs then there may be a role for protection to minimise the destruction of human and physical capital by giving industries the necessary time to adjust to new conditions of comparative advantage or to the state of the international business cycle.

5 Regulating the world economy: conditioning factors

The design and scope of active trade policies will be determined by the prevailing international institutional arrangements and the dominant forces shaping the world economy. This section considers such factors and how they will affect policy design and impact.

International trading regimes and institutions

The form of the international trading system may foster or impede economic growth (or both during different periods). Here we consider the impact of three regimes. First, the pre-First World War period, from 1870–1913, the era of the classical Gold Standard. Second, the interwar period which saw the rise of a reconstructed Gold Standard in the 1920s and its subsequent collapse in the 1930s leading to a series of discretionary and uncoordinated trade policies. And third the post-Second World War period which was dominated by the Bretton Woods system until its collapse in 1973 and which has been replaced by a number of attempts at establishing stability in trade and foreign exchange.

The classical pre-First World War Gold Standard survived due to the existence of 'negative' adjustment mechanisms, such as domestic deflation and migration, and the benefits of specific historical conditions, such as the level of international capital flows and the lack of labour resistance to unemployment and underemployment. The interwar Gold Standard was short-lived due to its structural faults. It created a system of asymmetric adjustment which imposed a deflationary burden on the weaker countries and amplified the impact of recessionary forces during the Great Depression. The Bretton Woods system accommodated a number of positive adjustment mechanisms such as capital controls and the widespread use of fiscal policy to regulate domestic demand. Its effectiveness, however, was ultimately undermined by the reluctance to use exchange rate realignments, and by the changing world conditions which undermined the central position of the US in the system. As with the Gold Standard systems, asymmetries developed which led to imbalances in world economic development. Of course, any international monetary system will face changes in global economic conditions; the point is that systems must therefore evolve and incorporate appropriate adjustment mechanisms.

The leading nation in the world economy has shifted during different epochs of international economic development. The pre-First World War era saw Britain, the first industrialised economy, as the dominant economic power. Increasingly, however, its relative position declined – the 'diminished giant' syndrome (Bhagwati and Irwin, 1987) – with the rising economic might of the US and Germany and others as 1914 approached. Figure 3.1 indicates that the UK's share of the output of the world's capitalist countries (measured as the aggregate output of Maddison's 16 capitalist countries) declined from 21.5 per cent in 1870 to 15.3 per cent in 1913 whereas the US share rose from 24.5 per cent to 40.8 per cent over the same period.[15]

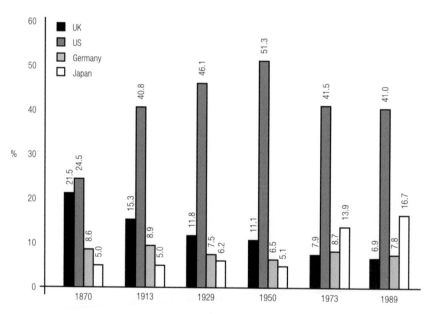

Figure 3.1 GDP shares of 'world' capitalist countries (benchmark years)

Sources: Authors' calculations from Maddison (1991).

Notes
1. 'World' is Maddison's 16 capitalist countries.
2. Data are measured using 1985 US relative prices and adjusted to exclude the impact of boundary changes.

In addition, the UK's share of exports declined from 37.2 per cent in 1870 to 27.0 per cent in 1913 (Figure 3.2).[16] During the same period the output of the US increased rapidly so that by 1913 its output share was more than two and a half times that of the UK. Furthermore, although the UK remained the largest exporter in 1913, its share of total exports was only 8 percentage points greater than that of the US and only 6 percentage points greater than that of Germany.

By 1929 the US share of the capitalist world's GDP was four times that of the UK's and it had overtaken the UK as the world's leading exporter.[17] Britain could not maintain its leading role in the international monetary system; indeed, it has been argued that this, combined with the reluctance of the US to assume leadership, resulted in global instability which exacerbated the depth and duration of the Great Depression (Kindleberger, 1973).[18] What is certainly true is that the post-Second World War 'Golden Age of Capitalism' was underpinned by the strength of the US economy, with the dollar thereby being able to act as the anchor to the international monetary system. As indicated in Figures 3.1 and 3.2, by 1950 the US accounted for over half of GDP, and a third of exports, of the capitalist countries. However, the growth of the world economy and the emergence of other economies, in particular Germany and Japan, was to undermine the US's relative position. By 1973, when the Bretton Woods system of fixed exchange rates collapsed, the US share of output had fallen by 10 percentage points since 1950 and its share of

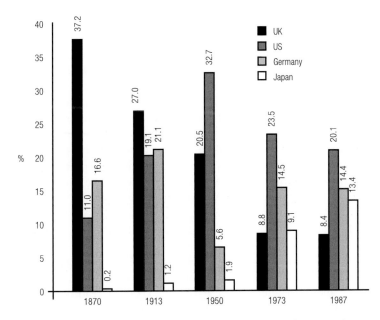

Figure 3.2 Export shares of 'world' capitalist countries (benchmark years)

Sources and notes: As Figure 3.1.

exports had fallen to less than the combined total of Germany and Japan. Figure 3.2 also indicates that the US share of exports has continued to decline since 1973 whereas the Japanese share has increased significantly. (As argued in the previous chapter, the problems faced by the Japanese economy over the course of 1997 and 1998 have not reversed this broad change in relative economic circumstances.)

The requirements of a balanced international monetary system are therefore twofold. First, it must accommodate a series of positive adjustment mechanisms that do not impose domestic deflation, and that allow participating countries to adjust to national-specific conditions. Second, these adjustment mechanisms must reflect the characteristics and dominant forces of the global economy; as such they need to evolve over time. For instance, an exchange rate realignment may be an appropriate mechanism, but its effectiveness will be contingent on the behaviour of exchange rate markets. These markets are now dominated by transactions for speculative rather than trade purposes and, as shown by the ERM debacle in the early 1990s, the volume of these speculative flows alone can force through exchange rate adjustments. This can deprive the monetary authorities of much of their discretion over the choice of exchange rate parity. One response to this has been the policy of 'a quick jump to monetary union' (Eichengreen, 1994). A more appropriate response, we would argue, would be the introduction of capital and exchange controls to counter the threat of speculative attacks; (a variety of such proposals exist – see for example Kelly, 1994, 1995; Eichengreen *et al.*, 1995; Arestis and Sawyer, 1999). At the very least, it is necessary to throw 'some sand' in the wheels of international finance (Tobin, 1978) in order to reconcile international economic stability with some domestic policy autonomy.

Fifty years after the establishment at Bretton Woods of what became the post-Second World War international financial system, the construction today of a new 'Bretton Woods' would thus need to provide the capacity for exchange rate adjustment, exchange controls, the coordination of capital flows and flexibility over the use of fiscal policy. International economic cooperation at present is, however, dominated by concerns with monetary and financial targets, the pursuit of which can impact adversely on the real economies of the participants; this was the experience of the Gold Standard regimes and, more recently, the ERM.

Globalisation

The 'globalisation' thesis can be interpreted as implying that it is no longer necessary for individual countries to pursue national trade policies (on which, see Chapter 2 above). Trade deficits, it is argued, can be readily financed by global financial markets. And since trade imbalances are the result of individuals' decisions to save or dis-save, such imbalances will in time be self correcting.[19] Porter (1994) paraphrases the globalisation thesis as follows:

In a world of global competition, it is argued, location is no longer relevant. Geography and political boundaries have been transcended. The firm, in particular, can shed its locational identity or dependence entirely.

(p. 35)

There have already been a number of critiques of such arguments, as well as of the other variants of the globalisation literature. In addition to the article by Porter see, for example, Costello *et al.* (1989) Chapter 2, Hirst and Thompson (1992), Martin (1994), Kozul-Wright (1995), Michie (1995) and Archibugi and Michie (1995a, 1995b). The important point for the present discussion is that the form taken by the processes described by some as 'globalisation' has been determined by the politics of the 1980s and 1990s and the balance of class forces both within the advanced capitalist economies and on a global scale.[20] Hence its characterisation as 'global neoclassicism' (Schor, 1992, p. 4).[21] This has been accompanied by a positing of national economic policy objectives as being to seek 'stability' where this is interpreted, perversely, as stability of policy instruments – interest rates, exchange rates, fiscal balances and so on – despite the fact that stability in these will provoke or exacerbate instability in real economic variables. We would argue that it is rather these real economic variables, of growth, employment and the like, which should be stabilised through the active use of economic instruments including where appropriate trade policy.

Regionalisation

Empirical evidence provides some indication that regionalisation has increased in the 1980s and 1990s (the issue is considered more fully in Chapter 4). The evidence, however, is not conclusive and suggests that the pace of change has varied across the postwar period and within blocs. In part this may reflect the conflicting impact of the increasing globalisation of the world economy on regionalisation. On the one hand, regional arrangements develop as both a defensive and aggressive response to intensified international competition. On the other hand, globalisation can counteract, or at least constrain, underlying trends towards regionalisation as it encourages extra-bloc trade. Despite the uneven and erratic process of regionalisation it is undoubtedly true that the world economy of today is dominated by three blocs, the policies of which will define the future path of the world trading system.

6 Feasible policies

The preferred policy framework would encompass a cooperative system which would allow countries to adopt active trade policies, deploy the coordinated use of fiscal and monetary policies and enable the effective redistribution of resources to regions and countries experiencing difficulties.[23]

First, on active trade policies, the aim would be to allow balance of payments constrained economies to alleviate such constraints and hence enable the expansion of domestic demand. By this route policies which act to reduce import *propensities*, if successful, may create the conditions for a sustainable increase in import *levels*. A rise in domestic incomes would encourage more imports of complementary, and subsequently competitive, goods. By allowing countries to develop competitive advantages, rather than relying on free trade to take advantage of their comparative advantages (thereby locking countries into these), the level of economic activity can be enhanced. Thus Japan's import levels are far higher today, after decades of various restrictions on imports, than might have been expected had a free trade policy been followed after the Second World War to take advantage of the comparative advantage of rice-growing and the like.[24]

Second, the coordinated use of fiscal and monetary policies would be required to avoid expansionary policies in individual countries leading to undue pressure on exchange rates, interest rates and inflation rates.[25] The increased integration of the world economy[26] and the dominance of speculative capital flows in foreign exchange markets limit the potential benefits, and create risks of unmanageable instability, of adopting 'Keynesianism in one country'.

Third, effective redistribution is required if the 'winners' in any trading arrangements are not to undermine their own position by allowing trade imbalances to exacerbate uneven development between economies. This danger will be exacerbated in particular within the EU with monetary union proceeding without fiscal policy also being transferred to an EU level, which would enable the normal operation of fiscal transfers to occur (for an analysis of which see Michie, 1993). Additionally, such fiscal transfers will have to be significantly increased as monetary union will effectively remove other means (interest rates, exchange rates, etc.) of dealing with national economic difficulties. Even at a global level, and in the absence of monetary union, coordinated policy action would need to allow for some system of redistribution, even if only via capital flows.[27]

Fourth, improved regulation of financial institutions. The dangers of unfettered and ill-informed speculative activities by many financial institutions has been illustrated in the recent crises in Asia and elsewhere. A new framework will require better information, tightening up the capital backing required by banks and security houses, and greater international coordination of regulating functions. (On the detail of such a new framework of global regulation see Robinson College Working Group, 1999.)

The possibility of the above scenario developing internationally in either the short or medium term appears, however, to be unlikely. First, the level of cooperation required would be significant, the 'rules of the game' would be complex and the commitment to a large transfer of resources between countries (as opposed to within countries) would face political resistance. Second, there is no longer any one nation with the economic and political power to take centre stage. The lead must come from the three dominant trading blocs. This itself presents additional difficulties as there is not only potential conflict amongst the three main players but those countries outside the main blocs may also be disadvantaged. And third, institutional reform would also be required, the most important of which would be to stop the International Monetary Fund (IMF) from pedalling the myths of monetarism and *laissez faire* economics as being the only effective means of economic management. (On which, see the various contributions to Michie and Grieve Smith, 1999, and in particular those of Singh, Grabel, Palley, and Braunstein and Epstein.)

In the absence of a global growth strategy the alternatives are to adopt expansionary policies at the regional or national level. The history of the 1930s indicates that these may be appropriate responses to a lack of coordination at the world level (Kitson and Solomou, 1991). As the experience of Maastricht and the ERM testify, though, regional blocs do not necessarily provide higher growth; outcomes depend on the objectives, implementation and coordination of macroeconomic policy. While there have been repeated exhortations for a coordinated European growth strategy over the past ten years and more, much of the coordinated action has instead been deflationary.

In the absence of expansionary regional initiatives, countries may have little option but to pursue independent growth strategies. Even at this level however, prospects will be tempered by the dominant forces in the world economy. Policies aimed at regulating product and labour markets to safeguard the interests of both consumers and workers could lead to attempts to relocate production by multinationals, hence the calls for common labour standards (on which see Sengenberger and Wilkinson, 1995). Demand management policies aimed at increasing output and employment could also lead to capital flight and a free-falling exchange rate. However, it needs to be remembered that this dual process may to some extent sort itself out: as the exchange rate falls, it makes capital flight increasingly costly to those who continue to sell the currency. In addition, it is not clear how long competitor countries would allow one economy to enjoy the massive gain in competitiveness which a hugely devalued currency would provide.

While the limits which global economic pressures place on national policies have increased, this does not undermine the case for national initiatives – indeed, it may imply that the optimal level of intervention, to expand demand and regulate capital and product markets, is higher. Additionally, and of key importance in considering the appropriateness of national versus international action, is the role that national policies may play in breaking the log-jam and encouraging action from others, whether by agreement or imitation. The Bretton Woods system, a major contributor to the 'Golden Age', emerged from the experience of the uncoordinated trade policy regime of the 1930s. If active trade policies today were to allow one or more countries to begin such a process, the end result could well be a higher level not only of world economic activity but also of world trade itself.

7 Conclusion

Currently the bulk of international trade theory is of the conventional neo-classical sort. This approach almost invariably indicates the superiority of free trade.[28] This result is derived from the misleading assumptions embedded in neoclassical theory. A more appropriate perspective is to accept that economic conditions vary amongst countries and across time. This suggests that the approach to trade policy should be more flexible than is allowed for in the free trade paradigm. Policy instruments need to be formulated in the context of prevailing economic conditions. Thus, governments should beware of the indiscriminate liberalisation of trade and international monetary arrangements.

4 Trade and growth

A historical perspective

There has developed a growing realisation that stability of income and employment calls for policies operating not merely on prices and the credit base but on the volume of effective demand; and this affords a new hope for stability on a wider front. While the synchronisation of national policies required under the gold standard conflicted at times with the demands of internal stability and was for this very reason gradually abandoned, a synchronisation of policies aimed at sustaining and steadying effective demand in the various countries would promote both internal stability and stability of exchange rates at the same time.

Ragnar Nurkse (League of Nations, 1944)

1 Introduction

The 'hope for stability' expressed fifty years ago by Ragnar Nurkse was central to the international monetary system conceived at Bretton Woods in 1944.[1] As discussed in Chapters 2 and 3 above, the collapse of the Bretton Woods system of fixed exchange rates in 1973 ushered in an era of global economic instability. This chapter raises in its concluding section some of the options for an appropriate policy response, although these are dealt with in more detail in other chapters. The starting point of any such discussion must, however, be a recognition that there are many new and unique features to the present world economic and political scene, without historic precedence. At the same time, however, there are lessons that can be drawn regarding the key issues of economic rivalry, dominance, leadership and blocs; of regionalism; of free trade and protectionism; and of currency stability.

The history of world capitalism has been one of dominant powers in relative economic decline being challenged by the growing economic – and, in the past, military – strength of newly emerging powers with growing world market shares and ambitions. This has led to leadership or dominance passing from one country (the UK) to another (the US) but not without an inevitable interregnum with no dominant power able to underpin a world monetary and trade system. The interwar period was one such interregnum and in many ways the new millennium is ushering in another. It is from this historical context that the chapter attempts to give an account of how we have arrived at the controlled chaos that characterises the world economy today.

The principle aims of this chapter are threefold. First, to document the relationship between the growth of world trade and world output since 1870. Second, to evaluate the effectiveness of alternative international monetary regimes. And third, to consider the trends in world trade and power that will shape the future path of the world economy and any attempts to foster global economic cooperation in the twenty-first century. These issues are considered sequentially in the following sections. Section 2 presents some of the mechanisms that link trade and growth. Section 3 presents some comparative statistics on the pre-First World War, the interwar, and the post-Second World War periods. Section 4 considers the role played by the differing trade policy regimes across these periods. One of the main issues which will shape the future of the world economy – 'regionalism' – is considered in Section 5. Section 6 considers the current state of the world economy and Section 7 evaluates what lessons might be drawn regarding future policy and institutional arrangements.

2 Trade and growth: the mechanisms

The postwar 'Golden Age of Capitalism' was founded on a stable international monetary system which helped ensure a rapid growth of trade and output. The benefits of international trade are well known and frequently cited. First, trade leads to specialisation, improving the allocation of resources. Second, trade, as an important and increasing component of demand, can raise output through export-led growth.

The potential impacts of increased trade are, however, not universally positive. Increased dependence on trade can make countries more vulnerable in general to external shocks – shocks which may be initiated by national or international factors but whose impact is transmitted through trade. More specifically, the distributional impact of exchange rate movements increases as economies become more open on capital and current account, with any given exchange rate movement causing a greater redistribution of income within the domestic economy.[2] Additionally, increased international integration may constrain the growth and weaken the economic structure of some trading nations. Whereas exports are an injection into the foreign trade multiplier, imports are a leakage. Thus, a high dependence on imports – a high import propensity – may constrain the growth of a domestic economy.

3 Trade and growth: some evidence

In this section we consider the growth of world trade and output in three periods. First, the pre-First World War period, from 1870–1913, the era of the classical Gold Standard. Second, the interwar period which saw the rise of a reconstructed Gold Standard in the 1920s and its subsequent collapse in the

1930s leading to a series of discretionary and uncoordinated trade policies. And third the post-Second World War period which was dominated by the Bretton Woods system until its collapse in 1973 and which has been replaced by a number of attempts at establishing stability in trade and foreign exchange.

Pre-1913

During the 1870 to 1913 period there was an almost continual increase in world trade and world output. As shown in Table 4.1 world trade increased by an average of 3.5 per cent per annum whereas world output increased by an average of 2.7 per cent per annum (see also Chapter 2, Figure 2.1). There were cyclical variations in trade[3] and output, and significant differences in national growth rates (see Solomou, 1988), but only in four years did world trade decline (1885, 1892, 1900 and 1908) and only in three years did world output decline (1876, 1893 and 1908).

The interdependence between world trade and growth is indicated by the high positive correlation between the two variables. Evidence on the volatility of the growth rates of output and trade is presented in Table 4.2 which gives figures on absolute dispersion (the standard deviation) and relative dispersion (the coefficient of variation). The long-term perspective suggests that trade growth during this period was less volatile than during the disrupted period of the 1930s and the post-Bretton Woods period but was relatively more volatile than during the Bretton Woods period itself. Similarly, output growth was less volatile than during the turbulent 1930s but was more volatile than during the entire post-Second World War period, including post-1973.[4]

Table 4.1 Growth of world output and world trade 1870–1999 (annual % growth rates, calculated peak to peak)

	Output	Trade
Pre-First World War 1870–1913	2.7	3.5
Interwar 1913–37	1.8	1.3
1913–29	2.3	2.2
1929–37	0.8	−0.4
Postwar 1950–99	3.9	5.8
1950–73	4.7	7.2
1973–90	2.8	3.9
1990–99	3.0	6.2

Sources: Authors' calculations from IMF (1998), Lewis (1981), Maddison (1962), and Wells (1993a).

Note
Including IMF projections for 1998 and 1999

Table 4.2 The growth and volatility of world output and world trade, 1870–1999

	Output			Trade		
	Mean average growth rate (%)	Standard deviation (%)	Coefficient of variation	Mean average growth rate (%)	Standard deviation (%)	Coefficient of variation
Pre-First World War 1870–1913	2.8	2.1	0.75	3.6	2.5	0.71
Interwar 1924–37	2.1	4.8	2.26	2.2	7.5	3.48
1924–29	3.7	0.8	0.22	5.7	2.2	0.39
1929–37	1.3	5.9	4.53	0.5	8.5	16.65
Postwar 1950–99	3.9	1.8	0.45	5.9	4.6	0.78
1950–73	4.7	1.6	0.34	7.5	4.2	0.56
1973–90	3.1	1.6	0.53	4.5	4.9	1.09
1990–99	3.0	0.8	0.27	6.2	2.3	0.37

Sources: As Table 4.1.

The interwar period

Discontinuities in growth and trade characterise the interwar period, with the relative stability of the 1920s followed by the turbulence of the 1930s. As shown in Table 4.1, during the 1913–29 period world trade grew at an average annual rate of 1.3 per cent, whereas output grew at an average annual rate of 1.8 per cent. Much of this slow growth can be explained by the disruptions and dislocations of the First World War. The international trading system was in considerable disarray and only recovered slowly; by 1924 the volume of world trade was only 7 per cent above the 1913 level. From 1924 onwards output and trade grew at a faster rate and experienced less volatility than in the pre-1913 period.

During the 1930s, or more precisely from 1929, the world economy suffered severe disruptions. The Great Depression of 1929–32 was the most severe depression in the world economy since the Industrial Revolution began. During these three years world trade collapsed at an average annual rate of 9.9 per cent and world output declined at an average annual rate of 6.2 per cent. As shown in Figure 4.1, the disintegration of the world trading system was reflected in a movement towards a more closed world economy, a

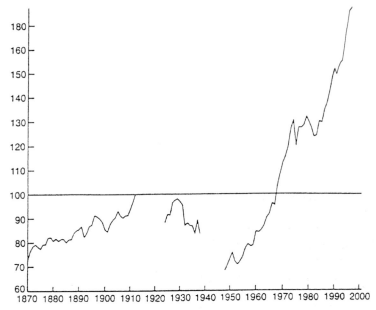

Figure 4.1 Index of the trade orientation ('openness') of the world economy, 1870–1999 (1913 = 100)

Sources: See Table 4.1.

Note
A rise in the index indicates that the world economy is becoming more open; a fall in the index indicates that the world economy is becoming more closed.

reversal of the 1920s trend towards increased openness. From 1932 there was a world recovery, albeit one with large inter-country variations. During the period 1932–37, world output grew at an average annual rate of 5.2 per cent and world trade at 5.8 per cent, although this failed to return trade to its 1929 level. For the 1919–37 period as a whole, as shown in Tables 4.1 and 4.2, growth of output and trade was very slow and, as expected given the experience of the Great Depression, highly volatile.

Post-Second World War

The postwar period is described, in terms comparable to the above discussion of the two previous periods, in Chapter 2 above. As described there, this was an era of increased international integration. This integration promoted openness despite the growing contribution of non-tradable activity to domestic output in advanced economies.[5] As shown in Table 4.2, trade and output were less volatile during this period than during any other period apart from the late 1920s. Moreover, comparison with the 1920s is not strictly appropriate as the Bretton Woods period was significantly longer – the stability of the system over 23 years being added testimony to its success.

The collapse of the Bretton Woods system disrupted this growing openness of the world economy. As shown in Figure 4.1 the post-Second World War trend towards a more open world economy was halted from the mid-1970s and only resumed from the mid-1980s.

4 Trade and growth: the role of trade policy regimes

Pre-1913

The classical Gold Standard formed the foundation of the international trading system in the pre-1913 period. From 1880, the four major industrial countries – Britain, France, Germany and the US – belonged to what was effectively a fractional reserve gold coin standard.[6] Under this system, notes and coins issued by government and commercial banks circulated alongside, and were convertible upon demand into gold coins. For many economists the growth of trade and output in the world economy can be attributed to the successful operation of the pre-1913 Gold Standard. It is argued that it was a system that provided stability and an automatic adjustment mechanism, via gold flows, to correct payment imbalances. For some, the main issue concerning the effectiveness of the classical Gold Standard is simply which monetarist adjustment mechanism it supposedly embodied, the Humeian price-specie-flow mechanism or its close cousin the monetary approach to the balance of payments.[7]

Others, however, have questioned the success of the system. First, the system did not actually operate according to the 'rules of the game' commonly supposed. Central banks, rather than allowing gold flows to adjust their domestic money supplies, intervened either by varying their discount rates or by expanding domestic credit (Bordo, 1992).[8] Second, the operation of the system depended not on gold flows but on a series of other adjustment mechanisms, such as deflation, migration, long-term capital flows and protectionism (Panić, 1992). The system did not provide an adjustment mechanism that ensured the attainment of internal and external balance. Any shock, domestic or international, which caused a deterioration in the balance of payments, required a tightening of monetary policy to maintain the gold parity. The impact of such a deflationary path is likely to have both price and quantity effects, the composition of which will depend on the structure of, and underlying conditions in, the domestic economy.[9]

The deflationary mechanism inherent in the classical Gold Standard depressed employment but widespread unemployment was prevented by migration. During the 1880s, 5 per cent of the British population emigrated and after Austria-Hungary joined the system in the early 1890s, 6.5 per cent of its population fled before 1910. Furthermore, the system was sustained by large international capital flows which financed the development of the weaker countries. Within the orthodox theoretical framework, the movement of capital is explained by interest rate differentials, which themselves reflect gold flows. A more realistic approach would have to also embrace the impact of underconsumption, capital market biases, government policies,[10] the co-movement of capital and population flows and the role of Empire(s) and the desire to obtain cheap food and raw materials. The prevailing economic, structural and institutional conditions therefore encouraged a transfer of resources from richer to weaker countries – a transfer that helped accommodate, at least in the medium term, the flaws of the Gold Standard system.

An additional adjustment mechanism was protectionism. During the nineteenth century there had been a movement, albeit erratic, towards free trade. Britain led the way with the repeal of the Corn Laws in 1846 and the Anglo-French commercial treaty in 1860. During the late 1870s, contemporaneous with the emergence of the Gold Standard, this trend was reversed and there was a shift to increased protectionism and in particular the widespread use of tariffs. In the main, this shift was a response to specific industrial factors. In the case of the protection of European agriculture it was a defensive response to cheap grain imports from North America and Russia. For manufacturing it was often a case of protecting young, infant industries. In Germany, for example, throughout the 1880s large parts of heavy industry, especially iron and steel, pushed for tariff barriers in order to compete with established British industries (Kitson, 1992). During the late nineteenth century the cumulative impact of tariff protection as an industrial policy was to provide domestic economies – that did not have recourse to nominal exchange rate realignment – with an alternative tool of external adjustment.

The picture often presented of the classical Gold Standard era is of a free-trade, low-inflation world. A sort of monetarist nirvana. In reality, the stability of the international system was founded on deflation in weaker countries and enforced migration. Limiting the adverse impacts of the system required resort to protectionism and the transfer of savings from the richer countries. Moreover, this transfer of resources was not the result of some automatic mechanism causing gold flows but resulted rather from the specific historical circumstances of the time.

The interwar period

Following the end of the First World War, the world economy was in considerable disarray. Initially the international trading and payments system was dominated by flexible exchange rates but from the mid-1920s the cornerstone of international economic management was a reconstructed form of the Gold Standard, the operation of which encouraged beggar-my-neighbour deflation and which, after 1929, became a vehicle for transmitting recession. It was replaced by the use of independent and uncoordinated trade policies including managed exchange rates and various forms of protectionism.

The failures of the interwar Gold Standard were more apparent than had been those of its pre-1913 predecessor. The earlier variant survived, despite its failings, because it accommodated a number of adjustment mechanisms to alleviate persistent trade imbalances, such as migration of labour and capital flows, and despite its deflationary bias and adverse effects on employment and wages, was not seriously challenged by organised labour. During the interwar period, however, there was not only an increasing political influence of organised labour but also a growing awareness of the impact of exchange rates – or more accurately of the monetary policies that accompanied them – on employment (Eichengreen, 1992).

As with the classical version, the success of the interwar Gold Standard depended on nominal convergence. However, its actual effect was to depress real variables such as output and employment and to undermine the capacity of individual governments to deal with domestic economic problems. As the main trading nations entered the exchange rate system with different domestic economic conditions it was apparent that the efficacy of the adjustment process would be central to the regime's impact. The option of adjusting the nominal exchange rate was effectively precluded. As the adjustment of real exchange rates was slow and erratic, only two adjustment mechanisms remained: first, changes in the level of demand, with deflation in deficit countries and reflation in surplus countries; and second, as in the classical Gold Standard, the financing of trade deficits by capital flows from countries with a balance of payments surplus.

Despite large capital exports from the US during the 1920s, the ultimate burden of adjustment was borne by domestic deflation. The surplus countries were reluctant to reflate. The classical adjustment mechanism assumed that gold flows would provide the means of changing the level of demand, with the impact falling on prices. As noted above, price adjustment was slow; in addition, the reflationary impact of gold flows into France and the US was negated by domestic monetary policy. Both countries, which by the late 1920s had accumulated 60 per cent of total world gold reserves, deliberately prevented these reserves from boosting their domestic money supplies. American policy makers were increasingly concerned with curbing stock market speculation whereas the French were wary of inflation. The prioritisation of domestic economic issues transmitted deflation abroad. Low import demand, particularly in America, led to widening balance of payments deficits in many of the key European economies.

The growth of world trade was therefore limited by the domestic policies of the surplus countries. Whereas these nations could choose whether to reflate or to pursue other domestic policy concerns, deficit countries had no such options. The entire burden of adjustment fell on them – they could either deflate to eradicate balance of payments deficits or they could borrow to fund them. The effective approach of the UK economy was the former and Germany the latter.

Deflation could be achieved either through allowing reserves to flow out, depressing the money supply and domestic expenditure – the classical mechanism – or by policies that directly affected the components of demand. In Britain it was interest rates that acted as the key deflationary tool. From 1923 there was a trend rise in the Bank of England's discount rate as the authorities adopted policies consistent with the return and maintenance of the exchange rate to the prewar parity. At the same time the general trend of other central banks' discount rates was downward (Eichengreen, 1991). The deflationary impact of the Bank of England's policy helped to keep the UK balance of payments in surplus and prevented the loss of gold.[11] The Bank of England also deployed gold market and foreign exchange operations to maintain its stock of international reserves (Moggridge, 1972). The impact on the real economy was to slow the growth rate, with the economy therefore failing to reap its growth potential (Kitson and Solomou, 1990). Despite the level of GDP in 1924 being significantly below what it had been in 1913, the rate of growth of the British economy from 1924 was significantly below the world average.[12] Similarly, unemployment remained persistently high, averaging just under 8 per cent over the 1924–29 period (Feinstein, 1972).

Unlike Britain, Germany maintained a persistent balance of payments deficit throughout the 1920s. Along with reparations, this deficit had to be financed and Germany became heavily reliant on foreign loans, particularly from the US. Although initially able to attract sizeable capital inflows, the rising debt burden undermined creditworthiness. Germany became increasingly reliant on short-term funds and by 1931 had accumulated net debts equivalent to 25 per cent of national income (Kitson, 1992). The subsequent concern about the German economy and the collapse of American lending abroad from 1928 led to capital flight, the loss of reserves, a credit squeeze and the raising of interest rates. Germany had been able to cope with its balance of payments constraint in the short term by borrowing; ultimately, however this only postponed the requirement to deflate.

Thus the deflationary bias of the Gold Standard not only failed to deal with the structural problems of constrained countries, it accentuated them. Countries which had entered the system with major structural problems, left the system weakened as a result of having had to accommodate the burden of adjustment by deflating their domestic economies. This not only lowered growth and raised unemployment, it also hampered long-run competitiveness. The dampening of domestic demand reduced the benefits of mass production and the exploitation of scale economies. Deflation to maintain external equilibrium thus raised unit costs, generating a further loss of competitiveness and world market share. Such a process of cumulative causation led the constrained countries to suffer a vicious cycle of stagnation. Locked into a fixed exchange rate system there were few policy options to reverse the process.

The operation of the Gold Standard thus hampered world growth in the 1920s; its shortcomings were also evident with the onset of the Great Depression, the severity of which can certainly be attributed to the operation of the Gold Standard; (see Chapter 5). The interwar Gold Standard placed a deflationary burden on deficit countries, and thus on the world economy as a whole, a burden which had persistent effects on productive capacity. The system failed to provide adjustment mechanisms to rectify payments imbalances which did not involve the loss of output and rising unemployment. Furthermore, the system restricted the policy options open to its members, limiting their ability to deal with changing domestic economic conditions or problems.

An analysis of inter-country variations in economic growth indicates that the pace of recovery during the 1930s was significantly dependent on countries untying themselves from the strictures of the Gold Standard and adopting independent expansionist policies. Exchange rate regime was not the only factor; some countries also reaped the advantages of increased protectionism and fiscal expansion. What is apparent, however, is that the cooperative regime failed and uncoordinated policies were a vast improvement. This is not the same as saying that coordination *per se* is ineffective. What was ineffective, however, was a coordinated regime which depended for its success on nominal convergence, but which led to adverse impacts on the real economies of some of the participants.

Post-Second World War

The design of the international trading regime established after the Second World War was formulated in the context of the perceived failings of the interwar system: the disintegration of world trade in the early 1930s and the subsequent development of uncoordinated trade policies. The system took its name from the conference held in 1944 at Bretton Woods, New Hampshire, which put into place the rules that would regulate the international monetary and trading system in the postwar world. The characteristics of the system were subject to dispute between the British delegation led by Keynes and the American delegation led by White, with Keynes arguing unsuccessfully that the system should put the onus on surplus countries to reflate rather than deficit countries to deflate. Nevertheless, the Bretton Woods era was, for a number of reasons, one of rapid economic growth, as has been extensively analysed elsewhere (see in particular Glyn *et al.*, 1990; Armstrong, Glyn and Harrison, 1991).

Within the Bretton Woods system every country had to peg its currency to gold or the US dollar (which, in turn, was pegged to gold). Before it could change its exchange rate a country would have to show that it faced 'fundamental disequilibrium'. This term lacked adequate definition although in effect it was interpreted as that condition where the exchange rate parity was inconsistent with acceptable levels of unemployment or inflation. There was a resistance to make general exchange rate realignments (one notable exception was the realignments made in 1949 following the sterling devaluation). Furthermore, the exchange rate adjustments that were made tended to be devaluations by deficit countries rather than revaluations by surplus countries. As with its Gold Standard predecessors, the Bretton Woods system did not function symmetrically; the burden of adjustment was borne by the weaker deficit countries, with the stronger countries accumulating increased reserves.

Despite its asymmetry, the Bretton Woods system was relatively successful because it accommodated a number of adjustment mechanisms and was anchored by US monetary hegemony.[13] Two of the principal adjustment mechanisms, which complemented each other, were first, the discretionary use of domestic monetary and fiscal policy and second, the use of capital controls. The case for capital controls had been made by Keynes, prior to the agreement at Bretton Woods:

> It is not merely a question of curbing exchange speculations and movements of hot money, or even of avoiding flights of capital due to political motives; though all this is necessary to control. The need, in my judgement, is more fundamental. Unless the aggregate of the new investments which individuals are free to make overseas is kept within the amount which our favourable trade balance is capable of looking after, we lose control over the domestic rate of interest.
> (Keynes, 1943, p. 275; quoted in Pivetti, 1993.)

The stability of Bretton Woods was undermined, though, by the relative decline of the US (evaluated in Section 6 below) and the increasing inconsistency between US domestic policies and the needs of the world economy. For most of the life of the Bretton Woods system US monetary and fiscal policies were directed at domestic targets (Kenen, 1992); there are parallels here with the problems faced within the European Exchange Rate Mechanism, with German monetary policy dictated by domestic rather than European needs. Furthermore, the need for the US to run balance of payments deficits to supply reserves to the rest of world such that its dollar liabilities exceeded its gold stock undermined the viability of the system (Triffin, 1960). A series of exchange rate crises in the early 1970s signalled the demise of the system, the end coming in early 1973 with the floating of the Yen and the currencies of the six members of the European Community.

The collapse of Bretton Woods was followed by floating exchange rates, albeit with various attempts at reintroducing a degree of exchange rate stability. The impact of floating exchange rates in practice has been to increase uncertainty and misalignments ('overshooting') in foreign exchange markets. The challenge for the new millennium will be to design a new framework for international economic stability which does not impose deflationary adjustment mechanisms on participating countries.

5 Regionalism and world trade

Regionalism can perhaps best be defined in terms of preferential regional trade agreements (RTAs) amongst groups of countries, or trade within broadly defined geographic regions such as Europe and North America. Regionalisation accelerated in the world economy in two periods; first in the 1930s and then again in the 1980s. During the 1930s the chaos in world markets led to an increased use of discriminatory trade policies and the *de facto* formation of trading blocs. These blocs, as indicated in Table 4.3, were usually centred on a dominant country. For countries such as the UK, The Netherlands and Italy, a growing proportion of trade during the period was conducted with their respective Empires (Kitson and Solomou 1991 and 1995). Furthermore, currency blocs also grew in importance as countries sought exchange rate stability and made extensive use of exchange rate agreements and exchange controls (particularly Nazi Germany – see Kitson 1992). However, despite the formation of trading blocs – or perhaps because of it, due to the dispersed location of Empires and Colonies – trade did not actually become regionalised on a geographical basis; the world did not see the development of 'natural' trading blocs. Table 4.4 shows the direction of merchandise trade in eight regions in 1928 and 1938. For most of the regions there was no increase in intra-bloc trade as a share of total trade, the one exception being Latin America.[14]

The first post-Second World War wave of regionalism was from the mid-1950s with the establishment of Regional Trade Agreements (RTAs) in the form of the original European Economic Community (EEC) and the European Free Trade Area (EFTA). The 1980s saw pressure for the formation of RTAs led by the US which negotiated a series of agreements culminating in the formation of the North American Free trade Area (NAFTA).[15] It is too early to discern the impact of the NAFTA agreement on intra-bloc trade. The

Table 4.3 The emergence of blocs in the 1930s

Country	Economic bloc	Imports from 'Economic bloc' as a % of country's total imports		Exports to 'Economic bloc' as a % of country's total exports	
		1929	1938	1929	1938
United Kingdom	British Commonwealth, colonies, protectorates	30	42	44	50
	Other countries of the 'sterling bloc'[1]	12	13	7	12
France	French colonies, protectorates and mandated territories	12	27	19	27.5
Belgium	Belgian Congo	4	8	3	2
The Netherlands	The Netherlands overseas territories	5.5	9	9	11
Italy	Italian colonies and Ethiopia	0.5	2	2	23
Portugal	Portuguese overseas territories	8	10	13	12
Japan	Korea, Formosa, Kwantung, Manchuria	20	41	24	55
Germany	Eastern Europe[2]	4.5	12	5	13
	Latin America	12	16	8	11.5

Source: League of Nations (1939), p. 186.
Notes
1 Sweden, Norway, Finland, Denmark, Egypt, Estonia, Latvia, Portugal, Thailand and Iraq.
2 Bulgaria, Greece, Hungary, Rumania, Turkey and Yugoslavia.

Table 4.4 Direction of merchandise trade in 1928 and 1938 (% shares, eight geographical regions)

	Africa		North America		Latin America		Asia		USSR		Continental		Non-Continental		Oceania	
	1928	1938	1928	1938	1928	1938	1928	1938	1928	1938	1928	1938	1928	1938	1928	1938
Imports from																
Africa	**7**	6	2	2	–	–	1	2	4	–	6	8	6	6	1	–
North America	10	12	**26**	**27**	38	34	16	19	21	33	14	11	22	22	27	22
Latin America	2	2	21	20	**13**	**18**	–	1	8	–	9	9	12	11	–	–
Asia	9	11	24	22	3	4	**46**	**45**	22	22	8	8	9	12	13	17
USSR	–	–	–	1	–	–	2	1	–	**4**	2	1	2	2	–	–
Continent (Europe)	43	44	17	19	30	31	15	17	39	30	**51**	**52**	35	30	11	10
Non-Cont (Europe)	28	25	8	8	16	13	18	13	2	11	8	9	**7**	**5**	43	43
Oceania	1	–	2	1	–	–	2	2	4	–	2	2	7	12	**5**	**8**
Total	100	100	100	100	100	100	100	100	100	100	100	100	100	100	100	100
Exports to																
Africa	**8**	**8**	2	3	1	1	3	5	–	–	6	7	10	15	2	–
North America	8	5	**23**	**20**	35	27	23	17	5	8	7	6	11	9	9	4
Latin America	–	–	14	15	**9**	**18**	1	1	–	–	6	6	10	9	–	–
Asia	3	5	11	13	–	1	**41**	**42**	19	15	6	7	21	16	12	9
USSR	2	–	1	2	–	–	2	1	–	–	1	1	1	1	1	–
Continent (Europe)	54	59	27	21	35	33	19	18	56	46	**58**	**57**	27	29	33	17
Non-Cont (Europe)	25	23	19	23	20	20	9	13	20	31	15	15	**10**	**9**	38	62
Oceania	–	–	3	3	–	–	2	3	–	–	1	1	10	12	**5**	**8**
Total	100	100	100	100	100	100	100	100	100	100	100	100	100	100	100	100

Source: League of Nations (1942).

Note
Figures in bold are the share of intra-regional trade in total trade.

evidence for the European Community (or as now called, depending on the context, the European Union), however, does show a rise in intra-bloc trade since 1960 although most of the increases occurred in the period up to 1973 with a later spurt from the mid-1980s (Lloyd, 1992).[16] The intra-bloc share of the EFTA members (the original six members) showed a moderate increase up to the mid-1970s, followed by a decline of a similar magnitude.

An alternative measure of regionalisation is the regional share of world trade. Figure 4.2 shows the shares of world imports of the three principal RTA blocs (with membership as at the time) since 1960. The combined shares of the European Community and EFTA have not increased significantly over the period (the total for all three regions jumps upwards in 1989 with the formation of the Canada–US free trade agreement). The share of the EC/EU has increased but this reflects expansions of membership.

In addition to the explicit role of RTAs, regionalism can occur through the increased *geographic* concentration of trade. Attention has been focused on the development of a tripolar world economy dominated by North America, Europe and the Pacific rim. There have been contrasting trends in intra-bloc trade since 1960 in these three areas: increasing in Europe and Asia but falling in North America since 1969.[17] Figure 4.3 shows the share of world imports of the three poles. It illustrates their dominance – they account for nearly four-fifths of world imports in 1989 – although it is noticeable that this dominance dates at least from the start of the period. The share of Europe has averaged over 40 per cent, although there was a fall from the mid-1970s until the mid-1980s. The share of North America has been relatively stable at

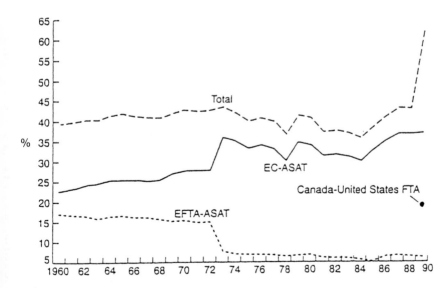

Figure 4.2 Shares of world imports of the three leading regional trade agreement blocs, 1960–90 (%)

Source: Lloyd (1992).

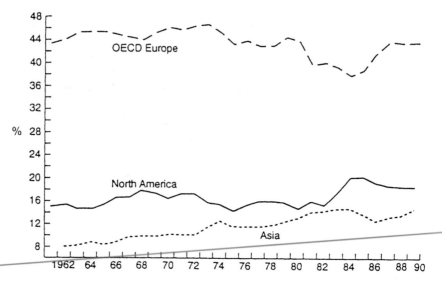

Figure 4.3 Shares of world imports of the three leading geographical trading blocs, 1960–90 (%)

Source: Lloyd (1992).

around 16 per cent, although there was an increase in the early 1980s. The most significant change has been the rapid growth of the Asian share of world imports, almost doubling over the period.

The evidence provides some indication that both RTAs and the development of geographical blocs has led to an increase in regionalism. The evidence, however, is not conclusive and suggests that the pace of change has varied across the postwar period and within blocs. In part this may reflect the conflicting impact of the increasing globalisation of the world economy on regionalisation. On the one hand, regional arrangements develop as both a defensive and aggressive response to intensified international competition. On the other hand, globalisation can counteract, or at least constrain, underlying trends towards regionalisation as it encourages extra-bloc trade. Despite the uneven and erratic process of regionalisation it is undoubtedly true that the world economy of today is dominated by three blocs: Figure 4.4, which indicates the distribution of world income in 1990, shows Europe, the US and Japan as the three clear concentrations. Although Japan accounts for a lower share of world income than either the EU or the US, Japan's GDP was 19 per cent higher than the EU average in 1990 (Figure 4.5), and with a faster growth rate than in either the US or the EU (Figure 4.6). Although Japanese growth has since stalled the picture remains of a world dominated by three blocs, the policies of which will define the future path of the world trading system.

An analysis of the trade and currency blocs of the 1930s indicates that

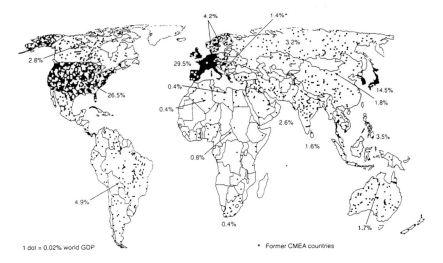

Figure 4.4 Distribution of world income, 1990
Source: Kitson and Michie (1995).

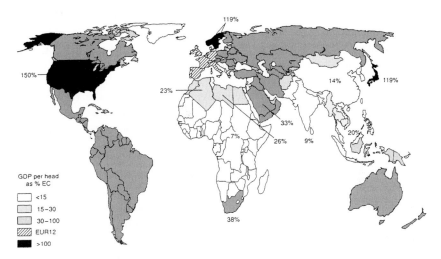

Figure 4.5 Income per head compared to the EC, 1990
Source: Kitson and Michie (1995).

different discriminatory regional arrangements had different impacts on the trading system – some blocs created trade while others diverted trade (Eichengreen and Irwin, 1993). In addition, there is no empirical support for the contention that discriminatory trade agreements led to a collapse in the level of multilateral trade (Kitson and Solomou, 1995). Likewise, an analysis of the impact of contemporary regional blocs provides conflicting results:

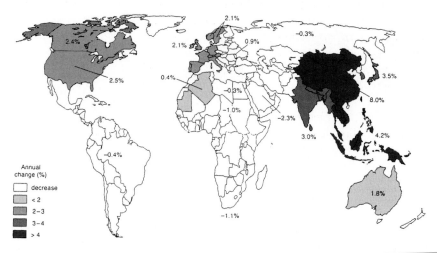

Figure 4.6 Growth of income per head, 1980–90
Source: Kitson and Michie (1995).

some studies have identified trade creation effects (Robson, 1984) while others have identified trade diversion effects (Pomfret, 1988). This conflicting evidence concerning the impact of regional blocs suggests that their overall impact will depend on the macroeconomic policies which they deploy. They can be a force for growth if they adopt expansionary policies, and in this context they can be particularly effective if they isolate the region from deflationary pressures which may emanate from the international trading system. If they merely replace a global form of monetarism with a regional form they will provide little benefit.[18]

6 Recent developments and immediate prospects

The key questions are first, what implications the present balance of international economic power will have for future developments politically and institutionally; and second, what if anything might replace the underpinning which was given to the world economic system by US dominance post-Second World War, and which had been given pre-First World War by British dominance, but which was lacking in the interwar period – without this underpinning, the Gold Standard eventually collapsed under the strains, even if these strains had been caused or at least exacerbated by bad institutional design.[19]

The 1994 Gatt agreement – the signing of the Uruguay round – ended seven years of negotiations and created the World Trade Organisation to police international trade, established in 1995. It is claimed that the freer trade in manufactures, services, textiles and agriculture which will follow what will be the biggest tariff cuts in history, will add $250 billion a year to world output over 10 years. Even on the assumption that such a figure might be plausible, there is some doubt as to what the differential impact would be, with suggestions that the benefits will be skewed towards the already industrialised countries. We have discussed above the dynamic links between trade and growth, but looking to the likely impact of the 1994 Gatt agreement, a key determinant of its effects on output will be the extent to which it impacts differentially on countries' trade balances, since if one or more countries or blocs are affected adversely, the resulting trade deficits may prove unsustainable, leading to deflationary policies being pursued to slow down the growth of import demand. The resulting slowdown in economic growth will also reduce the growth of trade – indeed, this latter result would be the purpose of the deflationary policies. From a static viewpoint it might be thought that reductions in output and trade brought about to correct imbalances caused by increased trade levels could not, logically, reduce world output levels below their initial levels; that is, could not reduce world output below what it was prior to the initial boost to trade. But this is, precisely, to ignore the dynamics of cumulative causation and the risks of countries – and even the global economy – slipping into a vicious circle of deflation. There is no necessary or logical floor to such a process, quite aside from the additional dangers which such imbalances carry of provoking trade wars and protectionism. Free trade is quite capable of creating the conditions for its own demise.

The immediate prospects for the world's trading imbalances, though, are dominated by global instability provoked – or at least illustrated – by the series of economic crises in East Asia during 1997 and 1998, and behind this, the continued combination of US deficits and Japanese surpluses. The resulting pressure from the US on Japan to open up its domestic market to American imports has led to fears from the EU that they will lose out in the three-way competition, with Japan opening up to US goods but not to European ones. And while the US deficit has led to pressure on Japan to open its markets to increased American imports, the trade balances between Japan, the US and the EU will also inevitably be influenced by the relative growth rates of the three. Countries (or blocs) with relatively high growth will often see their trade balances deteriorate as rising demand sucks in imports while export markets stagnate. Yet the opposite correlation may also be found, with successful economies enjoying both higher than average growth rates and trade surpluses. Europe's trade balance, on the other hand, is likely to do well, with a stagnant economy and correspondingly depressed demand for imports. That these deflated demand conditions apply equally to domestically produced goods means that the longer-term performance of Europe in export and domestic markets may be hampered by correspondingly weak investment and poor product and process development.

As for relative output levels, it is hard to envisage any of the world's countries or blocs emerging as an economically dominant power within the next generation or so, certainly not to the degree that Britain was pre-First

World War and the US was post-Second World War. Within the tripolar impasse with which the global economy is entering the twenty-first century, relative shifts in economic and political power will no doubt continue. In a four-nation poll (conducted in the UK, Germany, Japan and the US) reported in 1994, the strongest candidate for world leadership apart from the US was thought by people in the UK and Germany to be the EU and by people in the US to be Japan, while in Japan it was thought to be China.[20] Asked, 'Which country poses the biggest threat to world peace?', the most common reaction from those in the UK, Germany and the US was 'Russia', with Russia being outdone in people's minds as a military danger only in Japan, where the US was considered the greater threat.[21]

7 Some lessons

Conventionally, an evaluation of the history of the international monetary system has compared the efficacy of fixed versus flexible exchange rate regimes. This is a rather limited approach; the performance of alternative regimes depends not only on the exchange rate regime but on a range of other factors, including the power and impact of other adjustment mechanisms imbedded into the system.

The classical Gold Standard survived due to the existence of 'negative' adjustment mechanisms, such as domestic deflation and migration, and the benefits of specific historical conditions, such as the level of international capital flows and the lack of labour resistance to unemployment and under-employment. The interwar Gold Standard was short-lived due to its structural faults. It created a system of asymmetric adjustment which imposed a deflationary burden on the weaker countries and amplified the impact of recessionary forces during the great depression. The Bretton Woods system accommodated a number of positive adjustment mechanisms such as capital controls and the widespread use of fiscal policy to regulate domestic demand. Its effectiveness, however, was ultimately undermined by the reluctance to use exchange rate realignments, and by the changing world conditions which undermined the central position of the US in the system. As with the Gold Standard systems, asymmetries developed which led to imbalances in world economic development. Of course, any international monetary system will face changes in global economic conditions; the point is that systems must therefore evolve and incorporate appropriate adjustment mechanisms.

The management and regulation of the international monetary system should be seen as a dynamic process, not simply the establishment of a framework of static rules and codes. One of the key lessons of the performance of alternative international monetary regimes is that they become unstable when they fail to embrace, accommodate or regulate the dominant forces in the world economy. Such dominant forces are discussed above – but for many the most powerful, and possibly most pernicious, force is the globalisation of capital markets.

International capital markets are now dominated by speculative flows involving the short-term trading of financial assets and currencies. These markets are inherently unstable and threaten the growth of world income and employment. Exchange rate volatility and the rapid growth of 'hot money' have been associated with financial crises involving problems of debt repayment, banking insolvency and collapsing asset prices.

In many cases, the problems of volatile financial markets have been exacerbated by the premature liberalisation of capital markets in developing countries. Financial liberalisation has severely damaged the developing and transition economies with a series of crises in East Asia, Russia and Brazil which have led to mass unemployment and poverty. The 1997 East Asian crisis was almost totally unexpected – as was its severity and spread (contagion) (Singh, 1999) – but, perhaps by luck rather than design, the contagion did not spread, to any significant extent, to the industrialised countries. This has led to a failure in the West to recognise the severity of the crises: by the end of 1998 the combined unemployment in Indonesia, Korea and Thailand was estimated to be 18 million with millions more being pushed into dire poverty (World Bank, 1999). It was the poor and the most vulnerable in society that suffered from the 'mania, panic and crash'.

The international financial system requires major reform to resolve structural imbalances, to reduce its inherent instability and to manage crises (some of the reforms required are discussed in Chapter 3). One lesson of history, however, is that the regulatory framework needs to develop and change, and sometimes change quickly, to react to new directions in the international financial system. It is, therefore, fundamental that the institutional framework has an integrated and coherent structure that can develop with changing conditions. The current institutional structure does not fulfil these requirements and is in need of reform. The major international institutions are the International Monetary Fund (IMF), the World Bank, the World Trade Organisation and the Bank for International Settlements (BIS) – there are, however, a multiplicity of other international organisations which, although having little operational responsibilities, absorb a large amount of resources. This patchwork of institutions requires streamlining, perhaps under the auspices of the United Nations (on which see Robinson College Working Group, 1999).

The institution in most urgent need of reform is the IMF. It is an institution which calls for 'transparency' from others but whose internal affairs are riddled with intrigue and concealment. And, perhaps, of even greater concern are the economic principles and policy prescriptions of the IMF – *laissez faire* economics crudely applied to all economies in crisis and in need of help. The IMF adopts a standard and formulaic approach to all countries irrespective of their economic conditions, social structure or political framework. Thus, the IMF's response to the crises in East Asia, Russia and Brazil was to demand deflationary measures and institutional reform (in the Western 'image') in return for financial assistance. In the short term these demands made the crises worse and in the long term they threaten future prosperity. The IMF had demanded more privatisation, reforms of employment practices and changes to corporate take-overs rules. Such demands, which fail to appreciate that there are varieties of economic and social systems, are not only economically damaging but are undemocratic.

One of the important lessons of history is the need for the international monetary system to embrace change. But perhaps the most important lesson of history – and one that seems to be irrelevant to many of those dealing in the current global casino economy – is that financial markets do not create wealth. Those institutions that have a responsibility for global economic management must construct a policy regime that recognises that the purpose of finance is to facilitate real activity – output trade and employment – financial activity should not be seen as a desirable end in itself.

8 Conclusions

There are clear signs of the sort of policy responses which might be seen if present imbalances in trade and growth rates between countries continue. On trade, Clinton was elected on a platform which included 'managed trade', and while he has shown little sign of pursuing his election platform in office, disputes with Japan over the openness of the Japanese market to American goods have been a constant source of tension. On exchange rates, there are no signs of any imminent move to international exchange rate coordination.

On regional economic integration, the political experience regarding the Maastricht Treaty's ratification was mirrored in North America: during his election campaign, Clinton was critical of NAFTA, yet his first major policy action was to force it through in the face of widespread criticism, including that from trade unions. In Canada, the government, supporting NAFTA in its election campaign in face of criticism from the opposition, suffered perhaps the biggest election defeat in world history, being left with only two MPs, yet the incoming government, again, changed its tune and supported NAFTA wholeheartedly. This rise of regionalism is certainly, in part at least, a response to the new global competition. In some ways it can be seen as mirroring the response of countries and blocs to the previous demise of a global economic power capable of underpinning the world's economic, trading and currency arrangements: when Britain failed to reimpose her leadership role, via sterling's 1925 return to the Gold Standard, new economic blocs began to emerge capable of pursuing their own policy agendas. One key difference today is that there has not, as yet, been the recourse to the protectionism witnessed in the 1930s. Fears of a 'fortress Europe' and American 'managed trade' have so far remained in the background, with the World Trade Organisation promising ever freer trade. Whether this can form the basis of a stable economic environment on which new global institutional structures can be built will depend crucially on whether 'Third World' countries will be able to develop without recourse to the sort of interventionist measures which delivered economic development to the now industrialised countries, but which are now ruled out for others. If not, imbalances will be exacerbated and the go-it-alone responses seen in the 1930s may once again be seen as the best route for economic growth and development.

Part II
History versus equilibrium

5 Recession and economic revival in Britain

The role of policy in the 1930s and 1980s

1 Introduction

During the 1980s the discussion of economic policy became increasingly circumspect. The Governments of the Western industrialised countries – led by Britain and the US – abrogated their responsibility to maintain, or at least pursue, full employment and stable economic growth. Instead the focus of policy was redirected towards nominal variables, in particular inflation and interest rates, and the need for 'flexibility', especially in labour markets. The Chancellor of the Exchequer stated in 1980 that 'the main objectives of the Government's economic strategy are to reduce inflation and to create conditions in which substantial economic growth can be achieved', adding that 'overriding priority must be given to reducing inflation and strengthening the supply side of the economy' (House of Commons, 1980). The instability of the world economy during the 1980s and early 1990s has at last led to some, albeit piecemeal, revision to such a non-interventionist approach. Meetings of the G7[1] group of leading industrialised countries have at least stressed that jobs and growth are a top priority. The implications of this shift in priorities for economic policy have not, however, been clearly spelt out.

The fundamental dispute amongst economists over the role of economic policy centres on whether growth and employment can be maximised by relying on market forces and the price mechanism or whether there is a role for government intervention. The late 1970s and early 1980s saw the ascendency of free market economics. The propaganda and hype that went with Thatcherism and its other manifestations across the world economy, such as Supply Side Economics in the US, created a policy vacuum such that it was almost considered axiomatic that intervention in the economy would be harmful and destabilising. Expansionary fiscal policy, depending on how it was financed, would either reduce private sector investment or create inflation. The regulation of financial markets would create distortions in capital flows thus destabilising the monetary system. The regulation of labour markets, including unemployment benefits and minimum wages, would cause disequilibrium between labour supply and labour demand, leading to unemployment.

This free market approach gave credibility and credence to the economic policies pursued by the British Government during the 1980s. Throughout the decade a stream of publications extolled the allocative efficiency of the market mechanism and, in particular, the Thatcherite policies implemented in Britain (see, for instance Matthews and Minford, 1987; Walters, 1986).[2] At the same time, many economists and economic historians re-evaluated previous periods of economic policy in the light of the free market paradigm and the alleged adverse impacts of government intervention. The interwar period came under severe scrutiny with a number of critiques of government policies, particularly those concerned with international trade and the labour market (Capie, 1983; Beenstock, Capie and Griffiths, 1984; Matthews and Benjamin, 1992). Additionally, others have favoured the economic policies implemented during the 1980s when compared with those implemented during the 1930s. Broadberry and Crafts (1990a and 1990b) suggest that despite rapid economic growth in the 1930s interventionist economic policy impaired long-run performance by reducing competitive pressures. Conversely, they argue that policy during the 1980s, directed at reducing the role of the state and promoting 'competition', has improved long run economic growth by stimulating the supply side of the economy.

This chapter argues that economic revival in the 1930s was primarily policy-induced with little evidence of any significant adverse supply side effects. Conversely, economic growth in the 1980s can be attributed to the unintentional demand side effects of policy (such as the impact of financial liberalisation on credit expansion) and the impact of supply side developments that were largely independent of the Thatcher policy regime change. Thus this chapter argues that an analysis of economic policy must consider the underlying conditions prevailing in the economy during any given period or epoch.

This chapter is organised as follows. Section 2 compares the economic performance of the 1980s with that of the 1930s. Sections 3 and 4 consider various aspects of the economic policies pursued during the 1930s and Sections 5 and 6 consider similar issues for the 1980s.

2 Comparative economic performance

The paths of recession and recovery in the interwar period and during the 1980s were remarkably similar. As shown in Figure 5.1, which plots the path of Gross Domestic Product (GDP) for the 1930s and 1980s, the start of both periods was characterised by a severe downturn in economic activity. During the period 1929–31, the period of the Great Depression, British GDP fell by an average annual rate of 2.9 per cent, whereas during 1979–81 GDP fell by an average annual rate of 1.6 per cent. Following both recessions, there was rapid growth and sustained recovery, an annual growth rate of 3.0 per cent in the 1930s and 3.2 per cent in the 1980s.[3]

A major economic and social problem which persisted during both the

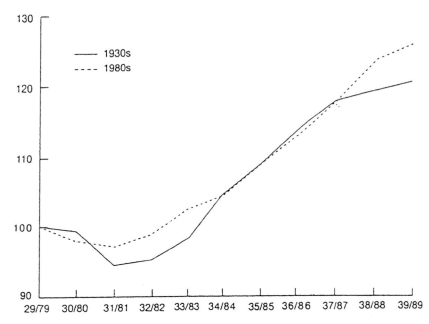

Figure 5.1 UK Gross Domestic Product in the 1930s and 1980s (1929, 1979 = 100)
Sources: Feinstein (1972) and CSO (1995).

1930s and 1980s was large-scale unemployment. Figure 5.2 plots the unemployment rate for both decades based on raw data: the 1930s figures are based on national insurance statistics and the 1980s figures based on more recent methods of counting. This graph suggests that the unemployment problem was more severe during the 1930s than during the 1980s. Unemployment peaked at 22.1 per cent in 1932 and averaged 16 per cent for the period (1929–38) whereas during the more recent period unemployment peaked at 13.7 per cent in 1983 and averaged 9.3 per cent for the period (1979–90). The usefulness of comparing the raw data series, however, is questionable as the methods of data collection have changed significantly since the interwar period (see Allin, 1993 for a description of the changes in the methods of counting). Even since 1979 there have been 29 changes to the method of estimating UK unemployment – all of which have reduced the total or left it unchanged.[4] The preferred method of counting during most of the 1980s and 1990s was the claimant count which has been severely criticised for underestimating the real level of unemployment; according to Wells (1994) the discrepancy is in the order of one million.[5] It is thus important to compare unemployment rates on a consistent basis. Figure 5.3 plots unemployment rates for both decades based on recent methods of counting. These adjusted figures show, contrary to conventional wisdom, that the unemployment problem was greater during the 1980s than during the

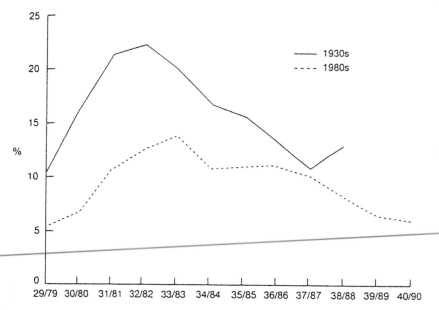

Figure 5.2 Unemployment rates in the 1930s and 1980s (%, raw data)
Source: Crafts (1991).

1930s. During the earlier period unemployment peaked at 10.6 per cent in 1932 and declined significantly afterwards, averaging 7.6 per cent for the period. Unemployment during the 1980s increased throughout most of the decade, reaching a peak of 11.1 per cent in 1986 and averaging 8.4 per cent for the period overall.

3 Policy during the 1930s

Macroeconomic performance

Like the start of the 1980s the early 1930s witnessed a deep and painful depression. Despite their similar magnitudes, however, there are important differences between the two economic downturns. Most importantly, the Great Depression which started in 1929 was a worldwide phenomenon. Conversely, the recession of the early 1980s was in the main an internal or domestic downturn in economic activity. This contrast reflects the different causes and propagating mechanisms of the two recessions and in particular the differing impact of policy.

The *causes* of the Great Depression are subject to continual debate. Many studies focus on domestic developments in the American economy which were transmitted to the world economy. Friedman and Schwartz (1963) have

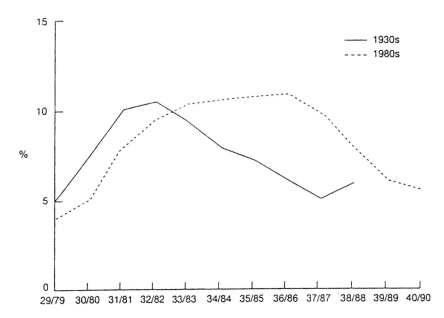

Figure 5.3 Unemployment rates in the 1930s and 1980s (%, consistent data)
Source: Crafts (1991).

emphasised tight monetary policy;[6] Kindleberger (1973) stresses the fall in consumption due to re-distribution of income from the agricultural sector where prices were falling; Romer (1990) considers the decline in the consumption of durables due to increased uncertainty created by the Wall Street Crash; Lewis (1949) considers the collapse of American capital exports; other policy factors include the alleged failure of fiscal policy to provide automatic stabilisers and the argument that the Smoot-Hawley tariff of 1930 initiated a mutually destructive trade war (Friedman, 1978; Capie 1992). Others have focused on the Great Depression as being initiated through changes and structural problems in the international economy (see for example Fearon, 1979).

As argued in Chapter 6 below, the *extent* of the Great Depression can be attributed to the operation of the Gold Standard (see also Eichengreen, 1992; Temin, 1989). The impact of adverse shocks, such as the recession in the US and the collapse in capital exports, were transmitted to the rest of the world through the exchange rate regime. As foreign loans were called in due to developments in the domestic economy, the gold flows to the US increased. The draining of reserves in the debtor countries accelerated and monetary policy was tightened to ensure gold convertibility. Thus the deflationary bias of the Gold Standard system resulted in a perverse reaction to adverse demand shocks. Rather than facilitating an expansion of demand to ameliorate the

Depression the system magnified the problem leading to a collapse in world trade.

There was no single cause of the Great Depression. The cumulative impact of structural problems, adverse demand shocks and policy mistakes, such as adherence to gold, all played a part.

The domestic recession in Britain was initially caused by a decline in exports although monetary factors were important during the later stages of the recession as the Gold Standard straitjacket led to rising real rates of interest. The impact of the Great Depression varied across countries: national income in the US collapsed by an annual rate in excess of 10 per cent between 1929 and 1932, whereas other countries such as Denmark and Norway witnessed little or no decline. These variations reflected national-specific factors. As shown in Figure 5.4, which plots the path of GDP for Britain and the world economy, Britain's depression, although severe in real terms, was relatively mild compared to the experience of the world economy; an annual output decline of less than 2 per cent compared to a world average of over 6 per cent. In part, this reflected the low dependence on agriculture and the stability of its financial institutions. Free-falling primary product prices severely affected the incomes of those countries that depended on agricultural output. Countries such as Britain with a relatively small agricultural sector suffered less direct adverse effects and also benefited from the terms of trade gain of lower import prices. The fragmented banking structures in Europe

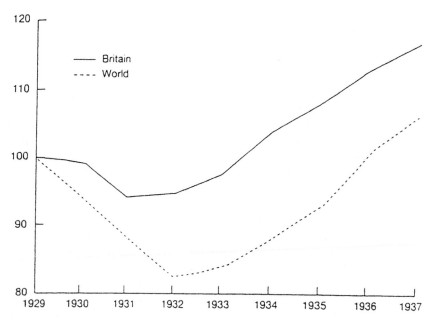

Figure 5.4 British and world Gross Domestic Product 1929–37 (1929 = 100)
Sources: Feinstein (1972) and Maddison (1982).

and the US led to a series of bank failures which caused greater chaos in capital and currency markets than was the case for Britain.

An additional factor which moderated the extent and duration of the slump in Britain and initiated the start of recovery was a shift in policy regime. A series of fiscal and balance-of-payments crises led to a number of macroeconomic policy changes starting with the suspension of the Gold Standard and the devaluation of sterling in September 1931. The devaluation of the exchange rate also allowed the Government to pursue a more expansionist ('cheap money') monetary policy. Additionally, the protection of manufactures was extended by the emergency Abnormal Importations Act in November 1931 and the Import Duties Act in February 1932.

The combination of these changes in trade and monetary policies increased aggregate demand for British products thus helping to promote recovery from the Great Depression. The suspension of the Gold Standard and the accompanying devaluation had a number of beneficial impacts on the domestic economy. First, it improved trade performance and alleviated the balance-of-payments constraint on growth. The competitive gain of the devaluation was particularly large in 1932. Taking Redmond's (1980) figure of a 13 per cent depreciation during 1931–32 Broadberry (1986) undertook an elasticities analysis of the policy change measuring the impact of the change in relative prices in the volume of exports and imports. The estimated improvement in the balance of trade, resulting from this competitive advantage, amounted to £80 million. Assuming a multiplier of 1.75, a 3 per cent increase in GDP can be attributed to the relative price effect, a large part of the turning point in 1932.

The second benefit of devaluation was that it removed the exchange rate constraint on monetary policy so that interest rates could be determined by domestic economic conditions rather than the need to maintain the exchange rate or to prevent excessive loss of reserves. The 'cheap money' policy has been identified as a permissive policy for economic revival (Richardson, 1967), especially important in stimulating a housing boom (Worswick, 1984).[7] The important contrast with the housing boom of the 1980s is that in the 1930s the main impact was a massive increase in the number of houses, whereas in the 1980s there was a massive increase in the price of houses.

Devaluation and the accompanying introduction of other expansionist policies led to a third, less mechanistic, benefit. Under the prevailing world conditions of uncertainty and monetary and financial turbulence, the reorientation of policy towards the domestic economy significantly improved business confidence. The prospect of a stable and growing economy encouraged home producers to increase, or at least bring forward, investment and expand production.

The extension of protectionism also led to increased demand for domestic products through a number of mechanisms (Kitson and Solomou, 1990). First, it improved competitiveness of domestic manufactures which reduced Britain's dependency on imported manufactures and encouraged the production of domestic substitutes. Second, the resulting increase in domestic incomes generated a demand stimulus for the whole economy. Third, the more favourable conditions for manufactures and the expanded domestic market allowed the exploitation of economies of scale and increased productivity.

There is no doubt that a number of policy initiatives contributed to the turning point from depression to recovery in 1932. These policy changes, however, also contributed to the strength of the recovery throughout the 1930s. As noted previously, there was a sustained increase in GDP from 1932 and, as shown in Figure 5.4, the rate of increase was similar to that of the world economy. This was a notable achievement as the British recovery followed a relatively *mild* depression whereas much of the world recovery was a cyclical bounceback in response to a *deep* depression.

Many of the mechanisms through which policy sustained recovery were similar to those discussed above that initiated the turning point from recession. There were, however, a number of differences, the most important of which was the dissipation of the relative price advantage of the devaluation of sterling due to the global collapse of the Gold Standard and a series of devaluations abroad – there was a large nominal devaluation of the sterling effective exchange rate between 1931 and 1932 but this advantage was subsequently eroded.[8] Although the competitive effect of the suspension of gold was moderated, the gains of the early 1930s may have provided long-term advantages as the short-term benefits of improved trade performance could be sustained through the establishment of distribution networks and customer loyalty. Throughout the 1930s Britain maintained a reduced propensity to import which increased the share of domestic demand for domestic products – although much of this improvement can be attributed to the benefits of protectionism which remained throughout most of the decade. Additionally, Britain's share of world export markets stabilised, whereas it had been falling for the previous 50 years; this however, did not lead to export-led recovery due to the low volume of world trade during the 1930s. Furthermore, and despite competitive devaluations abroad, breaking the exchange rate constraint on monetary policy allowed lower interest rates throughout the period.

The policy regime change initiated in 1931–32 was central to Britain's improved economic performance in the 1930s. There are, however, a number of additional factors which need to be considered. First, policy acted in the context of favourable supply conditions, such as the existence of a technological gap with the US which provided the potential for 'catching-up' growth and the development of new industries. Second, there were favourable demand shifts that were, at least in part, independent of macroeconomic policy such as the terms-of-trade shift in the early 1930s and the increased demand for housing. Third, firms and employees did not offset all the output effects of increased demand through increased prices and wages.[9]

It should also be noted that the policy-induced demand shift was not of the traditional Keynesian sort, that is, via expansionary fiscal policy. The 'Treasury View' and balanced budgets were the order of the day. Although the actual budget balance went into a small deficit during the Great Depression this was due to the operation of automatic fiscal stabilisers – such as falling tax revenue and increased expenditure on such items as unemployment benefits. In fact the Government attempted to limit the operation of the stabilisers through public expenditure cuts including cutting the standard rate of unemployment benefit. The discretionary component of fiscal policy, that which excludes the automatic component of stabilisers, was in surplus during the depression suggesting, from a Keynesian perspective, a deflationary fiscal stance during the depression (Middleton, 1981).[10] This tight fiscal policy was continued during the early 1930s and was only relaxed towards the end of the decade with the advent of rearmament.

Although the policy shift of the 1930s improved economic performance it has been argued that as it was a response to economic crisis, the shift lacked coherence, and was not discretionary but was forced on the authorities (Beenstock, Capie and Griffiths, 1984). This argument, however, overstates the case. Booth (1987) has argued that policy-makers had a coherent strategy which was to increase profitability through raising prices. Although, as we have argued, the impacts of policy changes were primarily through other mechanisms, namely output effects rather than price effects, this does not negate the fact that the policy shift had internal coherence. The increased management of the economy can be illustrated by looking at exchange rate policy. First, the timing of policy was important for moderating the recession and promoting recovery. Those countries that untied themselves from gold early were more likely to experience faster economic growth (see Chapter 6, below, and Newell and Symons, 1988). Furthermore, some countries, such as France, Belgium and the Netherlands, despite prolonged recession, were reluctant to leave gold. This suggests that leaving gold was not an automatic act, although those countries that remained locked into the system did so because of their fear of inflation (resulting from their recent history of inflation), whereas British policy was more concerned with raising the price level. Second, following the suspension of gold the exchange rate was not allowed to freely float but was managed through the newly created Exchange Equalisation Account. This allowed the monetary authorities to buy or sell sterling to offset movements in the exchange rate caused by private sector trading.

Some issues relating to productivity growth and long-run productive potential

Broadberry and Crafts (1990a and 1990b) argue that macroeconomic and industrial policy in the 1930s harmed the supply side of the economy resulting in a poor productivity performance, and left an anti-competitive legacy which hindered economic performance after the Second World War. This section argues that the first proposition is inconsistent with productivity evidence of the 1930s and the second proposition remains unproven.

First, under conditions of underutilised capacity – such as the 1930s – a policy which expands demand will result in the use of previously unemployed resources. Such resource mobilisation will outweigh any disadvantages of resource misallocation. Better to be misallocated than unemployed. With economies of scale, however, increased output will also lead to efficiency gains – there is no trade-off.

Competition is a dynamic process (see Chapter 9 below).[11] Appropriate economic policies depend on underlying economic conditions. Thus policy requirements will alter as market structures and behaviour develop. The interwar period witnessed the development of mass production techniques and increased mass consumption. Furthermore, during the early 1930s there was widespread excess capacity combined with a productive structure which required rationalisation and the exploitation of economies of scale through mass production. Policies such as devaluation and tariffs, by expanding the domestic market allowed producers to reap the advantages of scale. In addition, the objectives of industrial policy, to encourage rationalisation and cooperation in production, were appropriate to the underlying economic conditions. The problem was its flawed implementation. First, industrial policies were piecemeal in design. Second, rationalisation objectives were frequently formulated without credible sanctions if such objectives were not implemented. Third, the raft of industrial initiatives did not include an effective competition policy, in order to combine the reorganisation of production with effective competition in product markets.

The picture we have drawn of the policy stance in the 1930s is a broadly effective macroeconomic policy regime combined with a flawed industrial policy framework. Yet despite the limitations of industrial policy the supply side performed remarkably well during the decade – in part reflecting the benefits to the supply side of buoyant demand. Broadberry and Crafts (1990a), however, cite the superior productivity levels in the US as evidence of a 'supply side sclerosis' in the UK: the estimates of Rostas (1948) indicate that productivity in US manufacturing during the mid-1930s was 2.25 times higher than the UK level.[12] This is, however only a snapshot of prevailing productivity levels. As shown in Figure 5.5, the UK's productivity gap with the US was large and expanding since the Victorian period; and this compares with the period after 1950, which was one of almost continual catching up. More importantly, the only period prior to 1950 which showed any significant closing of the gap was 1929 to 1935. During the period the gap was closing by an average of 3.0 per cent a year, whereas in the immediate preceding period, 1925–29 it had been widening by 1.6 per cent a year. This picture of an improving productivity performance in manufacturing is also evident for the whole economy (see the GDP per person estimates of Maddison, 1982 and Broadberry, 1993). Thus, in the period allegedly

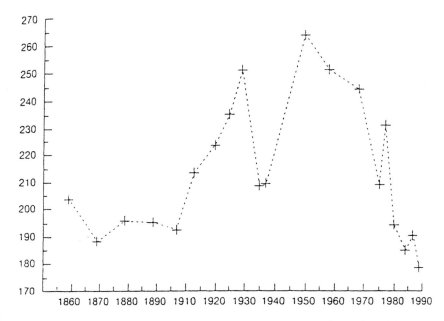

Figure 5.5 Manufacturing output per person in the US where the UK = 100, 1860–1990

Source: Broadberry (1993).

characterised by a policy-induced *retreat* from competition there was an *advance* in relative productivity performance.

The evidence on productivity trends is inconsistent with the pessimistic assessment of policy effects on the supply side. This conclusion is supported by examining the impact of increased protectionism on productivity performance. It is commonly contended in the economics literature that protectionism distorts market forces and lowers efficiency. In this vein it has been argued by Capie (1983) that the British tariff harmed the British economy during the 1930s. The productivity evidence, however, suggests that protectionism was associated with improved productivity performance. Table 5.1 shows the productivity performance of the newly protected industries (those protected by the legislation of 1931 and 1932) relative to non-newly protected industries (those protected by earlier legislation or those receiving no protection). In the pre-policy shift period, 1924–30,[13] productivity growth of the non-newly protected sector increased by 1.4 per cent a year, three times greater than the rate of increase of the newly protected group. During the policy-on period, 1930–35, there occurred a substantial turnaround: the productivity of the newly protected group increased by 2.7 per cent a year, whereas the annual productivity growth of the non-newly protected group, although greater than in the previous period, was only 1.5 per cent.

Table 5.1 Manufacturing productivity performance in the interwar period (industries newly protected in 1931–32 and non-newly protected industries)

	Newly protected	Non-newly protected
Productivity Level (1935 = 100)		
1924	85.1	85.4
1930	87.4	93.0
1935	100.0	100.0
Growth per annum (%)		
1924–30	0.45	1.43
1930–35	2.73	1.46
Inter-period growth differences (%)		
1924–30 and 1930–35	2.28	0.03

Source: Kitson and Solomou (1990).

If the policy shift of the 1930s did not significantly harm the supply side during that decade there is still the issue of whether it harmed the economy during the post-Second World War period – by creating institutional rigidities and by preventing the necessary structural change that would have accelerated long-term growth. This argument remains unproven. First, it is difficult to construct viable counterfactuals; economic performance post-Second World War was dominated by the impact of the war itself on the world economy and the new world order that was established. This discontinuity makes it difficult to isolate the impact of inherited structures and practices. Of related concern is how the policy changes of the 1930s affected the ability of Britain to fight the war. The protection of strategic sectors, such as iron and steel, may have been important in the development of the war economy. Second, even if the legacy of the 1930s policy regime was harmful, this is not a failure of the regime itself but a failure to adapt and transform the policies and institutions to the prevailing conditions in the postwar period.

The case for the policy changes of the 1930s is that they improved macroeconomic performance and, at the very least, did not harm the supply side. This is not an argument that it was an optimal policy mix. It was, however, an improvement on what went before it and in the next sections it will be argued that it was a more appropriate mix than the policy changes of the 1980s.

4 Policy during the 1980s

Macroeconomic performance

The 'overriding priority' of the Thatcher Government elected in 1979 was to squeeze inflation out of the economy. This objective, which stands in stark contrast to the 1930s objective of raising the price level, was to be achieved through macroeconomic policy.[14] The conquering of inflation was considered a necessary condition for economic success despite the lack of empirical support for such a relationship (see Stanners, 1993). The other strand of the growth strategy was to improve the supply side of the economy by decreasing the role of the state and promoting the role of the free market. This involved the deregulation of markets, the privatisation of state-owned industries, and reform of the trade unions.

It has been commonly contended that the Thatcher government implemented a monetarist experiment in Britain. In part this is true, as monetarism does place the control of inflation at the centre of macroeconomic policy – real variables such as output and employment are determined independently by the supply side. In its detail, however, the government's strategy was a mixture of libertarian economic ideology and inherited policy instruments.

The lack of consistency was reflected in the use of policy instruments. The foundation of macroeconomic policy was the Medium Term Financial Strategy (MTFS) which identified targets for money supply growth. The instruments initially deployed to achieve these objectives were interest rates and public borrowing (fiscal policy). However, this did not accord with orthodox monetarism which advocated that the money supply should be controlled directly.[15]

Monetary policy went through a number of transformations during the 1980s as indicated in Table 5.2. From 1979 to 1982 the Government myopically focused on attaining its preferred target for monetary growth – sterling M3 (£M3). To achieve this it pushed interest rates to record levels and attempted to implement massive cuts in public spending and public borrowing despite high and rising unemployment. Despite these deflationary policies the Government consistently failed to achieve its desired growth of the money supply. Figure 5.6 shows the deviations of actual £M3 growth from the mid-point of the target range. Monetary growth, using this

Table 5.2 Anti-inflation policy shifts since 1979

Period		Target	Instrument
1979–81	MTFS Mark I	£M3	Interest rates Public borrowing
1982–5	MTFS Mark II	£M1, £M5, £M0	Interest rates Public borrowing Exchange rates
1985–8	Exchange rate targeting	Exchange rate	Shadowing the deutschmark
1988–90	Confused targeting	?	Interest rates Public borrowing Exchange rates
1990–2	The ERM solution	Exchange rate	ERM solution
1992–7	Policy vacuum	?	?
1997–	Independent Bank of England	Inflation rate	Interest rates

Source: Kitson (1999).

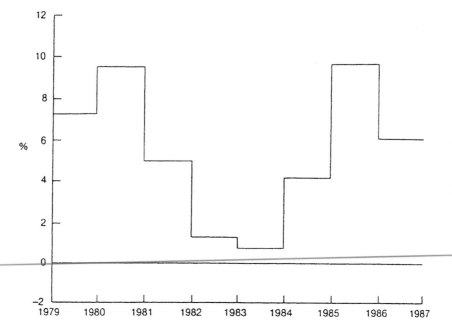

Figure 5.6 Deviations from money supply (£M3) targets, 1979–87 (%)
Source: Authors' calculations from Healey (1993).

indicator, consistently overshot its target, particularly in the early 1980s when most importance was attached to the £M3 indicator. There are a number of explanations for this failure.[16] In the meantime the deflationary impact of the Government's policies had plunged the economy into a deep recession. High interest rates discouraged both investment and consumption, and created cash flow problems for many companies leading to bankruptcies and plant closures. The tightening of fiscal policy removed the fiscal stabilisers which normally operate during a recession, further reducing consumption and public sector investment. Additionally, the high interest rates, combined with the popularity of the government's policies with the financial community and the high level of oil exports, led to an appreciation of the exchange rate (compared to the depreciated exchange rate of the 1930s). This led to a deterioration in trade performance – lower export growth and rising import penetration.

The impact of the Government's policies was to lead to annual average fall in GDP of 1.6 per cent between 1979 and 1981. Figure 5.7 plots the path of British and world GDP since 1979. When the British economy was in recession, the world economy was growing, albeit moderately, at an annual rate of 1.7 per cent (between 1979 and 1981). Thus, whereas the slump of the early 1930s was due to external forces, the slump of the early 1980s was due

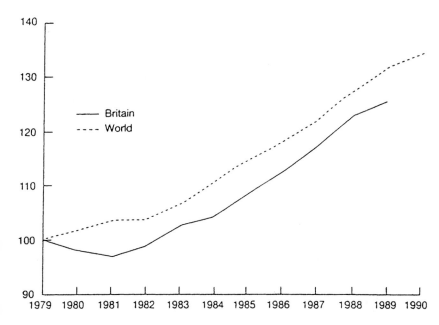

Figure 5.7 British and world Gross Domestic Product, 1979–90 (1979 = 100)
Sources: Wells (1993a) and CSO (1995).

to internal mechanisms, the most important of which were the deflationary policies of the Government.

From 1982 there was a move towards targeting a broader range of monetary indicators (such as M1, PSL2 (later M4), M5 and M0) as well as the exchange rate.[17] More pertinently, in the wake of the massive rise in unemployment there was a relaxation of interest rate and fiscal policy. Interest rates were reduced from a peak of 16.0 per cent in October 1981 to 8.75 per cent in March 1984. In 1982 and 1983 there were also a number of tax cuts. This change in policy stance, combined with the usual cyclical recovery mechanisms, generated a moderate revival in the economy. The economy started to grow from the first quarter of 1981, but it was not until the second quarter of 1983 that it surpassed the peak of 1979. Despite this economic growth permanent damage had been inflicted on the economy; high unemployment persisted and the severity of the recession had destroyed much of industrial capacity.

The mid-1980s witnessed another shift in policy as monetary targets were downgraded and the exchange rate took centre stage. The Chancellor of the Exchequer, Nigel Lawson, admitted in 1984 that the objective of stable prices had been postponed: 'There is no point kidding yourself, there is no point in self-delusion' (quoted in Healey, 1993, p. 137). The key domestic shock that occurred in the mid-1980s was a domestic credit boom, fuelled by a cycle of financial deregulation and accelerating house price inflation. The easy availability of credit, including mortgages, led to accelerating property prices, increasing the wealth of the private sector which led to increased consumption and boosted the demand for credit. Thus, the spiral continued. The credit boom did generate increased economic growth and a moderate fall in unemployment. Expansion emanated from the unintentional demand side effects of policy changes such as financial deregulation. Although the credit boom provided a short-term stimulus to output and employment it also fuelled inflation. This led to another shift in policy as the Prime Minister (and her advisors) and Chancellor disputed the appropriate indicators of monetary control – Thatcher favoured money supply targets and Lawson the exchange rate.

A clear strategy re-emerged with the entry of Britain into the Exchange Rate Mechanism (ERM) of the European Monetary System (EMS) in October 1990. Although entry to the ERM had initially allowed the government to cut interest rates it ultimately acted as an engine of depression. The inevitable collapse of the credit boom plunged the economy into recession. The increase in house prices was halted, credit availability was restricted, indebtedness increased and consumption fell. The UK's membership of the ERM removed the policy options to deal with this recession; the exchange rate was effectively fixed and interest rates had to be kept in alignment with German rates. Thus the UK pursued deflationary policies when domestic economy required policies for expansion and growth.

The UK's forced withdrawal from the ERM in September 1992 provided some stimulus to the economy through mechanisms similar to the withdrawal from the Gold Standard in 1931: a more competitive exchange rate and lower interest rates. However, this exit from the ERM was not the result of Government policy. Both the Government and the Labour opposition had been fully committed to continued membership even at an exchange rate that was clearly overvalued. Indeed, prior to the forced exit it was widely – and incorrectly – argued that interest rates would have to rise following a withdrawal to compensate for loss of credibility and confidence.

Some issues relating to the supply side, productivity growth and long-run productive potential

Despite the argument that macroeconomic policy was mismanaged there is still the case that the economic reforms of the 1980s transformed the supply side of the British economy creating the conditions for future prosperity. Here we consider four of the most prominent areas of supply side reform: deregulation of financial markets; deregulation of labour markets; the encouragement of entrepreneurship; and privatisation.

The deregulation of financial markets was seen as central to the efficient allocation of capital. One of the first measures was the abolition in 1979 of exchange controls over capital movements. This led to a large cumulative net outflow of capital (Coakley and Harris, 1992). Additionally, it removed one of the key instruments for retaining some control over the choice of both the exchange rate and domestic interest rates (on which, see Chapter 4 above).

On the domestic front the main developments were first, the reforms of the London Stock Exchange known as 'Big Bang', and second, the set of reforms which abolished the principal distinctions between banks and building societies. The former did improve the efficiency of the equity market although it did lead to excess capacity in security dealing which was to prove unsustainable. The latter was of greater concern as the increased competition in the banking system, in particular in the mortgage market, led to a credit explosion and rapid house price inflation. Although in the immediate short term this fuelled rapid consumption-led growth (throwing the Government's monetary targets into turmoil) it was creating the conditions which would hinder growth in the medium term. The credit explosion–house price spiral fed on itself – easily available credit stimulating house prices (far more than house construction – in contrast with the 1930s) thus increasing private sector wealth which in turn increased the demand for consumer credit. Despite proclamations of an 'economic miracle' the situation was unsustainable – this speculative boom was no different from any other. When the housing market collapsed the spiral went into reverse – falling house prices leading to declining wealth, increased indebtedness, reduced demand for credit and stagnant consumption. Furthermore, the property crash particularly affected new entrants to the market who were left with high mortgages and negative equity.

Thus the major impacts of financial deregulation were first to remove discretion over the setting of interest rates and exchange rates; and second to generate a consumption-led boom which had nothing to do with an 'economic miracle' and everything to do with unsustainable speculation.

The other 'market' to feel the brunt of deregulatory fervour was the labour market. The Government purported to tackle unemployment by reforms aimed at 'pricing workers back into jobs' and by squeezing benefits to force people off the dole queues. Attacking the rights of trade unions was central to this strategy. This took the form of expanding, rather than reducing the role of law (Deakin, 1992). A series of Acts reduced immunities, increasing the scope of common law regulation of strike activity. The 1982 *Employment Act* removed immunity of unions from liability in tort, narrowed the 'trade dispute' formula which had protected many forms of industrial action and strictly regulated the closed shop. Additional Acts, such as the *Trade Union Act* of 1984 and the *Employment Act* of 1988, added to this regulatory framework, undermining the basic rights of trade unions.[18]

The *Economist* has reiterated the received wisdom that, 'If the unemployed get almost as much on the dole as they could get in work, they will be discouraged from seeking jobs.' But how 'over-generous' are unemployment benefits? An OECD study reported in the same *Economist* article (26 February 1994) indicates that the replacement rate (the ratio of unemployment benefits to wages) fell from 43 per cent in 1972 to 28 per cent in 1980 and to 16 per cent in 1990. This *fall* in the replacement ratio was contemporaneous with a *rise* in unemployment – from 2.9 per cent in 1972 to 5.1 per cent in 1980 and to 5.8 per cent in 1990. And these estimates, which are based on the claimant count method of calculation, seriously underestimate the scale of unemployment and its increase over the period (Wells, 1994a). It cannot be argued therefore that higher unemployment was caused by higher levels of unemployment benefit (relative to earnings). On the contrary, unemployment increased as relative benefit levels fell.

Privatisation was a central element of government economic policy during the 1980s, and continued into the 1990s. It was argued that the privatisation programme would improve efficiency, widen share ownership and generate government revenue which would help reduce public borrowing. There is, however little evidence that the programme has achieved these objectives.

Although profits per employee improved, the evidence on the effect of privatisation on efficiency is, at best, ambiguous – there were productivity improvements in some privatised industries and not in others (Parker, 1993). Moreover, the productivity improvements that were observed were not a result of the privatisation process. Bishop and Kay (1988) concluded that 'The privatised industries have tended to be faster growing and more profitable, but it seems that the causation runs from growth and profitability to privatisation, rather than the other way around.'

Increasing individual share ownership was central to the creation of a 'property-owning democracy'. Yet despite extravagant marketing campaigns, the privatisation flotations have not deepened share ownership. Although, as the government has heralded, the proportion of adults holding shares has increased, the majority only hold shares in one company. Furthermore, the power of institutional investors has risen, as they have increased their proportion of shareholdings at the expense of the private investor.

The receipts from privatisation have raised funds for the Exchequer (although, somewhat bizarrely, the revenues are treated as negative government spending in the public accounts). Such revenues, however, have only made a small impact on the public sector borrowing requirement – which, on average, remained high throughout the early 1980s, despite the Government's expenditure cutting agenda, as rising unemployment led to increased expenditure and falling tax revenues. The impact would of course have been larger if the Government had not consistently set the flotation price below the market valuation. Moreover, not only are the revenue benefits of privatisation small, but they are also transitory – you can only sell the 'family silver' once.

Another aspect of the 'enterprise culture' has been the increased number of small firms and the expansion of self employment. Yet, the developments in the small business sector do not suggest that government policy has had a significant positive impact. Although the increased number of the self employed does seem to be a 1980s phenomenon, the growth of small firms reflects a trend that started in the 1960s (Storey, 1994). Moreover, much of the growth of the self employed is a response to 'negative' factors – workers pushed into 'entrepreneurship' by unemployment and the contracting-out strategies of large firms (Kitson, 1995). Additionally, although an increasing number of small firms are being created, the majority will not survive three years and very few will make a significant contribution to job generation. This may in part reflect the failure of small firm policy which has been introduced on a piecemeal basis and the adverse impact of macroeconomic instability of small firm performance (Small Business Research Centre, 1992).

5 Conclusions

Economic performance in the 1980s was poor: overall growth was modest and the short period of rapid growth was unsustainable; unemployment soared and became persistent; and the manufacturing sector stagnated. The so-called success stories were exaggerated: inflation was only suppressed by mass unemployment and the casualisation of the work force; and productivity growth was modest compared to that achieved in the 1960s, especially in the context of the potential for catch-up. Moreover, the policy changes of the 1980s have not created the foundations for future prosperity – the opposite in fact. Advanced economies require economic stability and effective institutions to promote investment in skills and capital equipment. These in turn require economic management to be concerned with stable growth of the real economy and the regulation and management of markets.

The 1980s experience was one of an economic roller-coaster, fuelled by the vagaries of deregulation, which harmed the long-run growth potential of the economy. Recessions were deeper than previous (at least pre-1974) postwar recessions – which led to large scale scrapping of capital and the laying-off of workers. This contrasts with previous recessions where as the long-term costs of abandonment were high (the cost of restoring capital equipment, severance payments and search and training costs), the moderate extent of the down-turns encouraged firms to maintain capacity while waiting for the cyclical upturn. Conversely, during the post-1979 recessions, the depth of the recessions encouraged firms to reduce capacity in order to minimise short-term costs and maximise the possibility of survival. Furthermore, as the domestic economy has, albeit falteringly, developed, the industrial structure has shifted to more segmented and niche product markets. These sectors require specialist capital equipment and sector specific skills. The loss of such factors due to recession may be more difficult to replace in a period of recovery. Also, it is not possible to rely on future investment to make good the position; the existence of sunk costs means that restarting operations will be expensive – requiring a higher yield to encourage the replacement investment. This alone indicates that governments should adopt suitable expansionary policies to ameliorate the potentially negative impact of external shocks and certainly should not use severe contractionary policies to counter inflation. The long-term costs of recessions place an increasing premium on maintaining stable economic growth.

6 The tale of two recessions

1929 and the Gold Standard, 1992 and the ERM

Of all bad-neighbourly conduct among trading nations, the worst is to go into a slump.

(Joan Robinson, 1966)

1 Introduction

Europe has been locked into mass unemployment for the past decade and more, with all the economic and social misery which goes with that. The blame is put alternatively on the 'world recession', the welfare state, inflexible labour markets – almost anywhere except on government economic policy. Yet the governments of the European Union deliberately pursued deflationary, low growth, high unemployment policies throughout the 1990s.

The resulting unemployment should come as no surprise. Policies similar to those of the ERM were pursued under the Gold Standard of the 1920s, with parallel results in terms of deflationary government economic policies and the creation of mass unemployment. It seems that nothing has been learned. The world economy only managed to pull itself out of the Great Depression in the 1930s by abandoning fixed exchange rates, cutting interest rates and boosting growth. Yet when similar policies were advocated prior to 16 September 1992, when Britain was forced out of the ERM against its will by the currency speculators, such policies were denounced as 'anti-European'. But it does the European partners of any of the Member States no favours to have that Member State's economy in recession.

Although Britain suffered a more severe recession than most other EU countries in the early 1990s, Britain's exit from the ERM, cutting interest rates and devaluing the pound sterling boosted Britain's economic growth over the rest of the decade as compared with most of the other EU countries. If the other Member States were to cut interest rates and abandon the Single Currency then Europe might cease to play such a deflationary role in the world economy. If such policies were pursued by the other Member States then their currencies too might devalue, so that actual relative exchange rates might end up more or less where they started. But it would be with lower interest rates, higher economic growth and lower unemployment.

Yet when similar policies were eventually pursued in the 1930s with some success in cutting unemployment, the Great Depression nevertheless left a legacy of high unemployment. So an additional lesson which should be remembered, or re-learned, is the need for an active policy towards returning to full employment. First, interest rate cuts alone are not enough; industrial capacity itself still has to be rebuilt.[1] And second, economic growth, while absolutely necessary for tackling unemployment is not in itself sufficient; employment creation policies are also necessary.[2]

Lessons from the Gold Standard

We argue in this chapter that the Gold Standard as a framework for exchange rate policy slowed world growth during the late 1920s and exacerbated the Great Depression of 1929–32. The subsequent demise of the Gold Standard enabled many individual countries to implement independent economic policies which stimulated economic expansion. Despite the resulting upswing, however, the legacy of the Great Depression remained in the form of persistent unemployment.

As with the experience of the ERM, the experience of the Gold Standard indicates that there are serious dangers, as well as potential benefits, in entering 'cooperative' systems with fixed exchange rates. Such systems may limit the ability to deal with domestic problems, encourage strong countries to grow relatively stronger and weak countries to grow relatively weaker and ultimately become non-sustainable. Similarly, destructive cooperation risks being aggravated by the adoption of the Single Currency and the so-called Growth and Stability Pact which not only remove discretion over national monetary and fiscal policy but remove any possibility of currency realignment.

In Section 2 below we consider the extent of the unemployment problem in the interwar world economy. Section 3 then evaluates the operation of the Gold Standard and its deflationary bias. Section 4 considers the benefits which came from leaving the Gold Standard in the early 1930s, including the freedom to adopt expansionary policies. Section 5 highlights some lessons for current policy formulation. And finally in Section 6 we draw some conclusions regarding the European Single Currency.

2 Unemployment in the 1920s and 1930s

That mass unemployment was a major problem in the interwar world economy is not a matter of great controversy; measuring the extent of the problem is more so. Figure 6.1 shows contemporary (ILO, 1940) estimates of world unemployment which, under the impact of recession, increased to nearly 25 per cent in 1932 before falling during the 1930s, although the level remained high; unemployment averaged 17.5 per cent during 1930–32 compared with 15 per cent during 1932–37. An alternative measure of labour market

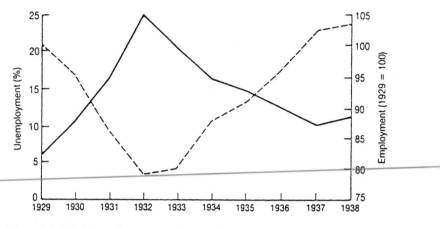

Figure 6.1 World employment and unemployment, 1929–38

Source: ILO (1940) Table 3.

Notes
1. Employment index excludes the USSR.
2. Unemployment series is the average of two series (A and B) presented in ILO (1940).

performance is employment change which is subject to fewer of the problems associated with estimating unemployment. Figure 6.1 therefore also shows world employment which from the peak in 1929 to the trough in 1932 declined at an annual rate of 7.6 per cent. Employment growth was rapid from 1932: the annual increase was 5.2 per cent, although it was not until 1937 that employment surpassed its 1929 levels.

Comparisons of national levels of unemployment are complicated by definitional problems and the paucity of consistent data. Table 6.1 provides a summary of the data from the two main sources: Galenson and Zellner's (1957) estimates of industrial unemployment and Maddison's (1991) estimates of industry-wide unemployment. The data are averaged over three periods: the period of moderate growth in the late 1920s, the periods of peak unemployment during 1930–32, and the recovery period 1933–37. As shown in Table 6.1, Galenson and Zellner's estimates tend to be twice those of Maddison for the European economies and 50 per cent greater for the other countries. The different definitional basis of the data is discussed in Eichengreen and Hatton (1988), who conclude that the actual economy-wide estimates of unemployment lie somewhere between the two sets of estimates.

Table 6.1 Average unemployment rates, 1924–37 (%)

	Maddison's estimates			Galenson and Zellner's estimates		
	1924–29	1930–32	1933–37	1924–29	1930–32	1933–37
Europe						
Austria	6.0	10.1	15.3	–	–	–
Belgium	6.4	8.6	8.2	1.3	11.2	15.7
Denmark	8.6	10.7	11.2	17.1	21.1	22.4
France	–	–	–	4.2	8.0	12.0
Finland	1.8	4.8	3.9	–	–	–
Germany	5.1	13.5	7.4	11.4	33.6	18.4
Italy	–	4.2	5.5	–	–	–
Netherlands	2.1	5.0	10.6	6.7	16.0	29.2
Norway	6.4	8.6	8.2	17.7	23.2	25.6
Sweden	2.6	5.0	6.1	11.0	17.0	15.9
UK	7.5	13.7	10.7	10.8	19.8	15.2
Rest of world						
Australia	5.9	16.7	12.6	8.1	24.3	15.8
Canada	3.1	12.8	14.0	4.8	18.8	19.1
USA	3.7	16.0	19.5	5.7	25.2	29.4

Sources: Maddison (1991), Galenson and Zellner (1957) and Lebergott (1964), as reproduced in Eichengreen and Hatton (1988).

There are further problems in comparing unemployment performance over time as methods of data collection change. This is illustrated in Figure 6.2 which presents two series of unemployment data for the UK for the period 1921–98, one based on standard data and the other based on more recent methods of counting. The adjusted figures illustrate that contrary to accepted opinion the extent of unemployment was greater in the 1980s than during the Great Depression; on this basis, UK unemployment reached 11.1 per cent in 1986 compared with 10.6 per cent in 1932.[3]

The limitations of the data cannot disguise the fact that unemployment was a major economic and social problem during the interwar period. Unemployment was a major cause of poverty driving families below the most basic of subsistence levels and leading to deteriorating health.[4]

Whichever series is used it is also evident that the major surge in unemployment came during the Great Depression, reaching a peak in 1932. The behaviour of unemployment in the 1930s depended on the strength of economic revival; however, what is apparent is that despite economic recovery and rising employment, unemployment was a problem that persisted in many of the major economies.

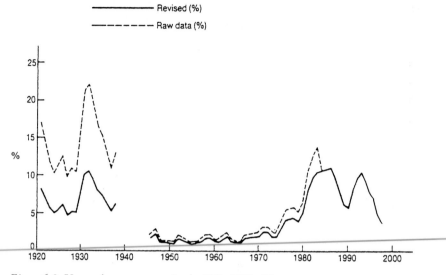

Figure 6.2 Unemployment rates in the UK, 1921–98

Sources: Crafts (1991) Table 41.3, p. 818 and Department of Employment, *Employment Gazette* (various editions), London: HMSO.

3 The Gold Standard: coordinated deflation

From the mid-1920s the cornerstone of international economic management was the Gold Standard. Founded on the questionable success of the classical Gold Standard in operation during the quarter century before the First World War, the 1920s variant was intended to bring stability into international trading relations and increase world prosperity.[5] It failed to achieve these objectives. Its actual effect was to depress real variables such as output and employment and undermine the capacity of individual governments to deal with domestic economic problems.

As shown in Figure 6.3, the restoration of the Gold Standard progressed throughout the 1920s. Austria stabilised in 1922, Germany and Sweden in 1924, Britain, Switzerland and the Netherlands in 1925, France and Belgium in 1926, and Italy and Poland in 1927. By 1927 the vast majority of trading nations had joined the system and the reconstruction of the fixed exchange rate system was in effect complete.[6]

The adjustment process integral to the Gold Standard created a severe deflationary bias for the world economy. To capture this bias the main trading countries can be broadly classified into those constrained and those unconstrained by their trade performance. Those countries that could maintain a sufficient level of exports, relative to imports, at a high level of

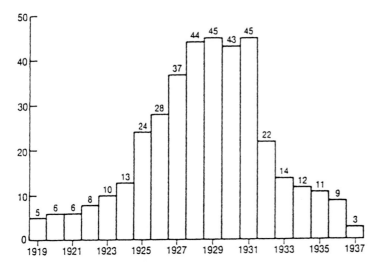

Figure 6.3 Number of countries on gold, 1919–37

Source: Eichengreen (1992) Table 7.1, pp. 188–191.

Note
The three countries on gold in 1937 were on the 'Qualified Gold Standard'.

economic activity were not balance-of-payments constrained. Such countries could pursue easier monetary policies or could accumulate increased reserves. Conversely, a country that could not maintain balance of payments equilibrium at a high level of economic activity had to reduce domestic demand in order to import only those goods and services which it could afford to finance.

The two key unconstrained countries were France and the US. France recovered successfully from the First World War, with an undervalued exchange rate helping to generate export-led growth. The US had become the world's leading economy during the late nineteenth century; its strength was based on huge natural resources of land and minerals, sustained investment which had significantly raised its capital stock, a large internal market and the development of an industrial structure that encouraged research and development and the exploitation of economies of scale.

The two major constrained countries were Britain and Germany, both of which emerged from the aftermath of war with severe economic problems. The British economy had been in relative decline since the 1870s. In addition, the commitment to return to gold necessitated tight monetary policies and the economy suffered a severe slump in 1920–21. The German economy, which had been rapidly expanding from the 1880s, had been devastated by the War. It lost financial and physical assets and reparations constituted a continual drain on its income and wealth.

The reconstructed Gold Standard, therefore, created a fixed exchange rate regime with members at different stages of economic development with different economic structures and different economic problems. Its prospects were not good.

Unrealistic assumptions

To be effective the Gold Standard depended on a process of automatic adjustment to correct payments imbalances. Under this system the price level would adjust in response to deficits and surpluses on the balance of payments. A deficit would lead to a loss of gold and a contraction in the money supply, leading to a fall in prices and the eradication of the deficit. Similarly, a surplus would lead to an accumulation of gold, a rise in the money supply and prices, and hence to a balance-of-payments equilibrium. But the real world did not work like this. The theory was based on various unrealistic assumptions, including the assumption that all the burden of adjustment would be borne by changes in prices rather than in changes in quantities produced.

As the main trading nations entered the exchange rate system with different initial conditions it was apparent that the efficacy of the adjustment process would be central to the regime's impact. The option of adjusting the nominal exchange rate was effectively precluded. The adjustment of the real exchange was slow and erratic. For the UK, most studies indicate a significant average overvaluation of the sterling effective exchange rate in the period 1925–31. Keynes's (1925) contemporary estimate of a 10 per cent overvaluation has proved to be a reasonable approximation of recent empirical estimates.

The result was lower growth and higher unemployment. Conventionally, it had been assumed that the unravelling of the price–quantity adjustment process would eventually return the economy to its previous position with only a temporary loss of output and jobs. However, the legacy of slow growth in fact lowered the long-run capacity of the economy itself.

The sluggishness of real exchange rate changes left two adjustment alternatives. First, changes in the level of demand: deflation in constrained countries and reflation in surplus countries. Second, the financing of the deficits of constrained countries by capital flows from the unconstrained countries. In fact the ultimate burden of adjustment was borne by domestic deflation. The surplus countries were reluctant to reflate. The classical adjustment mechanism assumes that gold flows will provide the means of changing the level of demand via prices. But price adjustment was slow, and the reflationary impact of gold flows into France and the US were negated by domestic monetary policy. Both countries, which by the late 1920s had between them accumulated 60 per cent of total gold reserves, prevented these reserves from boosting their domestic money supplies. American policy-makers were increasingly concerned with curbing stock market speculation whereas the French were wary of inflation. Deflation was transmitted abroad. Low import demand, particularly in America, led to widening balance-of-payments deficits in many of the key European economies.

The trade performance of the unconstrained countries is illustrated in Table 6.2. Their export growth was reasonable and close to the 5.7 per cent growth of world trade. Additionally, due to their reluctance to reflate, they were able to maintain large balance-of-payments surpluses throughout the 1920s. During 1925–29, France maintained a surplus that averaged over 2 per cent of GNP, while the US surplus averaged just under 1 per cent of national income. Table 6.3 shows that the US surplus was particularly significant, given the size of its economy, averaging 2.5 per cent of world trade compared to 1 per cent for the French.

The growth of world trade was therefore limited by the domestic policies of the unconstrained countries. Whereas these nations could choose whether

Table 6.2 Asymmetries in trade performance, 1924–29

	Annual average export growth (1924–29)	*Current account as a share of national income (average, 1924–29)*
Constrained countries		
United Kingdom	1.6	+1.5
Germany	11.3	−1.2
Unconstrained countries		
France	4.3	+2.1
USA	5.5	+0.8
World	5.7	−

Sources: Mitchell (1975, 1983); Carre, Dubois and Malinvaud (1976) and League of Nations (1939).

Note
Estimates for Germany refer to 1925–29.

Table 6.3 Current account surpluses as a percentage share of world exports, 1924–29

Year	France	USA
1924	1.7	3.5
1925	0.9	2.2
1926	1.2	1.5
1927	1.0	2.2
1928	0.7	3.1
1929	0.5	2.3
Annual average	1.0	2.5

Sources: Mitchell (1975, 1983); League of Nations (1939) and Kitson and Solomou (1990b).

or not to reflate, the constrained countries had no such options. The entire burden of adjustment fell on them – they could either deflate to eradicate balance-of-payments deficits or they could borrow to fund them. The effective approach of the UK economy was the former and Germany the latter.

Deflation could be achieved either through allowing reserves to flow out, depressing the money supply and domestic expenditure – the classical mechanism – or by policies that directly affected the components of demand. In Britain it was interest rates that acted as the key deflationary tool. From 1923 there was a trend rise in the Bank of England's discount rate as the authorities adopted policies consistent with the return and maintenance of the exchange rate at the prewar parity. At the same time the general trend of other central banks' discount rates was downward. The deflationary impact of such policies helped to keep the balance of payments in surplus and prevented the loss of gold.[7]

The Bank of England also deployed gold market and foreign exchange operations to maintain its stock of international reserves. The impact on the real economy was slow growth, with the economy failing to reap its growth potential (for more detail see Kitson and Solomou, 1990). Despite the level of GDP in 1924 being below that of 1913, the growth rate of the British economy was significantly below the world average.[8] Unemployment remained persistently high, averaging 7.5 per cent for the period 1924–29.

Unlike Britain, Germany maintained a persistent balance-of-payments deficit throughout the 1920s. Along with reparations this deficit had to be financed and Germany became heavily reliant on foreign loans, particularly from the US. Although initially able to attract sizeable capital inflows, the rising debt burden undermined creditworthiness. Germany became increasingly reliant on short-term funds and by 1931 had accumulated net foreign debts equivalent to 25 per cent of national income (for more detail see Kitson, 1992). The subsequent concern about the German economy and the collapse of American lending abroad from 1928 led to capital flight, the loss of reserves, a credit squeeze and the raising of interest rates. Germany had been able to cope with its balance-of-payments constraint in the short term by borrowing; ultimately, however, this only postponed the requirement to deflate.

The asymmetry in the adjustment processes showed in the relative trade performance of the two groups of countries during the 'successful' operation of the Gold Standard as illustrated in Table 6.2. The trading position of the constrained countries, the UK and Germany, differed significantly from that of the unconstrained countries. Although the UK managed to maintain a balance-of-payments surplus, its export performance was poor, exhibiting slow growth and a declining share of world markets. As Table 6.4 shows the UK share of world markets in 1929 was 3.2 percentage points below its 1913 level – the result of an average annual decline of 1.6 per cent. The German trading position was also in a precarious position, the deficit on the balance of payments averaging 1.2 per cent of national income between 1925 and

Table 6.4 UK and Germany's percentage
shares of world exports, 1913 and 1929

Year	UK	Germany
1913	13.9	13.1
1929	10.7	9.7
Average annual % change	−1.6	−1.9

Source: Lewis (1949: 90).

1929. Germany's export growth was rapid during this period, but this was catching-up from a very low postwar base and was boosted by enforced exports through reparations in kind. Despite this rapid growth, Germany's share of world exports in 1929 was more than 25 per cent below its 1913 level.

Competitiveness

Thus the deflationary bias of the Gold Standard not only failed to deal with the structural problems of constrained countries, it accentuated them. Countries which had entered the system with major structural problems, left the system weakened as they had to bear the burden of adjustment by deflating their domestic economies. This not only lowered growth and raised unemployment; it also hampered long-run competitiveness. The dampening of domestic demand reduced the benefits of mass production and the exploitation of scale economies. Deflation to maintain external equilibrium raised unit costs and generated a further loss of competitiveness and declining shares of world markets. Such a process of cumulative causation led the constrained countries to suffer a vicious cycle of stagnation. Locked into a fixed exchange rate system there were few policy options to reverse the process.

If the Gold Standard failed to maximise world growth in the 1920s its shortcomings were also evident with the onset of the Great Depression. The causes of the Great Depression are subject to continual debate, but key factors were certainly the cumulative impact of structural problems, adverse demand shocks and policy mistakes (on which, see Chapter 5 above). One such policy mistake was the constrained countries' adherence to gold.

And the severity of the Great Depression can certainly be attributed to the operation of the Gold Standard: the impact of adverse shocks, such as the recession in the US and the collapse in capital exports, were transmitted to the rest of the world through the exchange rate regime. As foreign loans were called in due to developments in the domestic economy, the gold flows to the US increased. The draining of reserves in the debtor countries accelerated and monetary policy was tightened to ensure gold convertibility. Thus the deflationary bias of the Gold Standard system resulted in a perverse reaction to adverse demand shocks. Rather than facilitating an expansion of demand to ameliorate the depression, the system magnified the problem leading to a collapse in world trade.

As countries moved into recession they needed the capacity to initiate domestic policies in order to insulate themselves from the collapse in the world economy. The structure, characteristics and paths of development of the major economies were different and thus the timing and the composition of the policy mix required was also different. The phasing of the depression of the major countries differed: there was approximately a three year gap between the onset of decline in Germany and that in Denmark.[9] Yet during this period economic policy was constrained by the Gold Standard, leaving little flexibility to deal quickly with domestic problems.

The impact of the Great Depression also varied across countries: national income in the US collapsed by an annual rate in excess of 10 per cent between 1929 and 1932, whereas other countries such as Denmark and Norway witnessed little or no decline. In part these variations reflected the speed with which countries left gold, although another major factor was the difference in economic structures and institutions. Britain's relatively moderate depression, an annual decline of less than 2 per cent compared to a world average of over 6 per cent, in part reflected the low dependence on agriculture and the stability of its financial institutions. Thus shocks had different national and sectoral impacts. Binding nations together in a fixed exchange rate regime made no allowance for this.

The Gold Standard's fault lines

The interwar Gold Standard system was structurally flawed. Even if cooperation between countries had managed to limit the deflationary bias, it would most likely have only extended the life of the system rather than preventing its ultimate demise. Indeed, had the system lasted longer, it might have resulted in divergent growth paths. Reflation in the stronger countries could well have led to faster growth of output and productivity, leading to a virtuous cycle of growth, but with deflation limiting the growth potential of the relatively weaker countries.

Also, the system combined together countries with different economic conditions and problems. These problems were not eradicated by the regime; rather they were accentuated. Discretion over the use of monetary, fiscal and exchange rate policy was removed.

And finally, the regime was not able to accommodate adverse economic shocks to the system; on the contrary, the operation of the international monetary system magnified the impact of any such recessionary forces. The regime was inappropriate for members with different economic structures and a recession phased differently amongst the international community.[10]

4 Economic Recovery in the 1930s

The extent and magnitude of the Great Depression put the Gold Standard regime under severe strain. A series of financial and balance-of-payments crises ultimately undermined the system, culminating in Britain's decision to abandon the Gold Standard and devalue in September 1931. This marked the collapse of the regime. Other countries quickly followed sterling off the Gold Standard, including most of the dominions and Empire, the Scandinavian countries, Canada and Japan. It was not until March 1933 that the US devalued, while a core of countries including France, Belgium and the Netherlands remained on gold until later in the decade. Devaluation was not the only uncoordinated trade policy implemented; tariffs and quotas were increased while many of the Central European countries including Germany and Italy resorted to extensive exchange controls.

Devaluation

Devaluation can have beneficial impacts through a number of mechanisms. First, it can directly alleviate the balance-of-payments constraint on growth. Shifts in relative prices and improved competitiveness can raise exports and depress imports. The conventional account of this process is that it is a 'beggar-my-neighbour' policy, as the improvement in trade performance is reflected in an improving trade balance for the initiating country and a deteriorating trade balance for trading partners. This account, however, ignores the effects of an independently pursued trade policy on the level of economic activity. Increasing exports and reducing the propensity to import will raise the level of demand in the domestic economy. With unemployment and excess capacity, such a policy initiative will raise output and employment as well as leading to an income-induced increase in imports so that there need be no change in the actual trade balance. Indeed, this is precisely the reason why, although Britain devalued and adopted widespread protectionism in 1931, the current account deficits persisted throughout the 1930s. If countries get locked into a pattern of trade which constrains domestic expansion, an active and independent trade policy provides one means of overcoming the problem without necessarily affecting adversely other trading partners.

The second benefit of devaluation is that it removes the exchange rate constraint on domestic policy, encouraging expansionist policies. In particular, monetary policy can be relaxed and therefore interest rates can be determined by domestic economic conditions rather than by the need to maintain the exchange rate or by the need to prevent excessive loss of reserves. For instance Britain's suspension of the Gold Standard allowed the government to pursue a more expansionist policy after 1932. This 'cheap money' policy has been identified as a permissive policy for economic revival, especially important in stimulating a housing boom. Conversely, the reason that the UK Government's claims on 16 September 1992 – that it would remain in the

ERM by raising interest rates as far as was necessary – lacked credibility was that raising interest rates by 5 percentage points in one day in the midst of the longest economic recession for 60 years was not believed to be a feasible policy option domestically.

Although a wide range of uncoordinated policies were implemented in the 1930s, including devaluation, it is possible to classify the major trading nations into different trade policy regimes (for a discussion of which see Kitson and Solomou, 1990). First, the sterling bloc that devalued with or soon after Britain and linked their currencies to sterling. Second, other countries who also devalued either early (before 1932) or later (1932 and after). Third, the exchange control group, who were reluctant to devalue for fear of inflation. And fourth, the gold bloc countries that remained, at least in the short term, committed to the system. Table 6.5 shows the average annual growth rate of output for the four policy regimes for various periods. During the 1929–32 depression, 'world' output declined by more than 6 per cent per annum. The sterling bloc exhibited the mildest contraction, with national income falling by an annual rate of less than 2 per cent per annum, and just

Table 6.5 Performance of different policy regimes during the interwar period: annual growth rate of output

	Depression	*Recovery*	*Inter-period*
Sterling bloc	−1.7	4.7	−1.6
(excluding Canada)	−0.5	4.7	−0.7
Other devaluers	−6.0	6.8	−2.5
early devaluers	−5.0	7.7	0
late devaluers	−7.1	5.9	−5.0
Exchange control	−3.5	4.5	−3.3
Gold bloc	−3.3	2.3	−3.7
World	−6.1	5.2	−2.8

Sources: Maddison (1991) and Mitchell (1975, 1983).

Notes
1 *Phases*
   Depression: 1929–32.
   Recovery:1932–37.
   Inter-period: Change in growth performance between two peak-to-peak periods, 1929–37 minus 1924–29.
2 *Countries in sample*
   Sterling bloc: Australia, Denmark, Finland, Norway, Sweden, United Kingdom and Canada.
   Other devaluers: Early devaluers are Brazil, Japan, and Mexico. Late devaluers are Colombia, Chile and the United States.
   Exchange control: Austria, Bulgaria, Czechoslovakia, Germany, Hungary, Italy and Yugoslavia.
   Gold bloc: Belgium, France, Netherlands and Switzerland.
3 Figures are unweighted averages.
4 'The world' is the weighted sum of Maddison's 16 capitalist countries.
5 For most countries the output measure used is real GDP.

0.5 per cent if Canada is excluded from the sample (Canada was particularly adversely affected by its large agricultural sector and its links with the US). This suggests that devaluation policies may have helped to mitigate the adverse effects of the depression. Leaving gold provided less help for the 'other devaluers' group although there is evidence that those who devalued early experienced a milder depression than those who delayed and devalued late. Thus, the timing of the policy response was important.

For the period of recovery, from 1932–37, most countries exhibited reasonable cyclical growth. The exception was the gold bloc countries. Constrained by their commitment to their exchange rate parities they had to adopt tight monetary and fiscal policies to maintain internal and external balance. Thus although output was depressed, the French government in the early 1930s adopted contractionary fiscal policies to prevent destabilising exchange rate speculation.

A simple comparison of growth performance during recovery can be misleading as it will include both a cyclical component (the automatic recovery from a deep depression) and policy induced effects. An alternative is to examine inter-period, peak to peak growth performance. Table 6.5 reports the change in the annual rate of growth of national income during 1929–37 relative to 1924–29: the results for the 'world' economy indicate a retardation of the growth path. This is consistent with other findings that the shock of the Great Depression had persistent effects on the level of output. The performance of the different policy regimes, however, provides important contrasts. The countries that devalued, particularly those that devalued early, experienced only a small (or zero) fall in trend growth. Those countries that had the limited benefits of exchange controls experienced a deterioration in annual growth of 3.3 per cent. The poorest performing group was the gold bloc, which had little flexibility to initiate policies for domestic recovery.

Further evidence of the striking contrasts in performance of different policy regimes is shown in Table 6.6, which presents figures for annual growth of industrial production. These indicate that those countries that devalued, and to a lesser extent those that introduced exchange controls, had a milder industrial depression, faster recovery and a better inter-period growth performance.

Table 6.7 presents some evidence on the unemployment performance of the different policy regimes showing that the high unemployment that developed during the depression persisted throughout the period of recovery. Only for the sterling bloc was there any fall in the unemployment rate; for the other regimes unemployment increased during 1933–37. In part this reflects employment lagging output, plus changing activity rates and demographic shifts. But it is also evidence of the persistent effects of the Great Depression, the long-term unemployed having difficulties re-entering the labour market.

Growth and improved economic performance during the 1930s were dependent on countries untying themselves from the strictures of the Gold Standard and adopting independent policies, with different exchange rate regimes created and with some countries also reaping the advantages of

Table 6.6 Performance of different policy regimes during the interwar period: annual growth rate of industrial production

	Depression	Recovery	Inter-period
Sterling bloc	−5.3	9.5	−2.0
(excluding Canada)	−3.7	9.3	−0.5
Other devaluers	−8.3	11.9	−2.1
early devaluers	−4.7	12.8	—
late devaluers	−11.8	11.0	—
Exchange control	−11.2	10.3	−4.1
Gold bloc	−10.9	6.0	−7.1

Sources: Mitchell (1975, 1983).

Notes
1 *Phases*: See Table 6.5.
2 *Countries*: As Table 6.5, except 'Sterling bloc' excludes Denmark from inter-period esti-
    mates. 'Other devaluers' excludes Colombia and Japan. 'Exchange control' group excludes
    Bulgaria, Yugoslavia and Hungary from inter-period estimates. 'Gold bloc' excludes
    Switzerland and includes Poland.

increased protectionism and fiscal expansion. What is apparent, however, is that the cooperative regime failed and uncoordinated policies were a vast improvement.

The role of wages

As always, there are some authors (such as Beenstock, Capie and Griffiths, 1984) who argue that it was wage movements that accounted for the cyclical fluctuations in output, both for the Great Depression and the subsequent recovery. It is true that real wages (adjusted for price changes) did move counter-cyclically over the 1929–37 cycle in Britain – rising relative to trend in the recession and then falling relative to trend during the recovery – but the causes of the output fluctuations lay elsewhere, and the timing of the wage fluctuations do not actually fit the claim that recession was caused by wage rises and recovery caused by wage cuts. We have shown elsewhere (in Michie, 1987) that this wage–output correlation itself does not in any case hold outside those particular years – a finding which reinforces the argument that the output and wage series are independently generated, with output influenced crucially by the level of demand for output, and wages by factors such as productivity levels and bargaining strength.[11]

5 The economic consequences of Mr Major

The similar experience of deep slumps and widespread unemployment has led to comparisons between the interwar period on the one hand and economic events in the 1990s on the other, including by analogy between the ERM and the interwar Gold Standard. Both resemble 'adjustable peg systems' in

Table 6.7 Performance of different policy regimes during the interwar period: average annual unemployment rate

	Depression 1930–32 (i)	Recovery 1933–37 (ii)	(ii − i)
Sterling bloc	10.3	9.5	−0.8
(excluding Canada)	9.9	8.8	−1.1
USA	16.0	19.5	+3.5
Exchange control	9.3	9.4	+0.1
Gold bloc	4.4	6.8	+2.4

Source: Maddison (1991).

Notes
1 *Phases*: See Table 6.5.
2 *Countries*: As Table 6.5, except 'other devaluers' excluded due to lack of data. 'Exchange control' group excludes Bulgaria, Czechoslovakia, Hungary and Yugoslavia.
3 French data are for benchmark years only.

theory, but rather less adjustable in practice; both failed to deal with external shocks; both suffered adversely from speculative attacks; and both limited the flexibility of domestic policy. As in 1931, Britain disengaged itself from the exchange rate system, allowed the exchange rate to fall, and introduced cheap money. As in 1931, policy reflected crisis management rather than any coherent strategy, although the benefits of devaluation were at least more fully discussed 60 years ago than they were prior to September 1992. Similarly, the French 'franc fort' policy of the 1980s and 1990s resembles the ultimately misconceived French commitment to gold in the 1930s.

Despite the historical similarities some important differences remain. International capital markets are now more integrated, making it more difficult to engineer unilateral reductions in interest rates. Recent British experience does show, however, that such unilateral action is still possible, with the leaving of the ERM allowing interest rate cuts despite claims prior to September 1992 that interest rates would actually have to increase in such circumstances to compensate for loss of confidence and credibility.[12] Also, the present economic problems faced by European economies have different causes and different characteristics from the interwar period. For instance, depressed demand in the British economy in the 1990s reflected the high level of debt in the private sector resulting from Government policy mismanagement and the impact of financial de-regulation in the mid-1980s. However, some important lessons can still be drawn.

First, macroeconomic policies which retard growth may have persistent effects on the real economy. Second, policies which are based on trying to achieve convergence of inflation rates and other monetary and financial indicators can have adverse effects on the real economy. This is particularly so when those policies fail to accommodate different initial conditions, or when they tend to have a deflationary bias, or when they fail to successfully accommodate economic shocks. The experience of the Gold Standard supports this warning, as does more recent evidence. Thus the notion, for example, that because Germany had a strong economy and a strong currency, imposing a strong currency on Britain would thereby strengthen the domestic economy, was fatally flawed. Causation runs from the real economy to the exchange rate not vice versa. Britain's decision to join the ERM at DM2.95 served to weaken Britain's trading sector and removed the policy options required to deal with domestic recession. As with the collapse of world trade in 1929, the problems of German unification and the Danish response to Maastricht produced a major shock to the exchange rate system.

One of the keys to economic growth during the 1930s was the use of independent and uncoordinated policies. This is not the same as saying that coordination itself is necessarily ineffective. What *is* ineffective is a coordination based on convergence towards monetary and financial targets which has adverse impacts on the real economies of the participants. During the 1930s, coordination based on structured reflation and the effective redistribution of resources to regions or countries of the world with difficulties would have been appropriate. The limitations of such policy packages is that the level of cooperation required is significant and the rules required are complex and not easily enforced. In the absence of such an agreed and enforced policy package, independent policies were the next best option, and as such proved successful during the 1930s. Unless current European economic policy is reorientated towards the objective of full employment, embracing an active industrial and regional policy, rather than with the myopic concern with zero inflation, the route forward must once again be based on independent national growth strategies which would not only allow countries to help themselves, but by doing so would help each other. Competitive deflation is the real 'beggar my neighbour' policy of the 1990s.

And third, despite economic revival in the 1930s, unemployment remained high. It was a constant source of poverty, disease and malnutrition. The implementation of a growth strategy today, whether it be of a national or European variety, is a necessary condition for tackling unemployment, but may not of itself be sufficient. It is important, therefore, first that the pursuit of market flexibility does not further erode the welfare state upon which the basic needs of so many depend; and second that policies for employment are pursued alongside those for economic recovery and growth. These need to include measures such as reducing the length of the working week and year; expanding employment-intensive public services and public works, such as a major environmental programme; and supply side measures on education and training, and on research, development and design to see through new products and production processes.[13]

6 Conclusions

The European economies in the 1930s experienced differing degrees of employment growth, and the cause of this growth also differed across countries. What was common to many of the countries, however, was the breaking of the exchange rate constraint on monetary policy. In addition, some countries benefited from fiscal expansion, a policy shift often associated with the publication in 1936 of Keynes's *General Theory*, although in reality it had more to do with rearmament and, in certain countries, fascist economic policies.[14]

Today, mass unemployment and economic stagnation have been brought about by monetarist policies pursued by governments in the European Union operating under the labels 'Conservative' and 'Socialist' alike. The operation of the ERM caused high interest rate policies, producing widespread unemployment throughout the 1980s in many of the participating economies. National income fell by 2.4 per cent in Britain in 1991 and growth remained negative throughout 1992. Unemployment rose to above 3 million and fell only after Britain was forced out of the ERM.

When Britain joined the ERM in October 1990, why, though, was an overvalued exchange rate, at DM2.95, chosen? The stated objective was squeezing inflation. What was not stated was the route by which it was hoped it would work, by deliberately making things hard for British firms, thereby forcing them to try to cut costs by cutting wages and introducing more intensive working practices. As detailed above, this is not the first time that governments have allowed the currency to be overvalued in this way. Winston Churchill as Chancellor took Britain back onto the Gold Standard in the 1920s at an overvalued rate, with Keynes warning at the time, in his pamphlet *The Economic Consequences of Mr Churchill*, of the disastrous likely consequences of this policy – consequences which were to include the General Strike of 1926. Similarly, the first Thatcher recession of 1979–81 was exacerbated by the high exchange rate caused not only by North Sea oil, but also by the high interest rates which followed from the government's monetarist experiment.

In the interwar period Britain was indeed forced to abandon the Gold Standard. And the exchange rate similarly fell after 1981, depreciating nearly 30 per cent by 1986, helping to fuel the recovery. Likewise, the overvalued rate at which Chancellor Major entered the ERM meant that our membership was always doomed to failure. Yet those who pointed this out at the time were dismissed out of hand. The leadership of all three major political parties supported continued membership at the overvalued rate. Even if this had been a genuine option, it would have been a disastrous one, but in reality it was not even an option.

But the problems of the ERM policy for the UK lay deeper than just having joined at the wrong rate. The ERM was a high unemployment mechanism for the European Union as a whole, but all the pressure was on the weaker economies to take action, rather than on the strong ones. And worse, that action was designed more to prop up the currencies of the weak economies than to strengthen their productive potential, which is the only sustainable basis for maintaining a healthy currency. Increased interest rates were demanded. These depressed investment plans and left the economy in question further weakened. Yet the weakness of the economy most probably underlay the weakness of the currency in the first place. So a weak economy produced a weak currency; the ERM then required the government in question to raise interest rates; and increased interest rates squeezed the country's economy, leaving it still weaker. If this high interest rate policy itself proved inadequate, then government spending cuts were required as well, further accelerating the cumulative process of relative decline.

Extending the ERM into a single currency risks locking the European Union into prolonged recession and unemployment. The 'independence' of the European Central Bank should certainly be opposed, as should the limits on public borrowing and the other monetarist and deflationary strictures of the post-Maastricht Treaty's Growth and Stability Pact. Full employment and improved economic welfare should be the aim, not the completion of some grand monetarist design.

7 Britain's industrial performance since 1960

Underinvestment and relative decline

1 Introduction

There has been considerable debate over the causes of 'deindustrialisation'.[1] The relative decline of manufacturing, and particularly manufacturing employment, and the corresponding relative growth of services, is prevalent in both slow and fast growing countries (see Petit, 1986). Since 1960 the share of manufacturing in total employment and GDP has fallen in the major OECD countries (with a concomitant rise in the share of services). This relative decline of manufacturing has led some to see the process as being some sort of an inevitable historical evolution. The argument that there are definable stages of economic development as advanced by Fisher (1935), Rostow (1960) and Kuznets (1966) have as a common feature that the final stages are characterised by a modern tertiary sector with growing preferences for service products.

A first explanation of this phenomenon is based on the proposition that there is a faster relative growth of labour productivity in manufacturing than in services. This will result in the costs of manufactures falling relative to services. Assuming that the demand for manufactures and services is relatively price inelastic, the share of manufacturing employment in total employment will decrease. Many studies including those by Baumol (1967), Fuchs (1968), Saxonhouse (1985) and Summers (1985) have presented evidence that productivity differences are the main source of the decline in manufacturing employment, although others such as Marquand (1979) dispute that services have low productivity.

Like much of the analysis of the service sector, the lagging productivity thesis is hampered by the data problems. In particular there are substantial difficulties in measuring productivity in services as in most cases no physical output is produced. In the UK, however, the evidence on relative price movements (assuming similar wage rates in manufacturing and services for the same occupation), and the suggestion that non-marketed service output may be overestimated (as such output is measured, in part, simply via wage bills) – so that service productivity may actually be lower than the official figures would suggest – does add support to the idea that differential productivity growth between the two sectors plays an important role (Gershuny and Miles, 1983).

A second explanation for the relative decline of manufacturing and the relative growth of services stems from the changing structure of demand as incomes increase. This explanation is relevant to the growth of personal or consumer services as opposed to intermediate or producer services, although the distinction is often arbitrary. It has been argued that, as their income elasticity of demand is greater than one, the growth in demand for services will exceed the growth of income. Gershuny (1978), for example, pointed out that in Britain wealthier households spent a greater proportion of their income on services; such relationships however seem to be unstable over time and suffer from definitional problems, as much of this service expenditure is on associated goods. Fuchs (1968) argued that the income elasticity of demand for services was only slightly greater than that for other products and was not a major explanation of the growth of the service sector. Similarly, Baumol *et al.* (1989) reject the demand explanation for the US, as during the past few decades manufacturing output has risen as fast as the output of services and Rowthorn and Wells (1987) have argued that demand for manufactures and services tends to increase at the same rate as economies reach industrial maturity. Additionally, superior productivity growth in manufacturing will create a widening price advantage which will help maintain the share of demand as income rises.

A third explanation for the relative 'decline' of manufacturing is the changing source of service provision, with activities which were previously undertaken by firms becoming increasingly contracted out (to the service sector). Fuchs (1968) found that changes in intermediate service production in the US accounted for 10 per cent of the total expansion of service sector employment.

Contracting out can also take place with consumer services, such as the increased use of restaurants and housekeepers, with such service sector activity replacing work which was previously done within the household but which did not appear in the national accounts. The evidence here, however, is mixed. Rising incomes may encourage the replacement of domestic activities with commercial equivalents, but conversely the opposite may happen due to increased leisure time and the relatively high cost of services. Also, manufactured products may replace or reduce the need for some services (the television replaces the theatre). Such a substitution effect led Gershuny and Miles (1983) to argue that we are moving towards a 'self service' economy.

The impact of 'contracting out' is complicated not just by the usual measurement problems but also because observing the net changes for the sector may reveal little about the significant changes within the sector. Some services may be internalised within firms and households while other services are contracted out. What is required is an understanding of both processes. The mode of service provision needs also to be considered in the context of changing economic, technological and institutional conditions. The recessionary and uncertain environment in the UK since 1979 led many firms in the UK to concentrate on 'core' or central activities, contracting out peripheral activities ranging from catering and cleaning to design. The impetus for this change, however, seems to differ between firms. Some responded to the contraction of markets by attempting to restructure their production processes in order to become more competitive in the long term; others by attempting to simply cut costs in the short term.[2]

As income rises and economies approach industrial maturity it can be expected that manufacturing employment shares fall and manufacturing (current price) output shares rise and then fall (Cosh, Hughes and Rowthorn, 1994). It is, however, important to recognise that the process of deindustrialisation may not just reflect positive factors, such as rising income and industrial maturity, but may also reflect negative factors such as an uncompetitive or small manufacturing sector. In this regard, negative deindustrialisation will not only be reflected in falling output and employment shares (although these shares may fall more rapidly in countries suffering negative as opposed to positive deindustrialisation) but in low growth (of manufacturing and total output) and an inability to maintain external trading equilibrium. Furthermore, it may be possible for positive deindustrialisation to lead to negative deindustrialisation – as shifting sectoral shares may result in the domestic manufacturing sector being unable to reap the benefits of rapid productivity growth.

The notion that the manufacturing sector is a dynamic engine of growth can be traced to the work of Lewis (1954), Kaldor (1966), Cornwall (1977) and others. The extension of the market for manufactured products would lead through the benefits of economies of scale to increased competitive advantage and hence to increased economic growth. The implication of this argument is that the service sector may expand both in terms of output and employment but if full employment is to be achieved there must be sufficient demand for manufactured products. And as noted by Godley (1986), Britain was the only advanced industrial nation since 1960 where the growth of manufacturing output was less than the growth of output of other goods and services – thus the relative decline in manufacturing output was a unique British phenomenon.

In neoclassical economics, divergences from 'equilibrium' are thought to be rectified through price adjustment and/or the correction of market failures. In reality, economies do not behave like this. First, history is important (as recognised in recent path dependent models) such that the quantity and quality of factors of production accumulated from the past determine what can be produced in the immediate future. This is inconsistent with conventional equilibrium theory which asserts that an economy is constrained by exogenous variables which remain stable over time (Kaldor, 1985). Additionally, it implies that it is difficult and expensive to reverse many economic decisions. If a factory is closed or if a market is lost it is difficult to regain the status quo ante. Second, the impact of economic shocks may not only have a once and for all impact on long-run capacity but may lead to cumulative changes. Thus as Allyn Young stated, forces of economic change are endogenous:

> They are engendered from within the economic system. No analysis, of the forces making for economic equilibrium, forces that we might say are tangential at any moment of time, will serve to illumine this field, for movements away from equilibrium, departures from previous trends are characteristic of it.
>
> (Quoted in Kaldor, 1985, p. 64)

The factor generating economic change for Young (1928) was increasing returns.[3] This led to Myrdal (1957), Kaldor (1972) and others identifying the twin processes of virtuous cycles of growth and vicious cycles of decline. For Kaldor, manufacturing acts as an engine of growth as it exhibits increasing returns while services are characterised by constant returns. As noted above, this proposition may be too simplistic as increasing returns are likely to exist in services (despite problems of measurement). This does not, however, diminish the importance of the cumulative causation analysis for understanding the diverging economic performance and prospects of different countries. First, divergences in countries' growth paths can develop as a result of differences – due to the size of the market – in the ability of competing countries to exploit increasing returns in their *tradable* output sectors; and the tradable goods sector remains dominated by manufacturing. Second, the cumulative processes will not only lead to differences in cost competitiveness but also to other non-price factors, such as product quality, customer service and technological development (see Kitson, 1997).

Growing economies, for instance, will be able to invest in capital and skills enabling them to improve processes and products. Conversely in economies suffering relative decline, a lack of investment and a dwindling skill base are likely to constrain future growth. For the latter this may take the form of a reduction of in-house training and/or a decline in support for external provision by training agencies so that the local infrastructure for skill generation is weakened. This, and the migration from the trade of workers in a position to do so, creates a skill shortage. The response to this, in the face of the decline in formal training, is the substitution of on-the-job instruction with a focus on a narrow range of specific skills to meet the firms' immediate needs, often accompanied by the exclusion of worker representatives from the training design and implementation processes. Consequently the skill content of jobs is diluted and this interacts with the deterioration of the terms and conditions of employment and the increasing pessimism about future prospects of the industry to discourage new entrants from traditional areas of recruitment. And any subsequent relaxation of hiring standards to meet the labour shortage serves to further reinforce the social downgrading of the job, the dissipation of skills, the loss of competitiveness and industrial decline.[4]

2 Manufacturing in the UK

As the House of Lords Select Committee on Science and Technology reported, 'Manufacturing industry is vital to the prosperity of the United Kingdom . . . Our manufacturing base is dangerously small; to achieve adequate growth from such a small base will be difficult' (House of Lords, 1991, p. 3). The relative decline of manufacturing in the UK has been greater than the norm for the OECD countries. In terms of per cent shares of value added, the UK manufacturing sector contributed 13.3 per cent less in 1993 than it did in 1960, compared to an average fall across the OECD of 9.3 percentage points. In terms of employment shares, the manufacturing sector's contribution fell by 19.9 per cent across the same period, compared to an average fall across the OECD of 7.3 percentage points.

The extent of the UK's decline is prima facie evidence that the UK is suffering from negative deindustrialisation. Manufacturing output in the UK is barely higher today than it was 25 years ago. The picture is one of rising output up to 1973, followed by a sharp fall to 1975 and subsequent recovery in the second half of the 1970s (generally taken as peaking again in 1979 although the annual index averages to a lower overall figure over 1979 than for 1978). The deep recession of the early 1980s was followed by a weak recovery, leading straight into the Lawson boom, taking manufacturing output to a new peak in 1989 before falling again in the early 1990s' recession. Despite the recovery from the recession of the early 1990s, and even talk of an overheating economy in 1999, manufacturing output is barely higher than it was in the second quarter of 1990, just before the recession began. And at the time of writing (October 1999), UK manufacturing is still suffering from the problems caused by an overvalued currency as a result of the interest rate policy imposed by the newly-independent Bank of England.

Meanwhile manufacturing productivity grew in every year apart from 1975 and 1980, even when output fell. There has therefore been an almost continual decline in manufacturing employment from its peak level in 1966. Table 7.1 compares, in summary form, the UK's manufacturing performance with its main competitors. The UK is the only one of the six with a lower average level of manufacturing output over the years 1979–89 than over the years 1973–79. Britain was also the only country to experience a fall in output between the years 1973 and 1979. Since 1979 the average growth returned to a positive, albeit generally lower rate than in any of the other major industrialised countries: between 1979 and 1989 output growth averaged 1.4 per cent (only France had a lower growth rate) and between 1989 and 1998 it fell to 0.4 per cent (with only Japan having a lower growth rate). A similar picture emerges for manufacturing employment. The UK was the only country to experience a fall in manufacturing employment between 1964 and 1973. While others saw employment fall between 1979 and 1989, and between 1989 and 1998 (with the exception of Italy), none did so at the rate experienced in the UK. During 1973–79 only Germany and Japan

Table 7.1 Manufacturing output and employment: international comparisons 1964–98
(average output and employment over each period, and average annual % growth during each period)

	1964–73	1973–79	1979–89	1989–98
UK: Output (1985 = 100)	95.1	105.3	101.2	118.1
Average annual growth	3.1	−1.0	1.4	0.4
Employment (millions)	8.254	7.481	5.759	4.366
Average annual growth	−0.8	−1.3	−3.4	−2.9
Italy: Output (1985 = 100)	66.4	88.7	103.4	120.2
Average annual growth	6.1	2.6	1.8	1.1
Employment (millions)	6.203	6.525	6.606	5.529
Average annual growth	4.3	0.2	−1.5	0.6
France: Output (1985 = 100)	72.4	97.8	103.7	113.3
Average annual growth	5.9	1.5	0.7	0.9
Employment (millions)	5.670	5.825	5.140	4.368
Average annual growth	2.1	−0.9	−1.7	−1.7
Germany: Output (1985 = 100)	73.4	90.2	99.5	118.5
Average annual growth	4.8	1.2	1.5	1.5
Employment (millions)	8.060	7.684	6.972	7.088
Average annual growth	0.8	−2.2	−0.5	−1.3
USA: Output (1985 = 100)	61.1	77.5	98.0	130.4
Average annual growth	5.2	2.7	3.0	3.5
Employment (millions)	19.123	19.824	19.465	18.587
Average annual growth	−1.7	0.7	−0.8	−0.4
Japan: Output (1985 = 100)	45.7	70.3	95.8	120.9
Average annual growth	11.9	2.0	120.9	−0.3
Employment (1985 = 100)	97.3	96.8	97.3	104.2
Average annual growth	1.8	−1.9	1.0	−0.4

Sources: OECD (various dates), *Main Economic Indicators*, and own calculations.

Notes
For employment, the figures for Italy include construction; there are definitional changes in the data for West Germany from 1970; the first period average for France is for 1968–73 (with the average annual growth also calculated between these years); and the figures for Japan are index numbers with 1985 = 100.

experienced a faster rate of job losses and, as indicated above, in both cases this was due to strong productivity growth rather than simply output loss as was the case for the UK. Looking at the four peak-to-peak periods, Britain was at the bottom of the league table of the six countries in three of the periods, and second bottom in the third.[5] This poor record on manufacturing output resulted in declining manufacturing employment.

Table 7.2 gives the growth of manufacturing output for the six countries between the years 1964 and 1998, with the UK firmly at the foot of the performance league: the average annual growth of manufacturing output was 4.5 per cent in Japan, 3.7 per cent in the US, 2.9 per cent in Italy, 2.3 per cent in France, 2.3 per cent in Germany, and only 1.1 per cent in the UK. Table 7.2 also reports the overall growth between 1964 and 1998, as well as for the other peak-to-peak periods. Taking the overall growth figure to 1998, it can be seen that while the level of manufacturing output was more than 116 per cent higher by the end of the period in Germany, and more than 353 per cent higher in Japan, in Britain the overall growth was just 47 per cent. Furthermore, in each peak-to-peak period, the growth of manufacturing output was much lower than that achieved in the other five countries (the only exception being between 1989 and 1998 when the UK's poor total growth of 3.9 per cent was better than the negative growth experienced by Japan).

An assessment of the UK's relatively poor growth rate performance must be tempered by consideration of different levels of income. It may be expected that growth rates will differ as countries have different per capita income levels. Countries with relatively low income levels may have relatively higher growth rates as they have the potential to appropriate technologies and organisational techniques from the leading countries. This process, even allowing for the fact that it may be both erratic and confined to countries at broadly similar stages of industrialisation, cannot explain Britain's inferior growth performance. The UK's poor growth rate has not just been associated with other industrialised countries catching up with the UK GDP level, but with those countries overtaking that level. In 1950 the UK was the second richest European economy, by 1973 it was seventh, and by 1992 it was eleventh. During the period 1950–73, the UK had the lowest growth rate of the 16 European economies. During the period 1973–92, when all growth rates slowed, its growth rate ranked joint twelfth, with only two countries having an inferior growth performance.

Three important points are clear: first, the decline in manufacturing employment in the UK can *not* be explained solely by shifts in consumption

Table 7.2 Growth of manufacturing output, 1964–99

	Average annual % growth	Total % growth from first to last year			
		1964–73	*1973–89*	*1989–99*	*1964–98*
UK	1.1	31.1	8.2	3.9	47.4
Italy	2.9	70.6	39.7	10.4	163.0
France	2.3	67.8	17.5	9.5	115.9
Germany	2.3	52.7	24.0	14.3	116.5
USA	3.7	58.3	58.1	36.8	242.3
Japan	4.5	174.1	69.2	−2.2	353.3

Sources: OECD (various dates), *Main Economic Indicators*, and own calculations.

patterns, nor by other sectors' requirements for labour. The loss of manufacturing jobs has been accompanied by a deteriorating performance in manufacturing trade and by a rise in unemployment. Second, manufacturing has not experienced rapidly rising output as a result of productivity growth, but on the contrary, a stagnant trend in output, with the productivity growth hence translating not into output growth but instead into job losses. Third, the poor performance of the manufacturing sector has led to slow growth in the economy as a whole.

3 Causes of UK deindustrialisation

Two alternative approaches have been adopted in analysing the deindustrialisation of the UK economy. First, the free market approach suggests that deindustrialisation reflects excessive government intervention in the economy combined with other 'market imperfections', most prominently trade unions, that prevent the efficient allocation of resources. Alternatively, deindustrialisation is seen as reflecting a lack of, or inappropriate forms of, intervention in the economy – most importantly the lack of a coherent industrial policy, an unstable macroeconomic policy, and the failure to deal with the problem of chronic underinvestment.

Prominent aspects of the free market approach have been the arguments that the public sector (or more specifically, the non-marketable sector) crowds out jobs from the private sector (or more specifically, the marketable sector) (see Bacon and Eltis, 1976) and that the increase of the wage share, due to the impact of corporatism, full employment and strong trade unions, has squeezed profits and thus investment (see Eltis, 1996). In the spirit of this approach some have argued that the Thatcher years transformed the supply side of the British economy, creating conditions for future prosperity. Crafts, for example, has argued that Thatcher's 'get tough' approach to trade unions had yielded significant benefits for the economy and that these might endure 'if the bargaining power of workers over manning levels remains weak' (Crafts, 1991).[6] And Metcalf (1989) argues not only that there was a decisive improvement in productivity in the 1980s but also that this was due in part to a weakening of trade unions. The 'Unions were the main reason . . .' thesis often forms part of a wider view, that unemployment is at heart a labour market problem. This includes the more recent line of argument, that the key to the problem lies in education and training.

The key evidence presented in support of the Thatcher shock is the improvement in productivity – see Crafts (1996) and Eltis (1996), and for an opposing view, Kitson and Michie (1996). Yet, we would argue, there was no productivity miracle during the 1980s – any such picture is a mirage. Certainly, labour productivity in manufacturing grew in the 1980s, but this was due largely to job cuts rather than increased output, and these jobs were not being lost in a period of full employment when the labour would be taken up productively elsewhere.

Additionally, the official productivity figures are constructed using a single price deflator for both output and input prices. Stoneman and Francis (1992) have shown that when the appropriate deflators are used, productivity growth is lower, at only a 34 per cent rise between 1979 and 1989 rather than the 51 per cent increase shown in the official figures. The figures for total factor productivity (TFP), which are intended to capture the increase in output above that resulting from increased quantities of capital and labour, are also questionable. First, the growth accounting approach which forms the basis for the construction of TFP measures usually assumes that factors of production are homogeneous, that markets are perfectly competitive (ensuring marginal productivity factor pricing), and that there are constant returns to scale. Second, there are significant differences in TFP measures depending on the approach adopted and the data used.

Furthermore, the productivity record must be considered in the context of the increased intensification of labour.[7] Nolan (1989) and Nolan and Marginson (1990) have argued that an increase in output per head as a result of increased labour input through the intensification of labour should not be defined as an increase in productivity unless the growth of output is greater than the increased input. Nolan (1989) and Nolan and O'Donnell (1997) have also gone on to argue, in our view persuasively, that far from paving the way for genuine productivity improvements, the Government's policies of deregulation and anti-trade union legislation impaired effective labour utilisation and competitiveness in product markets.[8]

Last, the productivity gains that have been made went disproportionately into increased profits rather than reduced output prices. The latter would have allowed increased market share, with higher output and employment than was in fact experienced, along with a healthier balance of payments and lower inflation. And the increased profits went disproportionately into dividend payments rather than investment.[9,10]

So while labour productivity growth in the 1980s returned perhaps to the rates experienced in the 1960s, these rates of growth were never satisfactory. UK productivity levels still lag behind the other leading industrialised countries. And in the 1980s the benefits of this productivity growth went overwhelmingly into cutting costs and employment rather than into developing new products and expanding output.

Our interpretation of this performance by UK manufacturing is that first it is one of relative failure and second such failure has been caused, at least in part, by underinvestment which reflects a failure to manage and regulate the economy efficiently. As shown in Table 7.3 manufacturing net investment in the UK (as a share of manufacturing output) has been declining since the early 1960s, with negative figures for the early 1980s and 1990s. The averages for the peak-to-peak periods also show declining investment: manufacturing net investment averaged £3,614 million (in 1990 prices) between 1964 and 1973 and only £359 million (1990 prices) between 1989 and 1996.

Table 7.3a UK manufacturing net investment, 1960–96

Year	£ million (1990 prices)	Expressed as a share of manufacturing output (%)
1960	4,000	5.5
1961	5,451	7.5
1962	4,446	6.1
1963	2,846	3.8
1964	3,729	4.5
1965	3,896	4.6
1966	3,931	4.6
1967	3,430	4.0
1968	3,936	4.2
1969	4,378	4.5
1970	4,967	5.1
1971	3,817	4.0
1972	1,947	2.0
1973	2,106	2.0
1974	2,985	2.8
1975	1,790	1.8
1976	1,004	1.0
1977	1,216	1.2
1978	2,747	2.7
1979	3,174	3.1
1980	1,671	1.8
1981	−993	−1.1
1982	−1,561	−1.8
1983	−1,746	−1.9
1984	−279	−0.3
1985	1,317	1.4
1986	531	0.5
1987	888	0.9
1988	1,881	1.7
1989	2,749	2.4
1990	1,712	1.5
1991	173	0.2
1992	−809	−0.8
1993	−1,253	−1.1
1994	−456	−0.4
1995	742	0.6
1996	11	0.0

The impact of this dismal record has been to leave UK manufacturing with an inadequate capital stock.

During all three peak-to-peak periods since the mid-1960s the growth of the UK's manufacturing gross capital stock has been inferior to that of the other major industrial nations.[11] This is most evident during the 1979–89 period, when although there was a worldwide slowdown in the growth of manufacturing investment, the UK was the only country of the five not to

Table 7.3b Averages for the four peak-to-peak periods, 1964–96

Period	£ million (1990 prices)	Expressed as a share of manufacturing output (%)
1964–73	3,614	4.0
1973–79	2,146	2.1
1979–89	694	0.6
1989–96	359	0.3

Sources: CSO, *Economic Trends Annual Supplement* (1994); CSO, *United Kingdom National Accounts* (various editions); CSO, *National Income and Expenditure* (various editions); and CSO, *Economic Trends* (1994), November.

Note
The net investment series has been calculated by subtracting capital consumption from gross investment. The capital consumption series was constructed by linking the various series published in *United Kingdom National Accounts* and *National Income and Expenditure*. These series vary in their coverage as they use different definitions of manufacturing due to changes in the SIC classification system. The linked series adjusts for this by using the ratio between new and old definitions in overlapping years. This constructed series was preferred to that published in *United Kingdom National Accounts*, as the latter is deficient due to the variable inclusion of leased items and some other apparent anomalies in the series.

experience any growth in the manufacturing capital stock (see Table 7.4). This has left a legacy of a relatively low level of capital in UK manufacturing.[12] Figure 7.1 shows that capital per worker in the UK is significantly below that of the USA and Germany; the gap with these two countries (and France) has been widening since the mid-1960s.

In addition to a lack of investment, much of that which has taken place has been cost-cutting rather than capacity enhancing. Thus while for the vast majority of OECD countries the growth rates of both total and industrial R&D were much higher in the 1980s than in the 1970s, the most notable exception to this was the UK (see Archibugi and Michie, 1995, Table 1). The dismal investment record of the UK economy since the 1960s has been a major cause of Britain's indifferent growth performance.[13] This lack of investment has constrained technological progress and the expansion of demand.[14] Furthermore, the cumulative effect of this record has resulted in British workers lacking the volume of capital equipment used by their main competitors. This capital stock gap is likely to widen as, through cumulative causation processes, the expectations that the manufacturing sector is not investing become self fulfilling. Additionally, the process of deindustrialisation will lead to further weaknesses in terms of skills deficiencies and continuing balance of payments problems.

The importance of education and training has recently been emphasised by endogenous growth models where the growth rate of productivity is associated with the level of education. An educated and motivated workforce is able to facilitate the development of, adapt more easily to, and exploit more fully, new processes and techniques of production. In the models of Romer (1986, 1990) increased education generates new technologies whereas for Lucas

Table 7.4 Growth of the manufacturing gross capital stock: international comparisons, 1964–89 (annual % growth rates)

	1964–73	*1973–79*	*1979–89*
United Kingdom			
Equipment	4.6	2.6	0.2
Structures	2.5	0.8	−0.5
Total assets	3.9	2.1	0.0
USA			
Equipment	4.2	5.0	2.4
Structures	4.9	2.6	1.4
Total assets	4.4	4.1	2.0
Germany			
Equipment	7.6	2.9	1.7
Structures	4.1	1.8	0.4
Total assets	6.1	2.5	1.2
France			
Equipment	7.8	3.5	1.7
Structures	8.4	6.6	3.4
Total assets	8.0	4.2	2.1
Japan			
Equipment	14.0	5.5	5.0
Structures	13.9	7.3	5.7
Total assets	14.0	6.0	5.2

Source: Authors' calculations from data in O'Mahony (1993).

Notes
'Equipment' includes all types of machinery, furniture, fixtures and vehicles.
'Structures' includes all types of buildings and other forms of infrastructure.

(1988) there will be positive externalities from education as a high level of human capital will encourage increased learning from others. A recent study of UK businesses (Kitson and Wilkinson, 1998a) revealed positive links between training, innovation and growth. Yet, a number of studies have illustrated the inadequacies in the provision of education and training in the UK. For instance, the OECD (1994) reports the relatively low rate of enrolment of 17- and 18-year olds in formal education and training programmes, and Marsden and Ryan (1991) and the Small Business Research Centre (1992) indicate significant dissatisfaction with the availability and quality of training provision. While lack of skills is therefore a problem for the UK economy, it must be stressed that training programmes alone are not enough; the lack of job opportunities itself stifles skill attainment and development. The stagnation of the manufacturing sector creates conditions for social deskilling which add to the spiral of decline, since a common response by firms to their declining fortunes is to cut back on training.

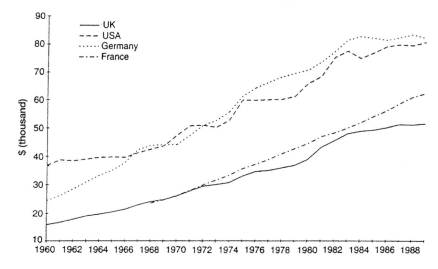

Figure 7.1 Gross capital stock per worker in manufacturing, 1960–89 ($'000, 1985 prices)

Sources: Authors' calculations from data in O'Mahony (1993) and OECD *Main Economic Indicators* (various editions).

Note
See notes to Table 7.4.

The historical legacy with which UK manufacturing has had to contend has included: a continued overseas orientation not only of the financial sector but also of Britain's multinational corporations; a disproportionate burden of military spending and the distorting effect this has had on R&D; and the continued inability of successive UK governments to modernise the economy. One manifestation of this legacy has been a failure to produce a sufficient volume of manufactured exports to pay for imports (at a reasonable level of economic growth). Despite assertions to the contrary by Chancellor Lawson (Lawson, 1992) and others, the balance of payments does matter. The loss of Britain's manufacturing trading surplus in 1983 and the subsequent annual trading deficit in manufactured goods does pose problems for the wider economy (on which, see Coutts and Godley, 1992; McCombie and Thirlwall, 1992; and Cosh, Hughes and Rowthorn, 1994). While Britain's balance of payments did benefit from the post-ERM devaluation, for the country's long-term trading position to be resolved, particularly at anything like full employment, will require a continual improvement in our industrial performance. The practically zero trend growth over the past 20 years will not do it. Neither could the service sector do it alone, as has been demonstrated for example by Cosh, Hughes and Rowthorn (1994); their modelling reveals that 'to offset the prospective manufacturing deficit would require a quite inconceivable increase in the exports of financial and miscellaneous services' (p. 29). Indeed, Crafts (1993) implicitly acknowledges that something is amiss, when he notes that the exchange rate needed to achieve full employment and trade balance at the same time has been falling since the early 1980s.[15]

4 Policies to reverse UK deindustrialisation

UK macroeconomic policy over the past 30 years has resulted repeatedly in an overvalued exchange rate and high interest rates, both of which are particularly damaging to manufacturing, while industrial policy has been ineffectual, with little attempt to use the public sector as a modernising force.[16]

The most obvious cases of sterling being overvalued as a result of macro-economic policy were first, the effects of the Thatcher Government's initial monetarist policies in 1979–80 and second, membership of the Exchange Rate Mechanism at an overvalued rate.[17] But the industrial policies of the 1964 Wilson Government were also sacrificed on the altar of defending the currency, as were those of the Callaghan Government in 1975.

Additionally, the high levels and volatility of interest rates have discouraged investment and business confidence. This was particularly apparent during the early 1980s when high interest rates created cash flow problems for many companies leading to bankruptcies and plant closures as well as contributing to the appreciation of sterling and the squeeze on exports. Interest rate policy during the 1980s has been identified as the main government policy which has impeded the growth of firms. The 1991 Cambridge survey (Small Business Research Centre, 1992)[18] into business performance, the most extensive since the 1971 Bolton study, indicated that a third of all firms surveyed identified interest rate policy as the most important negative government policy and half placed it in their top three policy concerns.[19]

The resulting instability to which the UK economy has been prone, particularly since 1979, has been worse than that experienced in other industrial nations, reflecting the UK Government's desire since 1979 to target nominal variables (inflation and interest rates) rather than real variables (jobs and output). Additionally, they have harmed the long-term growth potential of the economy. The depth of the recessions – they were much deeper than previous (at least pre-1974) postwar recessions – led to large scale scrapping of capital and the laying-off of workers. This contrasts with previous recessions where as the long-term costs of abandonment were high (the cost of restoring capital equipment, severance payments and search and training costs), the moderate extent of the downturns encouraged firms to maintain capacity while waiting for the cyclical upturn. Conversely, during the post-1979 recessions, the depth of the recessions encouraged firms to reduce capacity in order to minimise short-term costs and maximise the possibility of survival.[20]

We have stressed the negative impact of the economic shocks of the 1980s on the UK's long-run growth potential. Others have argued that the reduced bargaining power of workers and the creation of a more flexible labour market have had beneficial effects. This notion is based on a neoclassical view of the competitive process, where producers face a large number of competitors and price is the key indicator of competitiveness. (For a critique of the labour market flexibility thesis, see Michie and Sheehan, 1999.) In reality many firms have few effective competitors and the key factors which contribute to competitive advantage are product quality and the characteristics of the customer–client relationship (on which, see Chapter 9 below and Kitson and Wilkinson, 1998b).[21] Thus, in order to create and sustain a competitive economy, firms require stable economic growth to foster inter-firm cooperation and encourage innovation and product development and the upgrading of the skill base of the economy.

Part III

Public policy and corporate governance

8　From Welfare to Work?

*Michael Kitson, Jonathan Michie and
Holly Sutherland*

1　Introduction

According to an ex-Chancellor of the Exchequer of the UK, Norman Lamont,
unemployment is 'a price well worth paying' to keep down inflation. This was
echoed by the comment from the Governor of the Bank of England in 1998
that unemployment in the North of England was a necessary cost of keeping
down inflation – hence his being dubbed the Governor of the Bank of the
South of England.[1] The free-market policies pursued by successive Conservative Governments in Britain between 1979 and 1997 involved an additional
price – as well as that of high unemployment – namely, growing inequality
with a concomitant increase in poverty for many of those in work as well as
out of work. In this chapter we make an attempt to calculate just how great
this price has been – the price of high unemployment and increased inequality. The price involves a number of different costs, some more hidden than
others. Other work has evaluated the impact of unemployment on health and
crime, but the main focus of this chapter is on the fiscal costs. These costs
derive from the unemployed and the working poor receiving various forms of
benefit payments and at the same time paying less tax than they would were
they in reasonably paid employment.

Our main purpose in making these calculations is to evaluate an alternative
policy agenda involving a major public investment-led programme involving
around one million new jobs being created. Such a programme would be
ambitious and expensive. The public investment proposals outlined below
would involve a gross cost of up to £17 billion a year. Against this, however,
needs to be offset the savings in unemployment pay and other benefits, plus
the additional tax revenues which would be received with a million more in
employment. Together these have generally been assumed to amount to
around £9,000 per head, at least for those who were in receipt of unemployment pay. If this were the appropriate average figure for all the million
individuals, then the saving to the Public Sector Borrowing Requirement of
£9 billion would result in the net cost of such a Programme turning out to be
far lower that the gross cost of £17 billion, namely just £8 billion. Of course,
not all the million would have been in receipt of unemployment pay. But as

detailed below, one of the findings of our research is that the intuitive belief, supported by previous research, that the savings to the Treasury would be far lower if the individuals were not drawing unemployment pay, turns out to be quite false. On the contrary, those not in receipt of unemployment pay tend to qualify for higher levels of other benefits, so the net saving to the Treasury is rather similar regardless of whether the individuals in question were receiving unemployment benefit or not. So in terms of this distinction between those who were in receipt of unemployment benefit and those who were not, it would not be inappropriate to apply the above £9,000 figure to all the million people.

But a second empirical finding of the research reported in this chapter is that the overall gain to the Treasury of someone, on average, moving from being out of work to being in work, amounts to around £10,000 per head rather than the previously believed £9,000. Thus the net cost of the £17 billion programme would amount not to £8 billion but rather to just £7 billion.

Tackling the growth in inequality witnessed since 1979 by reintroducing a new top rate of income tax above £40,000 at 60 per cent – which after all was the rate which applied to the top income tax band during almost the entire Thatcher era – would raise more than £4 billion extra income tax revenues a year. This alone would therefore cover well over half the net cost of such a programme.

These figures suggest that maintaining high levels of unemployment and inequality involve far greater costs than has generally been realised. There is, in addition, strong evidence that unemployment: increases ill-health (Burchell, 1992); brings deteriorating psychological well-being (Oswald, 1997); and raises crime levels, especially domestic burglary (Dickinson, 1995; Wells, 1995). Unemployment has been a major cause of the alarming growth of inequality and poverty in Britain (and indeed in many other countries); in Britain, while the richest tenth of households have become 60 per cent better off since 1979, the poorest tenth are 20 per cent worse off. Wage inequality is greater than at any time since records began in 1886. Such inequality and poverty have detrimental effects on: the balance-of-payments constraint, with a transfer of resources to the better-off who import more (see Borooah, 1988); on the real economy as consumer spending is depressed and the pressure on firms to upgrade their production processes is weakened (Michie and Wilkinson, 1993); and on the government's own fiscal deficit (the Public Sector Borrowing Requirement or PSBR) (Michie and Wilkinson, 1994). Rising poverty means that the cost to the state of benefits and Income Support increases. A growing share of the income of the working poor is met not by their employers but by the taxpayers. This not only increases both the spread and the grip of the poverty trap (whereby any increase in pay by employers is matched by an almost equivalent loss of benefits from government); it also increases the burden on public expenditure. And if total government spending is constrained – for example by the European Union's 3 per cent formula in the Growth and Stability Pact – then this burden has to be met by public spending cuts imposed elsewhere, cuts which may well exacerbate unemployment.

In the face of these deeply entrenched problems, many doubt the ability of governments to generate jobs and tackle inequality. We take a more optimistic view. Governments can create jobs; moreover these can be high quality jobs that not only meet social need but also contribute to national economic prosperity. Furthermore, the cost of such a programme would be relatively modest.

This chapter is organised as follows: Section 2 outlines a public investment-led strategy for the UK that would create a million jobs. Section 3 then considers the fiscal and distributional implications of such a strategy. How the net costs of such a programme could be paid for is then discussed in Section 4. Our conclusions are stated in Section 5. The simulations reported in the chapter come from running the Microsimulation Unit's tax–benefit model POLIMOD; this model is discussed, along with the specific use we have made of it in the work here reported, in Kitson, Michie and Sutherland (1997).

2 A job generation strategy

Any strategy for job generation in Britain at the present time must be based on two essential components. First, there needs to be a substantial increase in investment in the tradable goods sector, and in manufacturing industry in particular, in order to boost economic growth and net exports (on which see Chapter 7, above). This is essential if we are to prevent full employment from resulting in a surge in imports that cannot be financed. It will also create orders for related service activities, as well as generating increased tax revenues to fund expanding public services. However, since manufacturing needs to achieve high levels of productivity to compete internationally, the potential for immediate job generation in this sector alone is limited. Second, therefore, any strategy to cut the dole queues requires increased investment, suitably targeted, in public services and infrastructure. It is not difficult to identify areas of enormous unmet social need, where there is work to be done and where jobs can be generated quickly: record housing waiting lists; investment in education and training lagging behind that of our competitors; hospital waiting lists at unacceptable levels, and an environment under increasing threat.[2]

Moreover, it is not difficult to identify obvious areas of enormous unmet social need, where there is work to be done and where jobs can be generated quickly:[3]

- Homeless people sleep on our streets, there are record housing waiting lists and millions of homes are in need of urgent repairs. Yet, at the same time almost 400,000 construction workers are on the dole.

- School classes are too large and investment in education and training lags behind that of our competitors, while teachers and other education workers get the sack.
- Hospital waiting lists are at unacceptable levels, while the numbers of nurses and other health care staff are cut.
- 'Care in the community' is little more than a fiction for many disabled and elderly people in desperate need of support. Yet the care staff necessary to provide that support are not being employed.
- Dirty streets and run-down neighbourhoods are in desperate need of attention, but little is being done.

These are just a few examples that demonstrate the need for increased spending on public services and infrastructure. We can all think of many more. An increase in public sector employment is therefore necessary both as an essential step towards full employment and to satisfy unmet social need. It also has other advantages. First, when private spending is sluggish an increase in public sector demand can give a welcome boost to the economy. Second, targeted public spending is less import-intensive and more labour-intensive than private sector spending; thus, a given increase in expenditure generates more jobs and has fewer adverse effects on the balance of payments if it comes through public spending (see Glyn and Rowthorn, 1994). Third, the UK lags behind the other major industrialised countries in terms of skills and capital investment (see Chapter 7, above) – key factors in determining the future performance of the economy – and the necessary investment in education and infrastructure is only likely to come via the public sector. And fourth, economic growth must be environmentally sustainable, but the pursuit of private profit is unlikely to ensure adequate environmental protection; improved public sector initiatives are therefore required.

Our aim in this chapter is to identify where and how one million full-time jobs could be created and the benefits these would bring. We have not sought to keep down the cost by focusing on part-time and low paid jobs. Jobs on poverty pay are not an acceptable alternative to unemployment. Clearly, however, there are people who *want* part-time work to suit their circumstances. If some of the increased employment opportunities identified below satisfy the demand for part-time jobs, then clearly the number in work will increase by more than one million.

The examples identified here are for illustrative purposes only. Clearly, other areas of public service provision could have been included, and there are many ways of constructing a package to create one million jobs. We would not argue that this particular split is necessarily the best; more detailed work would need to be done on the costs and benefits of the alternatives. However, what we have sought to do is to demonstrate that 1 million jobs on the road to sustainable full employment can be created relatively easily, that the benefits of such a programme are substantial and that the costs are modest.

Housing

The demand for council and housing association homes continues to outstrip supply. Independent studies have identified a requirement for at least 100,000 affordable new homes a year. In addition, more than three million – one in six – homes need urgent repairs costing more than £1,000. Moreover, poor housing conditions cause ill-health, currently estimated to cost the NHS £2 billion each year (Standing Conference on Public Health, 1994).

The cost of creating an additional job through increased housing expenditure clearly depends upon how such expenditure is used. Building new homes for rent incurs greater non-labour costs than expenditure on renovations and repairs. However, public investment in building new homes may be reduced by drawing in private capital if allocated through housing associations. If we take estimates of the average for all housing expenditure (Ball and Wood, 1994), it seems reasonable to assume a cost per job of the order of £25,000. On this basis, 150,000 jobs would therefore cost £3.75 billion. This could, for example, finance the building of 60,000 more homes for rent and bring 200,000 unfit homes up to standard (Foster, 1991).

Education and training

In the latest year for which statistics are available, 1992/93, total education expenditure by Local Education Authorities in England which could be considered staff-related amounted to £14.4 billion (CIPFA, *Education Statistics, 1992/93 Actuals*). Included here are not only the costs of wages and salaries, but also the costs of equipment and other staff-related current expenditure. Uprating for inflation gives an estimate of staff-related expenditure in current prices of £15.4 billion. This financed the employment of 470,000 full-time equivalent teachers and lecturers and 360,000 full-time equivalent other staff, such as support staff, supervisory staff, cleaners and caretakers. Three quarters of the former were full-time, while three-quarters of the latter were part-time. Assuming that any additional staff-related expenditure was divided between teaching and other staff in the present proportions, then the average cost per job in education and training may be estimated to be £19,000.

Increasing the number of those employed in education and training by 150,000 would therefore cost £2.85 billion. Any additional capital expenditure required would add to the cost. However, many schools and colleges have space that could be used if only they had the staff to do so. It is inconceivable that capital constraints would prevent substantial improvements to the quality of education and training as a result of this 18 per cent improvement in staffing.

The universal provision of nursery education for all 3- and 4-year olds, which the Labour Government is now introducing is estimated to have an annual cost of between £860 million (the National Commission on

Education) and £1 billion (the Department for Education). This package therefore allows for a major contribution to be made to this programme with resources still left to reduce student-teacher ratios and expand the number in full-time education and training. The latter would further reduce unemployment as people took up full-time places on education and training courses, and would also help to improve the skill base of the economy.

Health

The latest year for which a breakdown of revenue expenditure is available is 1993, when £13.6 billion went on salaries and wages (CIPFA, *Health and Personal Social Services Statistics for England, 1994*). Again, however, there are additional costs of employing extra staff – such as the need for additional equipment. This brings staff-related expenditure up to £16.6 billion which in today's prices would be around £17.6 billion. This financed the employment of 773,880 full-time equivalent staff. The cost per job in the health service may therefore be taken to be £23,000. An extra 150,000 jobs would therefore cost £3.45 billion. It would increase NHS employment by 16 per cent.

Personal social services/care in the community

In 1993/94 local authority social service departments in England employed 233,000 full-time equivalent staff, with a total current expenditure of £5.7 billion (CIPFA, *ibid.*). Uprating for inflation this figure rises to £6.0 billion. The cost per job is therefore £26,000. An extra 100,000 jobs would therefore cost £2.6 billion. This would increase employment in personal social services by 36 per cent.

Environmental projects

Environmental policy can take three main forms: regulatory measures (for example, the imposition of legal standards in relation to waste disposal or pollution); 'eco-tax reform' (shifting the tax burden towards energy use and pollution); and public spending to improve the environment. A green public expenditure programme could include environmental enhancement and clean-up activities. The cost of creating an additional job in these areas is approximately £24,000 (Jacobs, 1994); 100,000 jobs could therefore be generated for £2.4 billion.

Energy conservation

Investing in a programme of energy conservation can generate rates of return that alone would justify such investment. Payback periods of less than five years are quite common. But, of course, saving energy is good for the environment and, overall, energy conservation measures create jobs. Adjusting for inflation an earlier estimate of the cost per job of £17,000 (Boardman, 1991), the cost per job in this area may be assumed to be £18,000. So, 100,000 jobs could be created for £1.8 billion.

Additional jobs

The impact of the proposals outlined above, as shown in Table 8.1, would directly create 750,000 jobs. In addition, further jobs would be created due to the linkages between the above sectors and the rest of the economy. The income spent by those workers directly employed would create additional jobs throughout the rest of the economy and increased purchases would expand employment amongst suppliers. The size of these multiplier effects will depend on the way the expansionary programme is targeted and financed (as discussed below), but might lead to an additional 250,000 jobs, making around a million jobs in total.[4]

3 The fiscal and distributional impacts

The cost to the Exchequer of this sort of strategy, leading to the creation of a million new jobs, would be in the order of £17 billion. This would, though, be offset by savings to the Treasury from reduced unemployment-related benefit payments, and by increased tax revenues, leading to a far lower net cost for such a programme. To quantify these impacts we used the Microsimulation Unit's tax-benefit model POLIMOD which simulates the impact of tax and benefit regulations on the household income distribution (see Kitson, Michie and Sutherland, 1997, Appendix; and for further details, Redmond, Sutherland and Wilson, 1995).[5] Estimates of the savings in benefits and

Table 8.1 A proposal to create one million jobs

Sector	Jobs generated (thousands)	Cost per job (£'000)	Total cost (£ million)
Housing	150	25	3,750
Education and training	150	19	2,850
Health	150	23	3,450
Care in the community	100	26	2,600
Environmental projects	100	24	2,400
Energy conservation	100	18	1,800
Total direct jobs created	750	22.5	16,850
Additional indirect jobs created	250	0	0
Total new jobs	1,000	16.85	16,850

Source: Berry, Kitson and Michie (1995).

increased revenue from income tax, employer and employee National Insurance contributions, VAT and excise duties are provided. The results we obtain from such a modelling exercise will be influenced by the assumptions made on various sets of questions, and in particular the following two:

> First, who of those currently not working, take up the new jobs? Using the Family Expenditure Survey sample on which POLIMOD is based, we can break down the 'unemployed' into three groups: group one being those in current receipt of unemployment benefit (UB); group two being those self-reported unemployed or sick, and seeking work (not on UB); and group three being those that are 'unoccupied' (that is, not necessarily seeking work). Alternative rates of job take-up from the different groups are modelled. Throughout, we assume that the following are *not* available for work: people aged under 16 or over 59 (in the case of women) or 64 (for men); those in full-time education; people already in employment or self-employment; people on training benefits; parents of young children where there is no other non-working[6] parent (i.e. single parents and 'second earners'); and those in receipt of benefits which indicate that the person is not available for work (severe disability allowance, maternity pay, etc).
>
> Second, what rate of pay do they receive and how many hours do they work? The policy package referred to above, which we are here modelling, is intended to generate good quality, full-time jobs. We could have kept the cost down considerably by assuming that many of the new jobs would be part-time or low paid jobs (or both). We have not done this; instead, we assume that all the new jobs are reasonably paid and full-time.[7] So, we assume that the average new job pays average national earnings, consistent with the strategy outlined above,[8] but to capture the varieties of job opportunities the earnings distribution is allocated across the middle 50 per cent of the earnings distribution (between £215 and £398 per week).[9] The earnings levels generated are allocated at random to those taking up jobs and it is assumed that they all work 38 hours a week.

The new jobs that are generated are superior in terms of pay and hours to the jobs already being done by many of the lower paid in the sample. The simulation is based on the assumption that some of the new jobs will be taken by those currently employed, with others in turn moving into the posts being vacated; those taking up the newly vacated posts will also come not just from the unemployed and otherwise unoccupied, but also from others who, again, are already employed. This process will continue, as workers move up the earnings hierarchy, until all the net increase in employment is taken-up by the previously unemployed (or otherwise unoccupied, as categorised above).[10]

Table 8.2 summarises the results of modelling the impact on government revenue of the job generation policies, under various assumptions. For the

Table 8.2 The revenue impact of job generation under various assumptions (£bn per annum)

	Creating 1 million jobs (alternative job take-up assumptions)				Creating two million jobs
	A_a	A_b	B_1	B_2	C
1 Non-means tested benefits	0.76	0.76	1.02	0.26	1.05
2 Means tested benefits	2.16	2.16	0.33	2.63	4.47
3 Total benefits	2.92	2.92	1.35	2.89	5.52
4 Income tax	2.68	2.61	1.12	2.71	5.21
5 Employee NICs	1.30	1.26	0.54	1.30	2.52
6 Employer NICs	1.58	1.54	0.65	1.58	3.07
7 Total direct tax	5.56	5.41	2.31	5.59	10.80
8 Total direct revenue	8.48	8.34	3.66	8.48	16.32
9 Indirect tax	1.42	1.38	0.59	1.36	2.81
10 Total revenue	9.90	9.72	4.25	9.84	19.12
11 Number of households (000s)	976	953	406	923	1774
12 Mean revenue per household (£000s)	10.14	10.20	10.47	10.66	10.78

Source: Calculated using POLIMOD.

Notes
Rounding errors cause some columns to not sum precisely.
Total number of households: 23 million.
Assumptions for creating *one* million jobs:
  A_a The jobs are taken by 75% of the group currently in receipt of unemployment benefit plus 35% of the group self-reported unemployed or sick and seeking work (but not receiving unemployment benefit), with the remainder coming from the unoccupied group. There are a number of excluded groups (see text); here it is assumed that parents with children aged under 5 and where there is no other non-working parent are excluded.
  A_b As A_a except that it is assumed that parents with children aged under 11 and where there is no other non-working parent are excluded.
  B_1 All the new jobs go to people in receipt of unemployment benefit. These are fewer than one million, namely 406,000.
  B_2 As A_a except that the jobs are distributed in the same proportion to each of the unemployed groups: 20.8% of all those assumed available for work.

Assumptions for creating *two* million jobs:
  C The jobs are taken by 100% of the group currently in receipt of unemployment benefit plus 80% of the group self-reported unemployed or sick and seeking work, with the remainder coming from the unoccupied group. Parents with children aged under 5 and where there is no other non-working parent are excluded.

creation of one million jobs, four alternatives are shown – based on different rates of job take-up from different unemployed groups and alternative assumptions concerning working parents. In addition, option C shows the impact of two million jobs being created.

The first two rows of Table 8.2 show the effect of the expansion of employment on benefit payments (non-means tested and means tested), with the third row giving the sum of these. With a net increase of one million jobs, the expenditure saving on benefits is found to vary between £2.92 billion and £3.21 billion.[11] Rows 4 to 6 show the impact on direct taxation (and the seventh gives the sum of these), with this revenue increasing by between £5.44 billion and £5.56 billion. Row 9 gives the indirect revenue arising from indirect taxes on assumed increased spending; this ranges between £1.37 billion and £1.42 billion.[12] Indirect taxes can only be computed at the household level so row 11 shows the number of households affected (that is, households including one or more persons entering work) and row 12 shows the average revenue generated by these households.

The total revenue impact of a net increase in employment of one million turns out to be rather robust in the face of varying the assumptions concerning job take-up and working parents. The total revenue generated varies between £10.14 billion (assumption A_2) and £10.66 billion (assumption B_2). These totals significantly exceed 'official' estimates which put the annual cost, in terms of benefits and forgone taxes, of an unemployed claimant at £9,000.[13] Our results indicate that the average cost to the Exchequer of having someone unemployed or unoccupied is over £10,000 a year. This is significantly higher than had previously been believed. Two factors explain the difference. First, a common difference from our scenario is that previous estimates assume that the new jobs will be lower paid than would be the case with the public investment led strategy outlined here. (For example, the figures from the Employment Policy Institute are calculated on the assumption that the new jobs will pay only 80 per cent of average earnings.) Second, previous estimates, including those from the Treasury, do not fully account for the actual circumstances of the families of the unemployed, and the impact of the new employment on the benefits received and taxes paid. Previous estimates give even lower costs of unemployment for those not in receipt of unemployment benefit.[14] The cost of unemployment will be lower in these cases only if there is no significant entitlement to means-tested benefits and this is only likely to be the case if the unemployed person is the partner of someone who is in work with wages at a reasonable level. However, unemployment and employment are increasingly each becoming concentrated within households: it is likely that the partner of an unemployed person will also be without work (Gregg and Wadsworth, 1995). The savings on income support and housing benefit from one or both of these people finding a well-paid job will be at least as great as the savings from a person who is eligible for unemployment benefit becoming employed. Indeed, in cases where a recipient of unemployment benefit is the partner of an employed person, then the benefit savings from finding them a job will be *less* because income support will not have been payable in these circumstances. The notion that the combination of unemployment (without entitlement to unemployment benefit) and a partner in work is a relatively rare situation is borne out by our analysis using a sample of actual households. The insensitivity of our revenue estimates to our assumptions about the circumstances of people available to take up jobs shows that receipt of unemployment benefit (or indeed, registration as unemployed) is not a factor which determines the cost of a person not having a job. This is demonstrated by the proximity of the results for our two most extreme assumptions. If we allow only current unemployment benefit recipients to take the new jobs (B$_1$) the average revenue per household affected is £10,470 per year. However, if we allocate jobs proportionately to all groups assumed to be available for work (B$_2$) – only 21 per cent of each group, including those on unemployment benefit – the revenue effect is slightly *larger*: £10,660 per household. It is workless households who cost the most in terms of benefit payments: and it is increasingly people in these households who predominate among those available for work.

Table 8.2 also shows the revenue impact of creating two million jobs (assumption C). The overall revenue effect is £19.12 billion or £10,778 per job. This suggests that our results are fairly robust even over large variations in the scale of the expansion in employment.

The impact of the job creation strategy on income distribution is shown in Table 8.3. The gains are found to be greatest for the poorest households (in both absolute and percentage terms). For instance the households in the lowest (pre-reform) decile receive an average weekly gain of £20.65 compared to an average across all households of £5.95. Additionally, a greater percentage of poorer households benefit compared to those at the richer end of the distribution.

To demonstrate the robust nature of these results in face of the full-time/part-time split of jobs, instead of one million 38-hour jobs, we re-ran the

Table 8.3 The distributional impact of creating a million jobs

Decile of household net income (pre-reform)	Average £ gain per week	Gain as a % of pre-reform income	% of households benefiting
Bottom	20.65	25.9	15.0
2nd	12.20	8.5	8.3
3rd	4.79	3.3	4.0
4th	2.73	1.6	2.5
5th	4.89	1.8	3.3
6th	4.96	1.7	3.2
7th	2.93	0.8	1.6
8th	3.34	0.7	2.1
9th	0.90	0.2	0.6
Top	2.11	0.2	1.3
All	5.95		4.2

Source: Calculated using POLIMOD.

Note
The job take-up assumption is A$_a$ (see Table 8.2).

model on the assumption of 700,000 such jobs plus 600,000 19-hour jobs. It is assumed that each person selected for employment is equally likely to work full-time or part-time. If part-time, they work 19 hours for half the weekly pay they would have received on a full-time basis. People with children under 5 who were previously excluded from the new jobs are now available for the part-time jobs. Runs D(i) and D(ii) thus build on run A_a with two alternative assumptions. Assumption (i) keeps the same numbers drawn from the unemployed groups 1–2 as in run A_a (although some may end up in part-time jobs) and assigns the remainder of the jobs to group 3 and group 4 (the new group of parents) in the same proportion as each other, although only people who are not carer-parents of under-5s can get full-time jobs. Assumption (ii) concentrates more of the jobs (both full- and part-time) in the groups most likely to be seeking work, allocating the residual as before.[15] Table 8.4 shows the revenue effect of these schemes in relation to A_a, and Table 8.5 shows the distributional effect of D(i).

Creating more jobs at a lower average weekly wage produces higher savings on benefits but reduced gains in tax revenue. The overall revenue effect is much the same. More households benefit by a smaller average amount. Allowing the carer-parent of under-5s to have new part-time jobs has the effect of spreading the benefit (somewhat) higher up the household income distribution (the people in the new jobs are more likely to have working partners).

Table 8.4 The revenue impact of increased part-time/full-time employment (£bn per annum)

	A_a	D(i)	D(ii)
1 Non-means tested benefits	0.76	0.84	0.87
2 Means tested benefits	2.16	2.52	2.62
3 Total benefits	2.92	3.36	3.49
4 Income tax	2.68	2.44	2.41
5 Employee NICs	1.30	1.24	1.23
6 Employer NICs	1.58	1.40	1.39
7 Total direct tax	5.56	5.08	5.03
8 Total direct revenue	8.48	8.43	8.52
9 Indirect tax	1.42	1.44	1.41
10 Total revenue	9.90	9.88	9.93
11 Number of households (000s)	976	1207	1195
12 Mean revenue per household (£000s)	10.14	8.18	8.31

Source: Calculated using POLIMOD.

Note
Rounding errors cause some columns to not sum precisely.

Table 8.5 Distributional effect of D(i)

Decile of household equivalised net income (pre-reform)	Average gain (£ per week)	Gain as proportion of pre-reform income %	% benefiting
Bottom	20.39	26.3	17.6
2nd	8.29	6.0	8.0
3rd	5.10	2.7	4.9
4th	4.50	2.2	4.2
5th	5.84	2.0	4.6
6th	3.84	1.3	3.2
7th	2.02	0.5	1.8
8th	4.09	0.9	3.4
9th	2.01	0.4	1.3
Top	3.46	0.4	2.6
All	5.96		5.2

4 How to pay for one million jobs

The creation of the one million jobs described above would involve a net cost to the Exchequer of around £7 billion. This would allow public spending to be increased by a total of £17 billion, offset by savings in unemployment-related benefit payments and higher tax receipts which together would pay for £10 billion of the increased public spending. The obvious question that remains, though, is how is the net increase of £7 billion to be financed?

Since our primary aim here is to identify a short-term programme to create a million jobs, we will not consider longer-term measures to finance full employment, such as reducing the level of military expenditure to that of our EU partners. However, an estimated £6 billion from the sale of council homes was set aside for debt repayment, and while the Labour Government has since allowed for some of these capital receipts to be released, the balance might reasonably be used to fund the housing programme. If this amounted to say £3 billion then the remaining £4 billion cost of the programme could be funded by a combination of public sector borrowing and increased taxation. An increased borrowing of £2 billion is well within the annual margin of error of estimation of the Public Sector Borrowing Requirement. The orthodox view that increased borrowing – even on such a modest scale – would lead to an increase in interest rates and thus 'crowd-out' private investment has little basis in theory or practice. In a world in which capital markets are highly integrated, one would not expect UK government borrowing to exert significant pressure on interest rates, since the UK is a relatively small economy. When the PSBR for 1993–94 turned out to be £5 billion less than anticipated, interest rates did not come tumbling down. There need not therefore be undue concern that £2 billion of extra borrowing would increase interest rates and there is a strong case that the Government is not borrowing enough: in 1999 the Government's current budget is in surplus and the lack of government borrowing is leading to a shortage of government bonds.[16]

£2 billion in additional taxation can easily be found even without plugging tax loopholes, which, although essential, will take some time to implement. For example, £2 billion could be raised by reversing the New Labour Government's cut in corporation tax, which would still leave it significantly below the European average. Rates of inheritance tax and capital gains tax and tax reliefs could also be changed to mobilise such modest resources. Alternatively, a new 60 per cent band on taxable income in excess of £40,000 would raise over £4 billion a year. This is still a small amount compared to the £15 billion in tax cuts received by the top 10 per cent of income earners under the Tories, but it would allow the whole of the remaining net cost of the programme to be paid for with no additional borrowing whatsoever.

If, however, some increased borrowing was actually thought to be desirable in the first instance, then some of this increased tax take from the highest paid could be redistributed through the income tax system by raising tax allowances, thus helping to partially overcome the increased inequality in after-tax incomes engineered by successive Conservative Governments since 1979. We therefore modelled the effects of combining a new 60 per cent rate on incomes of £40,000 with an increase in the tax threshold, increasing the personal allowance by £1,000 per year.[17]

This increase in allowances has a direct cost of £5.385 billion, with some knock-on effects on means-tested benefits and indirect taxes. The distributional effects of this new 60 per cent top-rate of tax on incomes over £40,000 with an increase in allowances were then combined with the programme to increase employment along with the introduction of a minimum wage of £4.15 per hour.[18] The results are shown in Table 8.6.

Table 8.6 Distributional effect of increased employment, a minimum wage, a new top-rate of income tax plus increased allowances

Decile of household equivalised net income (pre-reform)	Average gain (£ per week)	Gain as proportion of pre-reform income %	% benefiting
Bottom	24.99	31.4	33.4
2nd	16.28	11.6	35.7
3rd	9.87	6.4	52.0
4th	8.62	4.7	63.1
5th	13.41	5.2	85.5
6th	13.55	4.6	93.1
7th	12.15	3.5	96.7
8th	11.76	2.8	97.5
9th	6.71	1.6	95.4
Top	−20.13	−2.5	74.4
All	9.72		72.7

The effect of increasing tax thresholds is to distribute more to the middle and upper end of the income distribution. Nearly all of these households are net beneficiaries, whereas the households at the bottom of the pre-reform distribution contain a lower proportion of taxpayers (even after the extra jobs and minimum wage). The most effective way of tackling inequality and poverty is thus found to be through direct job creation measures, along with the establishment of a national minimum wage. The best use of tax revenues from the highly paid is not, therefore, to fund tax cuts for the rest, but rather to fund the sort of programme outlined in this chapter.

5 Conclusion

Unemployment in the UK fell significantly following the forced withdrawal of sterling from the Exchange Rate Mechanism (ERM) in 1992. A lower exchange rate and lower interest rates boosted demand throughout much of the 1990s; although towards the end of the decade these benefits were reversed as a result of interest rate rises by the newly independent Bank of England. By the second quarter of 1999, unemployment, according to the claimant count measure, stood at 1.3 million (4.7 per cent of the workforce). For some the UK economy is now in a new era of full employment and combating unemployment has fallen down the policy agenda. This policy stance is mistaken and inappropriate. First, the official figures, and the claimant count in particular, underestimate the level of unemployment (by as much as one million according to Wells, 1994). Second, much of the fall in unemployment is a temporary benefit due to an undervalued exchange rate and this will be undone by the rise in the exchange rate at the end of 1999. Third, many of the jobs that have been created are part-time, casual, low paid and with a low skill content; any effective job generation strategy must be concerned with the quality of jobs as well as the quantity of jobs.

The gross cost of creating a million new jobs through a public sector led strategy, involving an expansion of good-quality jobs in the public services, would be nearly £17 billion. However, our modelling of the impact which these jobs would have on tax receipts from, and benefit payments to households indicates that the net benefit to the Treasury of this increase in revenues and reduction in expenditure would amount to more than £10 billion, leaving a net annual cost for the programme of less than £7 billion. This could easily be financed – it is less than 2.5 per cent of current tax revenues – with various options set out above; the introduction of a new 60 per cent income tax band at £40,000 would alone cover more than half the net cost (raising £4.2 billion a year).

An increase in public sector employment, in addition to help decrease unemployment, would provide other economic and social benefits. First, it would help to reverse the massive shift in income towards the rich that took place in Britain throughout the 1980s and 1990s. Reversing this by increasing employment and achieving a more equitable distribution of income would relieve pressure on public finances as people are raised out of state dependency and as the costs of administering the tax/benefit system fall. And second, particularly in the area of education and training, it would improve the stock of human capital and help to raise the long-term growth rate. Thus, while our modelling results would suggest that the initial costs of a public sector jobs strategy would in any case be rather modest, over the medium to longer-term even these costs would fall, as higher economic growth would raise tax revenues still further. Indeed, the public investment-led programme would lead to additional public revenues directly by way of rental income from the houses built and so on. Also, by providing enhanced public services, favourable political conditions would be created in which the case for increased taxes, should these prove necessary, could best be made.

Unemployment today is thus not the result of the working of immutable economic laws. There is no substance to the claim that if the worst off in society accept a cut in their living standards, long-term prospects would be restored; the opposite is more likely the case. Nor is unemployment the result of there being too little work needing to be done to employ all those who seek employment. Both private need and public squalor are on the increase.

Of course, governments are continually under pressure from business, the 'City' and elsewhere to cut back on public employment and public intervention in the economy. This needs, though, to be met by even greater pressure for progressive economic policies. In practical terms this means forcing government to expand public employment on improving the Welfare State and environmental programmes, as well as taking measures to increase the level of industrial investment and upgrade the productive infrastructure. Only in this way can we create the conditions for sustainable economic growth.

9   Markets, competition and innovation

1 Introduction

Although the overall growth rate of the UK economy in the 1980s and 1990s was similar to that of the other advanced countries, this is hardly an indicator of success.[1] Output per person is lower for the UK than for any of the other G7 group of countries, and it is also below the OECD average. This output 'gap' indicates a potential for 'catching-up' growth. Lagging countries, such as the UK, could in principle borrow and adopt new technologies and management techniques from leading countries. This should enable lagging countries to achieve superior growth rates compared to the leading countries, at least until the output gap is closed. We have argued in Chapter 7 above that this failure of the UK to catch up with the other industrialised countries is due in part at least to a failure of economic policy as well as to the debilitating grip of various institutional constraints.

Politicians of all hues pay lip service to the need to create a competitive economy. This is often presented, in Britain at least, as requiring deregulation and the 'freeing up' of markets. Behind such policy proposals often lies a picture of economic processes where firms compete in markets with large numbers of customers and competitors, and where keen prices and low costs are the key determinants of success. This misrepresents the character of the competitive process in most sectors. This chapter – using evidence from the innovation survey carried out by Cambridge University's ESRC Centre for Business Research (Cosh and Hughes, 1996) – shows that factors such as trust and cooperation can play an important role in competitive success and may actually be undermined by a policy approach which prioritises deregulation.

In the following three sections we report the reality of the competitive process as perceived, at any rate, by those firms responding to the CBR survey. Section 2 reports on the relatively small number of major competitors which most firms are dealing with – a far cry from a perfectly competitive world of price takers. The role of price competition is considered explicitly in Section 3, as against other forms of (non-price) competition. Section 4 then investigates the role of cooperation and innovation. In considering the theory of market competition, Section 5 argues that the empirical findings of the

CBR's work, as discussed in Sections 2–4, actually matches rather well with much political economy literature – albeit at odds with the 'Austrian' theory underpinning UK Government policy under the Thatcher/Major administrations. Section 6 discusses our findings in the context of competition theory. Finally, Section 7 discusses the policy implications, including the need in Britain for policies to tackle short termism and boost investment. This would be in stark contrast to the market-oriented reforms introduced since 1979 which have discouraged links between investors and firms. More immediately it would contrast with investment in manufacturing – which still dominates world trade – having fallen by 8 per cent in 1996 while public investment fell by 20 per cent.

2 The data

The analysis in this chapter is based on surveys carried out by the ESRC Centre for Business Research (CBR) at the University of Cambridge (and its predecessor the Small Business Research Centre).[2] These surveys were intended to provide a comprehensive picture of British business, considering such factors as competitive structures, employment and skills, innovation, finance and growth.

The first survey was conducted in 1991 and was designed to provide a sample of 2,000 independent businesses employing fewer than 500 workers, equally split between business services and manufacturing. The sampling frame used was the Dun and Bradstreet database (see Bullock, Duncan and Wood, 1996, for a discussion of the advantages and disadvantages of this database). Originally, 8,050 firms were approached. Of these, 1,880 were discarded as they were too large, subsidiaries, had ceased trading, or were otherwise outside the survey's scope. Of the 6,170 firms that were surveyed, 2,028 returned useable questionnaires, a response rate of 32.9 per cent. The results of this survey (SBRC, 1992) provided the first comprehensive analysis of the UK small and medium sized firm (SME) sector since Bolton (1971).

A second survey was conducted in 1993, using a short questionnaire focusing on a few key variables. A third survey was conducted in 1995. It is the results of this third survey, using a questionnaire similar in scale to the first survey, which forms the basis of most of the analysis in this chapter. Continued monitoring of the respondents to the original survey enabled identification of firms which had failed, or were failing. Of the original 2,018 respondents, 436 firms were excluded because of failure or because they were now outside the survey's scope. Of the 1,592 firms surveyed, 681 firms returned the full postal questionnaire, and 317 firms completed shorter questionnaires, a total response rate of 62.7 per cent.

In order to draw a comparative picture the respondents' characteristics are analysed according to a variety of categories, as follows: two sectors (manufacturing and business services); four size groups based on 1990 employment (micro, 0–9 employees; small, 10–99 employees; medium, 100–199 employees; and larger, 200 employees); three employment growth categories between 1990 and 1995 (stable/declining – zero or negative growth; medium growth – greater than zero but less than 35 per cent; fast growth – over 35 per cent); two innovation categories[3] (based on whether the firm innovated or not during the period 1992–95); and two collaboration categories[4] (based on whether the firm entered into a collaborative arrangement during the period 1992–95).

3 The competitive environment

Firms operate in a range of competitive environments. At one extreme firms may compete in atomistic markets, with a large number of customers and competitors, and where competition is driven by price and cost factors. At the other extreme firms may operate in monopolistic or monopsonistic markets with no effective competitors, or with only one customer. The evidence from the CBR survey indicates that, although firms operate in diverse markets, the norm is for increasingly segmented markets – with firms relying on a few main customers and facing a limited number of competitors.

Table 9.1 shows that in 1995, 33 per cent of firms relied on just one customer for 25 per cent or more of their sales. The most apparent contrast is by firm size – micro and small firms are more likely to depend on just a few customers for the bulk of their business. Additionally, innovating firms are less likely to be dependent on a single customer than are non-innovating firms; 31 per cent of innovating firms – compared with 38 per cent of non-innovating firms – depend on just one customer to provide 25 per cent or more of their sales. In general, then, most firms have just a few key customers – indicating the importance to these firms of fostering their relations with

Table 9.1 Concentration of sales (% distribution of firms)

% of sales for largest customer	less than 10%	10%–24%	25%–49%	50%–100%	No. of firms
Micro	19.7	38.2	29.2	13.0	169
Small	25.8	43.0	20.1	11.2	375
Medium	40.3	32.8	14.9	11.6	65
Large	41.3	34.8	15.2	9.7	44
Manufacturing	26.8	41.2	19.6	12.4	347
Services	26.6	39.5	23.5	10.4	309
Innovators	28.8	40.7	21.8	8.8	441
Non-innovators	21.7	40.1	20.7	17.5	206
All	26.7	40.4	21.4	11.5	656

Source: University of Cambridge, ESRC Centre for Business Research, 1995 Survey into Growth, Innovation and Competitive Advantage in Small and Medium Sized Firms.

customer-firms. Furthermore, as shown in Table 9.2 the majority of firms operate in rather segmented markets – with nearly two thirds of firms having fewer than ten serious competitors.[5]

So, for the bulk of British business, the notion that firms are competing with a vast array of other enterprises – like the concept of perfect competition presented in economic textbooks – is a myth. Most firms are operating in segmented and niche markets.

4 How firms compete

How firms compete also reveals that any notion that prices and costs are the key to competitive success is at best simplistic. As shown in Table 9.3, when firms were asked to identify the sources of their competitive advantage the key factors were 'personal attention to client needs', 'reputation', and 'product quality'. 'Cost advantage' was the lowest ranked factor, especially amongst those firms with the fastest rate of growth.

There are large and significant differences in competitive strategy between innovating and non-innovating firms. As shown in Table 9.3, in 1995 there are statistically significant differences between the two sectors for seven out of the eleven competitiveness factors. The largest differences, in terms of rank as well as scores, were for product design, flair and creativity, product quality, specialised expertise or products, and range of expertise or products; all these factors were more important for innovating firms than they were for non-innovating firms. Further evidence of the differences in competitive factors is provided in Table 9.4, which shows the percentage of firms rating the factors as 'very significant' or 'crucial'. Innovating firms were far more likely to rank highly such factors as product design, flair and creativity, and specialised expertise or products compared to non-innovating firms.

Overall, innovating firms stress the importance of higher-order qualitative factors which require investment in skills and technical capability. Conversely, in terms of rankings, they put less emphasis on cost and price factors compared with non-innovating firms. These major differences were also evident in other surveys which assessed competitive advantage in different periods (Kitson and Wilkinson, 1996). This suggests that such differences do not merely reflect the contrast between firms that innovate and those that do not, but they also reflect differences between those firms that intend to innovate, or are receptive to such developments, and those that do not or are not.

One of the important ingredients for achieving competitive success appears to be to establish effective collaboration with others – customers, suppliers, higher education establishments and so on. Such collaboration allows firms to expand their range of expertise, develop specialist products, and achieve various other corporate objectives.[6]

Table 9.2 Competitive structures (% distribution of firms)

Number of serious competitors	All	Manufacturing	Services	Innovators	Non-innovators	Collaborators	Non-collaborators
0 (monopoly)	3.3	2.9	3.6	2.5	5.0	2.0	4.3
1–9 (highly segmented)	61.3	69.1	52.4	60.9	63.9	60.5	61.2
10–49 (partially segmented)	27.3	23.6	31.5	29.3	20.6	29.0	26.3
50–99 (partially atomistic)	2.6	1.2	4.3	2.5	3.0	3.6	2.1
100 + (highly atomistic)	5.5	3.3	8.2	4.8	7.5	4.8	6.2

Source: University of Cambridge, ESRC Centre for Business Research, 1995 Survey into Growth, Innovation and Competitive Advantage in Small and Medium Sized Firms.

Table 9.3 Assessment of key factors which contribute to competitive advantage

| | All | | Average score and ranking | | | | | | | | Average score and ranking | | | | | |
| | | | Manu-facturing | | Services | | Innovators | | Non-innovators | | Stable/declining | | Medium growth | | Fast growth | |
	Score	Rank	Score	Rank	Score	Rank	Score	Rank	Score	Rank	Score	Rank	Score	Rank	Score	Rank
Personal attention to client needs	4.4	1	4.3**	1	4.6**	1	4.4	1	4.5	1	4.5	1	4.4	1	4.4	1
Established reputation	4.2	2	4.1*	3	4.2*	2	4.2	=2	4.2	2	4.2	2	4.1	3	4.1	=3
Product quality	4.1	3	4.2**	2	4.0**	4	4.2**	=2	3.9**	4	4.1	3	4.3	2	4.2	2
Speed of service	4.0	4	4.0	4	3.9	5	3.9*	5	4.1*	3	4.0	4	4.0	4	3.9	5
Specialised expertise or products	3.9	5	3.8**	5	4.1**	3	4.0**	4	3.7**	5	3.9	5	3.9	5	4.1	=3
Range of expertise or products	3.6	6	3.5	=6	3.6	7	3.7**	6	3.4**	7	3.6	6	3.5	6	3.7	6
Price	3.4	=7	3.5**	=6	3.2**	=9	3.3**	9	3.5**	6	3.4*	7	3.4*	7	3.2*	=8
Flair and creativity	3.4	=7	3.0**	10	3.7**	6	3.5**	7	3.0**	9	3.2**	=8	3.3**	8	3.6**	7
Product design	3.2	9	3.2	8	3.2	=9	3.4**	8	2.7**	11	3.2	=8	3.2	=9	3.3	10
Marketing	3.1	10	2.9**	11	3.3**	8	3.2**	10	2.9**	10	3.0	=10	3.2	=9	3.2	=8
Cost advantage	3.0	11	3.1**	9	2.9**	11	3.0	11	3.1	8	3.0	=10	3.1	11	2.9	11
Range (highest score – lowest score)	1.4		1.4		1.7		1.4		1.8		1.5		1.3		1.5	
Total responses (No.)	652		350		302		208		437		341		140		157	

Source: University of Cambridge, ESRC Centre for Business Research, 1995 Survey into Growth, Innovation and Competitive Advantage in Small and Medium Sized Firms.

Notes
** Significant at 5% level.
* Significant at 10% level.
F-test of difference between groups.

Table 9.4 Competitive advantage: factors rated very significant or crucial (% of respondents)

	All	Inno-vators	Non-innovators	Collabor-ators	Non-collaborators
Personal attention to client needs	90.1	88.9	93.2	87.4	91.9
Product quality	85.2	87.6	78.9	87.0	83.7
Established reputation	83.4	82.7	84.9	82.2	83.9
Specialised expertise or products	75.2	79.1	67.5	80.5	71.7
Speed of service	75.2	73.5	79.9	66.0	81.8
Range of expertise or products	60.9	64.2	54.3	62.6	59.4
Price	46.8	43.6	53.3	37.8	53.0
Flare and creativity	50.1	55.1	39.5	55.4	45.8
Product design	51.8	57.5	35.7	58.0	47.0
Marketing	38.5	41.0	33.8	45.1	34.6
Cost advantage	34.3	33.8	34.9	26.9	38.9

Source: University of Cambridge, ESRC Centre for Business Research, 1995 Survey into Growth, Innovation and Competitive Advantage in Small and Medium Sized Firms.

5 Collaboration, innovation, and corporate performance

Innovation is a key element in long-term economic growth. And, collaboration is one of the most important means of fostering innovation. As shown in Figure 9.1, half of the innovating firms in the CBR survey had entered into collaborative partnerships, whereas only one in six of the non-innovating firms had entered into such arrangements. Also, collaboration is particularly important for firms facing foreign competition; as the process of globalisation continues (see Chapter 1 above) such collaborative behaviour may become more important as domestic firms face stiffer competition in both home and overseas markets.

Figure 9.2 shows that firms undertake collaboration for a range of reasons. The four most important were to help expand the range of expertise and products, to assist in the development of specialist services and products required by customers, to provide access to UK markets, and to provide access to overseas markets. The process of collaboration allows firms to exploit economies of scale and scope. The reason given for collaboration that has shown the greatest increase since 1990 (from 29 per cent to 38 per cent) is to help keep current customers. This suggests that collaboration may have increased for defensive reasons – perhaps in response to increased domestic and international competition.

Figure 9.3 shows the reasons for collaboration according to whether firms were innovators or non-innovators. In general, innovating firms are more likely to collaborate for all reasons compared to non-innovating firms. The one exception is to help keep current customers, suggesting that non-innovators

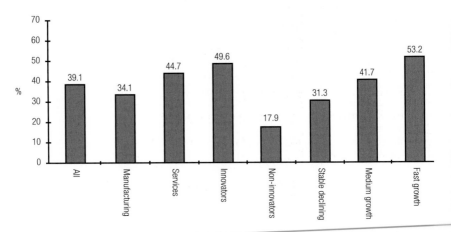

Figure 9.1 Percentage of firms entering into formal or informal collaborative partnerships

Source: University of Cambridge, ESRC Centre for Business Research, 1995 Survey into Growth, Innovation and Competitive Advantage in Small and Medium Sized Firms.

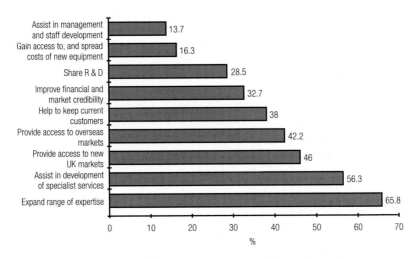

Figure 9.2 Reasons for collaboration (percentage of firms giving these reasons)

Source: As Figure 9.1.

are more defensive in regard to maintaining market share. Additionally, and not surprisingly, the reason for collaboration for non-innovators that has shown the greatest fall is the sharing of research and development.

The overall impact of increased innovation and collaboration is improvements in both output and employment growth rates – for individual businesses as well as for the economy as whole.[7] In terms of employment, fast

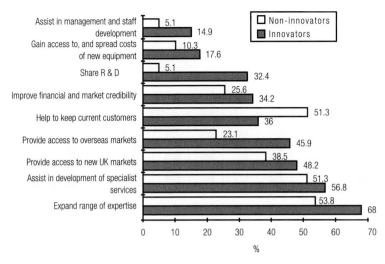

Figure 9.3 Reasons for collaboration: innovators and non-innovators

Source: As Figure 9.1.

growth firms were almost twice as likely to have collaborated compared to firms with negative or no growth. Figures 9.4a and 9.4b give the distribution of employment growth in first, innovating and non-innovating firms and second, collaborating and non-collaborating firms; as shown in Figure 9.4a, innovating firms were far less likely to have zero or negative employment growth than were non-innovating firms. Conversely, innovators were far more likely to have achieved fast growth in employment. Figure 9.4b indicates a similar picture in the contrast between collaborators and non-collaborators – superior employment growth being shown by the collaborators. Figures 9.5a and 9.5b, and 9.6a and 9.6b, show that this superior performance of innovating firms and of collaborating firms is also apparent in terms of turnover growth and in terms of the growth of profit margins.[8]

6 The theory of market competition

What might explain these results, of market competition apparently benefiting from cooperation? The issue of whether the competitive environment promotes innovation or cut-throat pricing has been discussed independently by Lazonick (1991) who argues that the key determinant of whether or not the firm's decision makers choose an innovative strategy is the extent to which 'they control an organisational structure that they believe provides them with the capability of developing productive resources that can overcome the constraints they face' (Lazonick, 1991, p. 328). Such structures include not only the internal organisation of firms themselves and their relationships with the public authorities but also networks of relationships between firms in a particular industry or cluster of industries.[9]

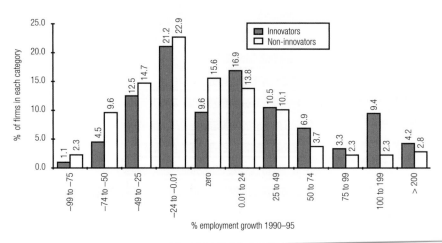

Figure 9.4a Employment growth, 1990–95 (%): innovators and non-innovators
Source: As Figure 9.1.

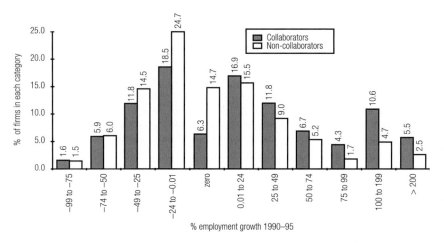

Figure 9.4b Employment growth, 1990–95 (%): collaborators and non-collaborators
Source: As Figure 9.1.

Lazonick's emphasis on the need for control over the requisite organisational structure derives at least in part from his own work as an economic
historian, particularly his work relating to the failure of the British cotton
industry to innovate in the late nineteenth and the twentieth centuries. Referring to a period of stagnation following the end of the post-Second World
War boom, Lazonick characterises the situation in the following terms:

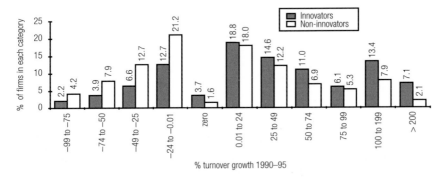

Figure 9.5a Turnover growth, 1990–95 (%): innovators and non-innovators
Source: As Figure 9.1.

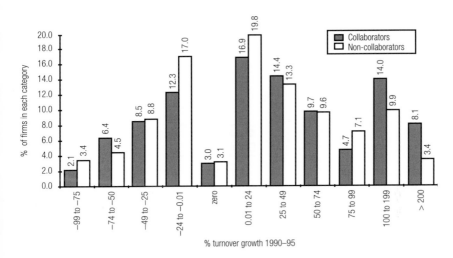

Figure 9.5b Turnover growth, 1990–95 (%): collaborators and non-collaborators
Source: As Figure 9.1.

The fundamental problem was an industry mired in its own highly competitive and vertically specialised structure, lacking any internal forces to set organisational transformation in motion.

(Lazonick, 1986, p. 35)

The vast majority of businesspeople in the cotton industry had neither the incentive to participate nor the ability to lead in the internal restructuring of their industry [. . .]. Given this absence of leadership

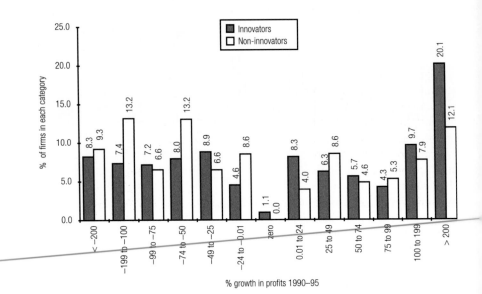

Figure 9.6a Growth in profits, 1990–95 (%): innovators and non-innovators
Source: As Figure 9.1.

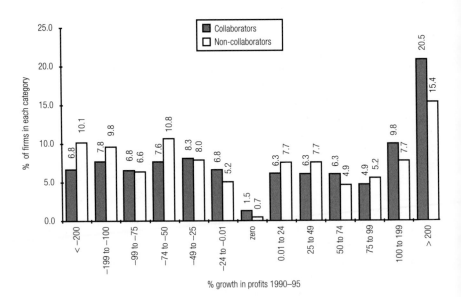

Figure 9.6b Growth in profits, 1990–95 (%): collaborators and non-collaborators
Source: As Figure 9.1.

from within private industry, what was required was the visible hand of co-ordinated control not the invisible hand of the self-regulating market.

(Elbaum and Lazonick, 1986, pp. 10–11)

The issue of the relationship between industry structure and the capacity for innovation is a complex one. On the one hand, there is evidence that forms of long-term relationship between independent firms may be superior to vertical integration as a means of coordinating the activities required for innovation especially where these activities involve a high degree of technological 'strangeness' (Gomes-Casseres, 1994, p. 63). These new forms of alliance are prevalent in high technology industries. There are indications that they contribute most to innovative performance when they involve a dense network of interpersonal relationships and internal infrastructures that enhance learning, unblock information flows and facilitate coordination by creating trust and by mitigating perceived differences of interest (Moss Kanter, 1994, p. 97).[10]

These points regarding information flows and so forth were also brought out by Dore (1983) in his discussion of the 'obligated relational contracting' found between Japanese firms. This involves long-term trading relations in which goodwill (with 'give and take') is expected to temper the pursuit of self-interest, although this and other labour market practices have since come under strain, especially following the relatively slow economic growth of the 1980s.[11] In his 1983 article Dore argued that such relations were more common in Western economies than is generally recognised. While it may be objected that relational contracts lead to price distortions and hence to a loss of allocative efficiency, they do lead to high levels of other kinds of efficiency. Specifically, 'the relative security of such relations encourages investment in supplying firms', 'the relationships of trust and mutual dependency make for a more rapid flow of information', and 'a by-product of the system is a general emphasis on quality'. This discussion links to a number of classic papers (such as Richardson, 1972, and Mariti and Smiley, 1983), with Dore citing Macaulay's 1962 paper as demonstrating that relational contracting is indeed valued by firms in the US as well as in Japan.[12]

With these apparent benefits of collaboration, why don't more firms enter into such arrangements? In part the answer may lie in the short termism that prevails in many firms and industries, and a financial system more geared to quick pay-back periods and a high priority to maintaining dividend payout levels than to long-term investment commitments.[13] In particular, the attempt to squeeze productivity growth out of UK firms during the 1980s and 1990s via the intensification of competitive pressures allied with the opening up of cost-cutting competitive avenues may have had two contradictory effects. First, recording what have been interpreted by some as impressive and welcome productivity growth figures (Crafts, 1996; Eltis,

1996), while at the same time undermining the conditions for long-term, sustainable economic development.

7 Policy implications

The fostering of collaborative structures may be an important element in creating a competitive and successful economy – an economy capable of closing the output gap with its major competitors.[14] This opens up a very different policy agenda than that which was pursued in the UK during the Thatcher and Major Governments of the 1980s and 1990s. Instead of the 'freeing up' of labour and product markets through policies of deregulation and casualisation we need new industrial innovation, and macroeconomic policies which will: develop new forms of corporate finance and create effective mechanisms of corporate governance; provide a modern productive infrastructure which private firms can utilise, in many cases in a cooperative fashion; ensure a macroeconomic regime conducive to the creation of new industrial capacity, including low interest rates and a competitive exchange rate; ensure the expansion of employment opportunities so that investment in education and training will translate into the increased output levels which in the long run will repay such investments; and promote productive cooperation and industrial innovation. On this last point of promoting innovation, innovation policy should distinguish the different determinants of innovation between types of innovating firm so that the particular policy targets can be more effectively hit.

Further reading

We have given references in the text and notes for more detail on the material covered in the various chapters. However, some of the key readings for anyone wanting to follow up on the main debates would be as follows.

On the debates around 'globalisation' see in particular Hirst and Thompson (1996) and the various authors collected together in Michie and Grieve Smith (eds)(1995, 1999). All three of these books take a rather sceptical view of the 'globalisation' thesis, although they do also give detailed descriptions of the opposing arguments, along with full references. On the particular idea that it is the globalisation of technology which is driving these processes, in the face of which individual governments can only play the role of King Canute, see the various authors within Archibugi and Michie (eds) (1997b, 1998), Howells and Michie (eds)(1997), and Archibugi, Howells and Michie (1999). On the UK's economic performance in the interwar period, see Kitson and Solomou (1990).

On the UK's relative industrial performance, see the four-way debate in the *Economic Journal*, referred to in Chapter 7, from which that chapter is taken. And on what policies the New Labour Government might take to tackle unemployment and inequality, in addition to Chapter 8 above, see the Kitson, Michie and Sutherland (1997) paper cited in that chapter.

Notes

1 Introduction and overview

1 The British 'public' schools are not state schools – quite the contrary, they are the private, elite schools such as Eton, and other, less well-known, fee-paying institutions.
2 It should be stressed that the present book does *not* aim to be a textbook. It is a collection of essays on different economic issues, mostly with a strong policy relevance. The discussion in the text refers to textbooks simply to illustrate that the approach of *this* book, which is to be global in outlook, historical and inter-disciplinary in approach, and to maintain a clear policy focus, is rather different than most books on economics, and most particularly different from the usual textbook approach. While we would not, therefore, recommend the present book in place of a textbook, we would suggest that it could be a useful supplement to such a text, particularly for courses which want to introduce greater realism and policy relevance than is usually the case.

2 Globalisation, unemployment and government policy

1 Thus:

> Many over-enthusiastic analysts and politicians have gone beyond the evidence in over-stating both the extent of the dominance of world markets and their ungovernability. . . . we have a myth that exaggerates the *degree* of helplessness in the face of contemporary economic forces. . . . It is *not* the case currently that radical goals are attainable: full employment in the advanced countries, a fairer deal for the poorer developing countries, and more widespread democratic control over economic affairs for the world's people.
> (Hirst and Thompson, 1996, pp. 6–7, emphasis added)

2 On which, see the various contributions in Michie and Grieve Smith (1999), and in particular Braunstein and Epstein.
3 Japanese economic policy also shifted towards austerity in 1981. It is true that the Japanese budget deficit continued to increase, but this was due to depressed tax revenue (see Itoh, 1994, p. 37).
4 M. Kalecki (1943), 'Political Aspects of Full Employment', in *Selected Essays on the Dynamics of the Capitalist Economy*, Cambridge: Cambridge University Press, 1971, p. 144.
5 Maddison's (1962) figures for the whole world economy indicate that in 1929 the US had 14.7 per cent of world export markets whereas the UK had 8.6 per cent.
6 Sawyer (1995) discusses these processes of vicious cycles and uneven spreading of

benefits as among the factors which have made full employment a relatively exceptional state of affairs under capitalism.

7 See Chapter 8 for further discussion of these issues.

8 See Rowthorn (1992) for an analysis of government spending in Britain during the Thatcher era. His Figure 12.1 gives international comparisons for 1969–89.

9 Japanese aid flows are now second in scale only to the US, with the six biggest recipients of Japan's aid being in East Asia. As ever, 'aid' is not unconnected with trade: a third of Japan's aid to its East Asian neighbours is used to finance infrastructure spending that supports trade, including ports and transport systems, all the better for receiving Japanese goods.

10 Karl Marx and Frederich Engels, *The Communist Manifesto*, 1848.

11 Kalecki (1932): see particularly pages 53 and 61; cited by Glyn and Rowthorn (1994), p. 198, note 13.

3 Trade theory and policy

1 The data series we constructed for world output and trade showed consistently high correlation statistics between the two series, both for levels and growth rates, as follows:

	Levels	*Growth*
1870–1913	0.9962	0.5062
1924–37	0.8469	0.8713
1950–90	0.9950	0.7688

Of course this says nothing about causality, which is discussed in the text. Our data series on world output is based on constant price GDP series from Maddison (1991, Table 4.7) for 1870–1950 (computed from annual growth rates of 16 countries) and from Wells (1993a, Appendix) for 1950–90. Our series for world trade was based on volumes of world exports from Lewis (1981, Appendix III, Table 4) for 1870–1913, from Maddison (1962, Table 25) for 1913–50, and from Wells (1993a, Appendix) for 1950–91; see Chapter 4 for further discussion of these data series. We are grateful to the late John Wells for providing us with unpublished data, used in the construction of these series.

2 The deflationary effect of deficit countries losing purchasing power while the surplus country deliberately curtails the equivalent boost to demand, with trade imbalances thus causing deflation overall, is not just a logical possibility. Rather, it is an accurate description of what West Germany, for example, was pursuing through its mercantilist policies combined with tight monetary policies, on which see Joan Robinson (1966), discussed further in Michie and Wilkinson (1995).

3 Krugman (1994b) argues that the attempt by mainstream economic theorists to incorporate increasing returns to scale into trade theory did not take place before the late 1970s because these economists were constrained by available mathematical techniques:

> Since economics as practised in the English-speaking world is strongly orientated toward mathematical models, any economic argument that has not been expressed in that form tends to remain invisible. While many economists no doubt understood that increasing returns could explain international trade even in the absence of comparative advantage, before 1980

there were no clean and simple models making the point. As a result this idea was often left out of textbooks and trade courses and even good trade theorists often seemed unaware of the possibility.

(Krugman, 1994b, p. 3)

4 There are many arguments in favour of managed trade in addition to the relatively narrow 'economic' ones we make here, such as the environmental objection to the waste of resources in transporting goods internationally which could instead have been supplied locally (see Lang and Hines, 1993).

5 Kaldor (1985, pp. 8–9) outlined the stylised facts approach as follows: 'One should subordinate deduction to induction and discover the empirical regularities first, whether through a study of statistics or through special inquiries . . . In comparison with the high-sounding principles of the great systematizers, this kind of inductive-deductive theorizing may appear pedestrian. But it is far more likely to lead to a better understanding of how capitalist economies work than the all-embracing principles of the great system-builders who, in the field of economics at any rate, are more likely to obstruct the progress of knowledge than to promote it.'

This use of the term differs somewhat from that of many econometricians, as illustrated in van der Ploeg (1994, p. xxii):

These discussions are followed by a presentation of stylized facts (unit roots, triangular arbitrage, cointegration, fat tails, skewness, volatility clusters etc.).

6 For an analysis of Britain's industrial performance since 1960 which confirms the dangers which underinvestment in the traded goods sector represents, not only by leading to deindustrialisation directly, with inadequate investment in the manufacturing sector, but also by exacerbating wider economic problems through the balance of payments effect, see Chapter 7.

7 This argument has similarities with that advanced by Thirlwall (1979). Thirlwall, however, assumes that income elasticities (for exports and imports) are constant over time so although countries' growth rates differ, due to the balance of payments constraint, they do not diverge. Our suggestion is that due to cumulative causation processes, including the Verdoorn effect, the income elasticities may shift and this may lead to diverging growth rates. This process will, of course, be affected by any countervailing processes of convergence such as appropriating technology and production systems from the leading country or countries. We are grateful to Jonathan Perraton for comments on this point.

8 Hahn and Matthews give a rather unconvincing explanation as to why it took them eight years to write their obituary of Kaldor for the *Economic Journal*, and then proceed to write less than two sides.

9 See the discussion by Thirlwall (1994).

10 Krugman (1994c) is concerned that those implementing trade policy (particularly in the United States) are underqualified 'policy entrepreneurs'. He argues that politicians have 'delivered the policies of a great and sophisticated nation into the hands of snake-oil peddlers'. Additionally, in complaining at Ira Magaziner's choice of experts for the health care task force, Krugman writes that

this may have reflected a number of factors, but it is probably not irrelevant that anyone who, like Magaziner, is strongly committed to the ideology of competitiveness is bound to have found professional economists notably unsympathetic in the past – and to be unwilling to deal with them on any other issue.

(p. 43)

11 For a critical analysis of the Delors' White Paper see Grieve Smith (1994).

12 See the various chapters in Michie and Grieve Smith (1995), and in particular those by Singh and Zammit, and Eatwell.

13 Reproduced in Henderson (1986), pp. 65, 70.

14 Sutton (1994, p. 41). He even goes on not only to say: 'It is clear that the intellectual map has changed; the question is, how are we to proceed?', but to admit that 'we are, in this area, witnessing at least a wobble in the paradigm which has dominated economic analysis for the past generation'.

15 These data do not cover the whole world economy. They are useful, however, in providing internally consistent comparisons over time of the changing shares of output amongst the group of countries covered.

16 As with the GDP data, the export data series will underestimate the total of world exports. Using more comprehensive series (Lewis, 1981), the share of UK merchandise exports is seen to have declined from 18.9 per cent in 1870 to 13.7 per cent in 1913. Although these shares are lower, the rate of decline is very similar.

17 Maddison's (1962) figures for the whole world economy indicate that in 1929 the US had 14.7 per cent of world export markets whereas the UK had 8.6 per cent.

18 This argument has been challenged by Eichengreen (1992) who argues that the problems of the interwar monetary system were primarily due to lack of cooperation amongst central banks rather than the absence of an effective hegemonic power.

19 For a discussion and criticism of this idea that trade deficits have been made unimportant, see Coutts and Godley (1992, pp. 60–67) and McCombie and Thirlwall (1992, pp. 68–74).

20 For an interpretation of slow growth and high unemployment as a policy choice in face of these class interests, see Singh (1992).

21 For a discussion of this 'global neoclassicism', which exposes several weak links in the chain – both theoretical and practical – which, according to the new orthodoxy, necessarily ties domestic economic policy to the dictates of international financial markets, see Harris (1995).

22 On which, see Chapter 6 which argues that the international monetary arrangements of the 1920s slowed world growth during the late 1920s and exacerbated the Great Depression of 1929–32, and that the subsequent demise of the gold standard enabled many countries to implement independent policies to stimulate economic expansion.

23 For a specific proposal, of a new multilateral, rule-based trade proposal which would reward nations for high levels of development achieved relative to their economic means, see DeMartino and Cullenberg (1995).

24 The policy package advocated by the Cambridge Economic Policy Group in the 1970s included the use of import controls with precisely this goal, of allowing an expansion of the economy which would result in a rise rather than a fall in import *levels*; see for example CEPG (1979). For a discussion of the possible use of active trade policies to permit the pursuit of national full employment policies in Europe see Eatwell (1994).

25 For an analysis of the Mitterrand Government's initial experience of reflation see Halimi *et al.* (1994).

26 For an empirical investigation into the historical trends of world trade integration see Chapter 4.

27 It was such capital flows that explained much of the success of the operation of the pre-First World War Gold Standard, on which see Chapter 4.

28 This consensus has of course continued to be challenged, as indicated in the various references already cited. See also Kirkpatrick (1995) who concludes that trade liberalisation

does *not* work anywhere, regardless of the economic and socio-political condi-tions in the reforming country; that initially unfavourable circumstances *do* affect both the form and the outcome of the reform process, and that liberalization *does* often have short-term drawbacks. The empirical evidence of the 1980s does not confirm the pro-liberalization arguments, and govern-ments have good reason to be apprehensive about the consequences of a liberalization programme.

(p. 38)

4 Trade and growth: a historical perspective

1 Although, as discussed by Panić (1995), there were significant differences between the system that was conceived and the system that was actually implemented.

2 See Frieden (1994, p. 82) who also argues that it is the internationally oriented economic groups within any country which will in general prefer fixed exchange rates, while domestically based groups will prefer floating rates.

3 For instance the growth of trade accelerated from the early 1900s to 1913.

4 Eichengreen (1994) examines the volatility of GDP across countries during the operation of different exchange rate regimes. He concludes that 'There is no evidence that output volatility increased with the shift from pegged to floating rate regimes after 1972: if anything the opposite may have been true' (p. 172). This conclusion may be dependent on Eichengreen's use of standard deviations (of detrended series) as the measure of volatility, since the transition to floating exchange rates led to lower growth of world output (see Table 4.1) and a lower mean growth rate for most industrialised countries.

5 During the post-Second World War period there was an increase in service sector activity in both the private and public sectors, much of which was not internationally tradable.

6 There have been a number of alternative forms of gold standard in history, for a discussion of which see Schwartz (1986).

7 See the arguments in favour of the price-specie-flow mechanism by Huffman and Lothian and arguments in favour of the monetary approach by McCloskey and Zecher, both contained in Bordo and Schwartz (1984). The essence of the dispute is whether gold flows cause, in the first instance, price adjustments (the price-specie-flow mechanism) or expenditure adjustments (the monetary approach). There is thus disagreement over whether there can be transitory changes in rela-tive prices – the invariance of the law of one price – but both retain the remaining monetarist assumptions.

8 According to the monetary approach, the rules were inconsequential due to perfect arbitrage in goods and capital markets.

9 In response to a shock, the unravelling of the price-quantity adjustment pro-cess will not necessarily lead to a return to the initial position; shocks can have persistent effects as well as altering and undermining the dynamics of growth.

10 Protectionism, through tariff-jumping, was one such policy which encouraged foreign direct investment during this period (Bairoch, 1976; Bloomfield, 1968).

11 The UK balance of payments on current account was in surplus from 1924 to 1929 apart from 1926 when the impact of the General Strike resulted in a small deficit (see Feinstein, 1972). The adverse impact of the overvaluation on com-petitiveness, however, led to smaller surpluses than had been achieved in the immediate prewar period.

12 During the period 1913–29, Britain's growth rate of 0.7 per cent per annum was approximately one third of the world average (Kitson and Solomou, 1990).

13 The system was also supported, particularly during its early life, by resource flows from the US to Western Europe and Japan (in the form of Marshall aid and other official transfers). While these flows helped to stabilise the international economy their primary motive was to act as a bulwark against the spread of communism.

14 The shares of intra-bloc trade are a crude indicator of regional trade bias as they can be affected by the number of countries in the bloc, the openness of each country, the commodity composition of trade and variations in transactions costs. Anderson and Norheim (1993) construct an index which adjusts for these factors. This index shows only a small increase in geographical intra-regional trade for the world economy from 1928 to 1938 (Anderson and Norheim, 1993, Table 2.2).

15 See Bhagwati (1993), who argues that the USA, frustrated at the slow progress of the GATT talks, turned to regionalism instead.

16 The intra-bloc share of the original six members of the EC increased up to the early 1960s but subsequently it declined until the mid-1960s. This possibly reflected the trade diversion impact of new members to the bloc.

17 The intensity of intra-regional trade index constructed by Anderson and Norheim (1993, Table 2.2), for various benchmark years, shows a continuous rise for Western Europe during the post-Second World War period, a rise for North America until 1979 followed by a subsequent decline, and a decline for Asia since 1958. The apparent contradiction of the latter with the intra-bloc share evidence is probably due to the intensity index adjusting for the fast growth of the Asian economies.

18 This is quite aside from the additional issue of what the effects would be of adopting a single currency in these areas; Bayoumi and Eichengreen (1994) find that the North American Free Trade Area (NAFTA) is even less of an optimum currency area than is the European Union (EU), because while most of the anticipated benefits apply with equal force, the underlying disturbances are more diverse across members of NAFTA and hence the costs of abandoning the exchange rate instrument are likely to be higher. For a detailed analysis see Moss and Michie (1998).

19 Not that bad institutional design is simply the result of technical inadequacies; more likely it is caused by the underlying economic disparities themselves, with the stronger powers in a position to dictate that the brunt of adjustment mechanisms be borne by the weaker powers rather than by themselves, which would actually be more rational for the global system (and therefore, indeed, for the long-term interests of the dominant powers themselves, if only they could be forced to act in their own long-term interests instead of, at every turn, having to be forced to by pressure from, or fear of, outside forces).

20 Answering the question, 'Which will be the strongest candidate for world leadership apart from the US?', the percentage responses were as follows (reported in the *Guardian*, 2 April 1994):

In the UK:	West Europe, 32; China, 23; Japan, 19; Russia, 10
In Germany:	West Europe, 53; Japan, 19; China, 13; Russia, 3
In America:	Japan, 28; West Europe, 26; China, 25; Russia, 11
In Japan:	China, 38; Japan, 24; West Europe, 12; Russia, 5

21 Answering the question, 'Which country poses the biggest threat to world peace?', the percentage responses were as follows (reported in the *Guardian*, 2 April 1994):

In the UK: Russia, 20; Middle East, 15; US, 11; China, 9
In Germany: Russia, 27; Middle East, 10; Ex-Yugoslavia, 9; Israel, 6
In America: Russia, 17; Middle East, 11; China, 9; Ex Yug., 6; Iraq, 6
In Japan: US, 22; Russia, 21; Korea, 13; China, 4

5 Recession and economic revival in Britain: the role of policy in the 1930s and 1980s

1 The G7 is the Group of Seven leading Western industrialised countries (with the addition of Russia it will become the Group of Eight).
2 The exaggerated claims of many of these publications may reflect the fact that they were written during the late 1980s boom – a boom which was a speculative bubble which was to burst leading to a major economic slump.
3 The economic slump. The growth rate in the 1930s of 3.0 per cent covers the period 1931–39. If the shorter period, 1932–37, is used – a period which allows a more accurate trough-to-peak measure, then the annual rate of GDP growth is increased to 4.3 per cent. The 1980s growth rate is for the period 1981–89, a reasonable approximation of the trough-to-peak period. The 1980 period is also influenced by oil output which increases the level and growth rate of GDP.
4 More recently, the Government has shifted to using the International Labour Organisation's (ILO) method of measuring unemployment which overcomes some of the inadequacies of the claimant count.
5 On the political misuse and manipulation of data see Harcourt and Kitson (1993).
6 Cooper (1992, p. 2125) makes the acute observation that Friedman and Schwartz 'having never met a central bank they liked, of course attributed the severity of the depression to the perverse behaviour of the Federal Reserve Board'.
7 For an examination of the strengths and limitations of this argument see Kitson and Solomou (1990).
8 As well as the appreciation of the nominal exchange rate from the mid-1930s due to competitive devaluations abroad the real exchange rate also appreciated due to higher domestic inflation.
9 The idea that recovery was caused by decreased wages is, however, quite misplaced – see Michie (1987, p. 123).
10 It is questionable whether the actual budget balance or the discetionary budget balance (sometimes referred to as the constant employment budget balance) is the best measure of fiscal stance. In addition there is the issue of how budget deficits affect private sector expectations and confidence. In the context of the early 1930s, prior to the establishment of Keynesian demand management policies, budget deficits were associated with economic instability and inflation. Thus, their psychological impact on private sector expectations was likely to lead to reduced investment. The fiscal orthodoxy of the 1930s may, therefore, have contributed to recovery, albeit not through the mechanisms ('crowding-out') of orthodox economics.
11 See also the theories of Marx (1867–94), Schumpeter (1942), Downie (1958) and Clark (1961).
12 The UK estimates are for 1935 and the US estimates are for 1937. The gap is based on an unweighted average of total factory trades.
13 The benchmark years, although not ideal, are necessary due to data limitations as the productivity figures are based on information contained in the Censuses of Production of 1924, 1930 and 1935.
14 The Government's approach is captured in the views of Nigel Lawson, one of the architects of the economic strategy:

The views I had arrived at, and which I continue to hold today, could be summarised in terms of two interconnected reversals of post-war conventional wisdom. The first is the conviction that the recipe for economic success is the greatest practicable market freedom within an overall framework of firm financial discipline – precisely how that discipline is best applied is a second order question, though important, and one which was to prove surprisingly explosive. . . . The second reversal is that . . . instead of seeking to use macroeconomic policy to promote growth and microeconomic policy to suppress inflation, the Government should direct macroeconomic policy to the suppression of inflation and rely on microeconomic (or supply-side) policy, such as tax and labour market reforms, to provide the conditions favourable to improved performance in terms of growth and employment.

(Lawson, 1992, p. 9)

15 In his evidence to the House of Commons Treasury and Civil Service Committee Friedman (1980) argued that:

Trying to control the money supply through 'fiscal policy . . . and interest rates' is trying to control the output of one item (money) through altering the demand for it by manipulating the incomes of its users (that is the role of fiscal policy) or the prices of substitues for it (that is the role of interest rates). A precise analogy is like trying to control the output of motor cars by altering the incomes of potential purchasers and manipulating rail and air fares. In principle, possible in both cases, but in practice highly inefficient. Far easier to control the output of motor cars by controlling the output of a basic raw material, say steel, to the manufacturers – a precise analogy to controlling the money supply by controlling the availability of base money to banks or others.

16 The failure to achieve the desired monetary targets can be explained by either operational problems of monetary control or theoretical objections to the existence of an exogenously determined money supply. In terms of the former, it has been argued that the Government failed to use the appropriate instruments; that financial liberalisation led to breakdown of the relationship between £M3 and inflation; and that the relationship between £M3 and inflation broke down when £M3 was used as a target variable as agents searched for other sources of money (Goodhart, 1975). In terms of the latter, it has been argued that in a credit money economy the money supply is endogenous and therefore it is impossible to control (all forms) of the money supply directly (Kaldor, 1980).

17 In the 1982 Red Book it was stated that:

The exchange rate is a route through which changes in the money supply affect inflation. It can also be an important influence on financial conditions. External or domestic developments that change the relationship between the domestic money supply and exchange rate may therefore disturb the link between money and prices, at least for a time. . . . They are a reason why the Government considers it appropriate to look at the exchange rate in monitoring domestic monetary conditions and in taking decisions about policy.

18 Regarding the more general claim that deregulation is required to promote the sort of flexibility necessary for a dynamic economy, see Tarling and Wilkinson (1997) and Michie and Sheehan (1999).

6 The tale of two recessions: 1929 and the Gold Standard, 1992 and the ERM

1 On which, see the various contributors to Michie and Grieve Smith (1996).
2 On which, see Chapter 8, below.
3 See Chapter 5 above for further discussion.
4 See Harris (1988). That unemployment has continued to cause psychological and other health problems is well illustrated by Burchell (1992) who demonstrates graphically how mistaken is the idea that people choose to be unemployed because of generous welfare payments.
5 For a detailed discussion of the classical Gold Standard see Panić (1992). 'The reconstructed Gold Standard consisted of various types of commodity money regimes. The commonest was the gold exchange standard, where central banks held some fraction of their reserves in foreign exchange rather than entirely in precious metals. Other types of regime included the gold bullion standard, the gold coin standard, the qualified standard and the silver standard.'
6 As each country declared a parity against gold this immediately established a network of fixed exchange rates.
7 The balance of payments on current account was in surplus from 1924 to 1929 apart from 1926 when the impact of the General Strike resulted in a small deficit. The adverse impact of the overvaluation on competitiveness, however, led to smaller surpluses than in the immediate prewar period.
8 During the period 1913–29, Britain's growth rate of 0.7 per cent per annum was approximately one third of the world average (see Kitson and Solomou, 1990).
9 The last major country to go into recession (in the first quarter of 1931) was Spain which had a flexible exchange rate.
10 In his study of the Gold Standard and its lessons for European Monetary Union, Miça Panić (1992) demonstrates that monetary union today could prove even more damaging than was the Gold Standard, given the massive scale of migration undertaken in the 1930s (which is unlikely to be accepted today), and the huge investments in colonial countries which again are unlikely to be mirrored by equivalent capital flows today.
11 For evidence on the statistical correlations, and a discussion of the cyclical behaviour of wages and its policy implications, see Michie (1987).
12 And with the late John Smith, then leader of the Labour Party, arguing that leaving the ERM would not assist in the reduction of interest rates.
13 See Chapter 8 below for a detailed discussion of employment creation measures. See also Glyn and Rowthorn, 1994.
14 The relation between the *General Theory* and fascist economic policies is discussed by Keynes himself in his preface to the German edition of 1936. The version which appears in the *Collected Works of John Maynard Keynes* (published by the Royal Economic Society) is not complete, omitting, for example, Keynes's statement that his theory is 'applicable to situations in which national leadership is more pronounced' (see Schefold, 1980).

7 Britain's industrial performance since 1960: underinvestment and relative decline

1 See for example Singh (1977, 1987) and Rowthorn and Wells (1987).
2 The experience of contracting out was analysed in detail by the ESRC's 1992–97 'Contracts & Competition' Programme, on which see Deakin and Michie (1997a, 1997b) and Milne (1997).
3 New models of economic growth also stress endogeneity due to externalities in the production of innovations. Endogenous technical progress, within a

neoclassical framework, was postulated by Arrow, with further developments by Romer (1986 and 1990) and Lucas (1988) amongst others. Unlike the traditional neoclassical model of growth (Solow, 1970), the new models may allow for divergences in growth (as in Kaldorian models) depending on the extent to which there are international spillovers of knowledge and technology.

4 These points are argued in more detail in Wilkinson (1992) and Michie and Wilkinson (1995).

5 The reasons for France's particularly bad performance during 1979–89 are analysed in detail in Halimi *et al.* (1994).

6 Indeed, Crafts (1988) claims that the industrial missions organised by the Anglo-American Council on Productivity between 1948 and 1952 had identified restrictive labour practices as posing the major obstacle to the 'Americanisation' of British industry, while in fact these reports pointed rather to the shortcomings of management (see Coates, 1994; Nolan and O'Donnell, 1997; and Tiratsoo and Tomlinson, 1994).

7 For a discussion of which, see Deakin, Michie and Wilkinson (1992).

8 See also the discussion of these issues by Deakin (1992) and Brown (1992), and by Nolan *et al.* (1997).

9 See Glyn (1992) and Cosh, Hughes and Rowthorn (1993) where these last, distributional points are analysed in depth.

10 The following report is typical:

> Among appropriations, dividend payments rose by 17 per cent in 1990, a lower growth rate than in the preceding two years (27 per cent in 1989 and 33 per cent in 1988), but one that was still surprisingly rapid. The dividend payout ratio, defined as the ratio of dividend payments to total income after deducting tax and interest payments, rose to 56 per cent in the fourth quarter of 1990 and 64 per cent in the first quarter of this year.
> (Bank of England, *Quarterly Bulletin*, August 1991, p. 364)

11 The gross capital stock series is from O'Mahony (1993) which presents estimates of internationally consistent data constructed using standard US service lives.

12 The estimate of the UK capital stock level may be an overestimate as the collapse of manufacturing in the early 1980s led to substantial capital scrapping which was not incorporated into official figures (see Oulton and O'Mahony, 1994).

13 Rowthorn (1995) shows that low investment over the past 20 years, especially in manufacturing, has been a significant factor in the rise of unemployment throughout Western Europe; as indicated above, this has been a particular problem in the UK.

14 Scott (1989 and 1992) emphasises, in contrast to much of new growth theory, that all types of investment, not just certain kinds (R&D expenditure, investment in education, etc.) create and reveal new investment opportunities (on this, see Kitson, 1998). Additionally he stresses, in the spirit of Keynes, that investment responds to demand and the expectations of the growth of demand. The important two-way relationship between investment and demand is overlooked in many recent discussions of economic growth which ignore demand constraints on the level of economic activity. Investment can increase, as well as respond to, the level of demand, affecting the scale of production as well as its organisation and technological efficiency. And through Verdoorn effects, increased scale can itself boost productivity.

15 This point is made by Wells (1993a), p. 56. Crafts (1993) cites the estimates of Church (1992) which suggest that the Fundamental Equilibrium Exchange Rate

(FEER) has been falling at a trend rate of 1.5 per cent per annum. This implies an annual terms-of-trade induced reduction of GDP growth of 0.4 per cent – a significant proportion of the UK trend growth rate.

16 As Postmaster General from October 1964 to August 1965, Tony Benn concluded the following:

> This highlights in my mind one of the great difficulties of being a socialist in the sort of society in which we live. The real drive for improvement comes from those concerned to make private profit. If, therefore, you deny these people the right of extending private enterprise into new fields, you have to have some sort of alternative. You have to have some body which wants to develop public enterprise but our present Civil Service is not interested in growth. It is geared to care and maintenance.
>
> (Benn, 1987, p. 264, diary entry for 28 May 1965)

17 See for example the arguments of the Cambridge Economic Policy Group published in the *Observer* on 19 April 1992 and denounced the following week (26 April) by the *Observer*'s own Adam Raphael in a piece entitled 'Beware the siren devaluers who lure us to ruin'; see also the reply from Coutts, Godley, Michie and Rowthorn in the *Observer* of 3 May 1992.

18 The Cambridge survey was undertaken during the spring and summer of 1991 and provides a national stock-take of approximately 2,000 enterprises. The sampling framework, and the respondents, was split equally between manufacturing and the rapidly expanding business service sector (for further details see Kitson, 1994, and Small Business Research Centre, 1992). For detail of subsequent survey work by the ESRC Centre for Business Research, which broadly reinforces the points being made here, see Chapter 9 below.

19 In the Cambridge survey, firms were asked to identify which government policies hindered or helped their business in the previous ten years. Overall, firms believed that government policy had hindered their performance. What was noticeable was the high proportion of firms that considered that they had received no help from government policy during the past decade. Nearly a third of the firms surveyed did not identify any significant help from government policy during the previous ten years.

20 The contrasting impacts of mild versus deep recession can also lead to contrasting productivity changes. With mild recessions we tend to observe 'Okun's Law' with a *short-term* productivity loss associated with a fall in output. With deep recession we observe a 'shock effect' with a short-term gain in productivity due to the shedding of labour and capacity.

21 The 1997 Cambridge survey indicated that 44 per cent of manufacturing firms had fewer than five competitors and 71 per cent had fewer than ten competitors (Kitson and Wilkinson, 1998b). The survey also showed that personal attention to client needs, product quality and an established reputation were the most important factors which contributed to the competitiveness of manufacturing firms. Price was ranked tenth out of 11 identified factors. Again, see Chapter 9 below for other survey results which reinforce these general findings.

8 From welfare to work?

1 When Eddie George, Governor of the Bank of England, was asked in October 1998: 'Are you saying that unemployment in the north-east is an acceptable price to pay to curb inflation in the south?' he replied, 'Yes, I suppose in a sense I am. It is not desirable, but the fact is that we can only affect through monetary policy the state of demand in the economy as a whole' (quoted in the *Financial Times*,

22 October 1998). Tony Blair defended the Governor the next day in the House of Commons.

2 Glyn and Rowthorn (1994) point out that there is a third route to increased employment levels (in terms of numbers in work), namely having the total amount of paid work available in the economy shared out among more people through cuts in working time. They make the case, however, for the importance of also pursuing a programme of greater government expenditure on public services and infrastructure, and show how such a programme can increase employment in a situation where conventional Keynesian measures are inappropriate for balance-of-payments reasons, which they believe represent the immediate constraint in many economies such as the UK.

3 As our starting point we use the public sector strategy outlined by Berry, Kitson and Michie (1995, 1996) to create a million new jobs. A range of other proposals have also been suggested including those by Coutts and Rowthorn (1995), Holtham and Mayhew (1996) and, in the European context, Glyn and Rowthorn (1994).

4 If the multiplier turned out lower then a net increase of one million jobs would require a slightly larger programme, but the difference in overall cost would be small. Even if the programme had to be increased by 10 per cent, the net additional cost would be well under £1bn a year. As indicated in the text, we have at a number of stages of the analysis chosen deliberately cautious assumptions (e.g. ignoring the savings in administration costs which other estimates of the savings brought about by reducing unemployment have included). So it may well be that the net cost of a slightly larger programme would still be less than the overall figure we arrive at.

5 POLIMOD uses 1991 Family Expenditure Survey data which are Crown Copyright and have been made available by the Office for National Statistics (ONS) through the Economic and Social Research Council Data Archive and are used by permission. Neither the ONS nor the Data Archive bear any responsibility for the analysis or the interpretation of the data reported here.

6 Where working is defined as at least 8 hours a week.

7 In reality some would be part-time, so to this extent our estimates of the net cost of such a programme are too high. The cost would actually turn out rather lower than we suggest since the pay which the newly taken-on workers receive over and above the income they were already receiving while out of work would be likely to be less for two part-time workers combined than for one full-time worker. However, in this case the fiscal gain from increased tax revenues would also be somewhat lower. So the net difference between whether the jobs are taken as full-time or (more) part-time is likely to be small (and far less than is assumed by some when part-time jobs are presented as a relatively cheap job-creation option, since this misses the point that the additional tax revenues in such a scenario will be correspondingly lower). This is illustrated by the simulations we ran with part-time jobs, reported below.

8 The average national weekly wage is £290.5. The weighted average weekly (Full Time Equivalent) wage taking the largest three sectors in Table 8.1 combined – housing, education and training, and health – comes out at £312. It is not possible to calculate average wages in all sectors, nor for the additional jobs created through multiplier effects, but these latter jobs would most probably start at below the national average. Thus while the assumption of average weekly earnings may if anything slightly underestimate the level of wages and hence the positive revenue impact of the job generation programme, the net effect would be marginal; even were the average wage to turn out to be much different from average earnings, which is most unlikely, additional simulations which were run with both higher and lower average

earnings suggested little net effect (as reported and discussed in Kitson, Michie and Sutherland, 1997).

9 Since there is no way of actually knowing in advance exactly what the pay will be for all the new jobs – since some of these are generated through multiplier effects and so will depend on what people happen to decide to spend their increased incomes on, and the distribution of earnings in these sectors – we did re-run our simulations with different assumptions regarding the actual pay levels for the new jobs, and found rather similar results to those reported here; (see Kitson, Michie and Sutherland, 1997).

10 Our costings therefore assume that the characteristics of the unemployed, such as family composition or housing tenure, are similar to those of the low paid.

11 Results are given to the nearest £10 million; this is not intended to imply that they are necessarily statistically significant to this degree of precision.

12 We make the assumption that all the increase in income is spent on the same goods as during unemployment. The assumption that none is saved will tend to inflate the revenue estimate. On the other hand it is likely that a higher proportion of the new income will be spent on goods on which VAT is charged than was the income during unemployment.

13 The estimate of £9,000 per claimant was given by Gillian Shepherd, then Education Minister, to the House of Commons Select Committee on Employment in October 1992 and a similar figure has been estimated by Piachaud (1994). Figures produced by the Unemployment Unit (Convery, 1996) estimate the revenue cost per claimant at only £7,420 in 1994/95 and £7,960 in 1995/96. Our estimates show that unemployment is a greater cost to the economy than previous work had suggested, despite the fact that some previous estimates had included savings in administration costs as unemployment falls which we have not done. Were these to be added to our estimates, the savings from a reduction in unemployment would be even greater than we have here suggested, and the corresponding net cost of a job creation programme even lower.

14 The Unemployment Unit estimate is as low as £4,000 in 1995/6.

15

Groups	Assumptions		
	A_a	$D_{(i)}$	$D_{(ii)}$
1	0.75×406	0.75×406	0.80×406
	$= 305,000$	$= 305,000$	$= 325,000$
2	0.35×1519	0.35×1519	0.40×1519
	$= 532,000$	$= 532,000$	$= 608,000$
3	0.057×2866	0.123×2866	0.093×2866
	$= 163,000$	$= 353,000$	$= 267,000$
4*	none	0.123×1069	0.093×1069
		$= 131,000$	$= 99,000$
Target total	1 million	1.3 million	1.3 million

* Group 4 includes people not working who are parents of under-5s (either lone parents or partners of working parents) who otherwise would be included in groups 1 to 3. They are assumed to be available for part-time work only.

16 The public finances are now in the ridiculous situation whereby there is excess demand for government bonds particularly by pension funds, yet instead of issuing bonds to finance new capital projects at relatively low rates of interest, the Government is paying much more for capital by increased use of the more expensive Private Finance Initiative (PFI). (On the weaknesses and costs of the PFI see Kitson, 1998.)

17 No change is made to the additional married allowances, but single age allowance is also increased by £1,000. The thresholds to the standard and higher

rates are *reduced* by £1,000 so that they cut into incomes at the same point as currently. We are simply increasing the band of income on which no tax is paid, at the expense of the 20 per cent band. The change has the same cash value to each taxpayer (£200 per year), except where taxpayers already pay less tax than this.

18 The impact of such a minimum wage is discussed in Kitson, Michie and Sutherland (1997).

9 Markets, competition and innovation

1 Particularly given the scale of North Sea oil production and employment, and the contribution made by North Sea oil to Britain's trade account and Government revenues over these decades.

2 See Bullock, Duncan and Wood (1996) and Cosh, Duncan and Hughes (1996) for more detail of the surveys. See also Wood (1998).

3 Firms were classified as innovators or non-innovators on the basis of their answers to the following questions:

 (i) Has your firm introduced any innovations in products (goods or services) or processes during the last three years which were new to your firm?

 (ii) If you introduced a product (process) innovation was it, to the best of your knowledge, already in use in other firms either in (a) your industry or (b) other industries? If you made more than one product innovation please answer with respect to your most important product (process) innovation.

4 Firms were classified as collaborators or non-collaborators on the basis of their answer to the following question: Has your firm in the last three years entered into formal or informal collaborative or partnership arrangements with any other organisations?

5 There is some evidence of fewer competitors in manufacturing than in services, although there is no clear pattern in the differences between innovators and non-innovators, or between collaborators and non-collaborators.

6 This issue of collaboration between firms raises a separate issue not discussed in the current chapter, namely the question of when collaboration becomes collusion, and how this is (and should be) handled in the context of competition policy. Oughton and Whittam (1996) contains an interesting discussion of the relation between cooperation between firms on the one hand and competition policy on the other, combined with an analysis of the benefits to be had from reaping internal and external economies of scale. Cooperative external economies of scale enable small and medium sized enterprises to pool fixed costs which can result not only in greater efficiency but also, by overcoming entry barriers, thereby increase competition. Thus public sponsorship of such cooperative industrial activities should not be seen as necessarily at odds with promoting competition. But a failure to appreciate this point could lead to a simple-minded competition policy failing to promote such cooperation – or even outlawing it – thus actually undermining the conditions for healthy competition. On these issues of competition policy, see also Deakin, Goodwin, and Hughes, 1997, and Anderman, 1997. This discussion also cuts across the distinction that can be made between the different views of the innovation process – and the roles played within this by competition on the one hand, and large firms able to fund R&D on the other – within Schumpeter's *Capitalism, Socialism and Democracy* (1947) and *The Theory of Economic Development* (1961), on which see Michie and Prendergast (1997).

7 Note that our data are all for small and medium sized enterprises. There is a mass of evidence to suggest that collaboration between firms of roughly comparable size tends to be of a very different nature from that between large and small firms

where the power relations are quite different. We are grateful to Keith Cowling for making this point. See also the discussion by Oliver and Blakeborough (1998).

8 For further discussion of these employment, turnover, and profit data see Cosh, Hughes and Wood (1996) and Cosh and Hughes (1996).

9 These points are argued in more detail by Michie and Prendergast (1997) on which this section draws.

10 For further discussion of the role of trust see the March 1997 Special Issue of the *Cambridge Journal of Economics* on Contracts and Competition, and in particular the Introduction by Deakin and Michie and the papers by Arrighetti, Bachmann and Deakin; Lane; and Burchell and Wilkinson. See also Deakin and Michie (1997b), Deakin, Goodwin and Hughes (1997), Michie (1997), and Deakin and Wilkinson (1997).

11 A point taken up by Dore (1998).

12 This literature is discussed in more detail in Buckley and Michie (1996).

13 An additional problem of a principal–agent nature may occur where the financial sector is dealing with networks or other alliances of firms, the legal definition of which may not be entirely clear; we are grateful to Laurence Harris for drawing this point to our attention. The socio-legal context of contracting and some of the implications of this for competitive performance are discussed by Deakin and Michie (1997b).

14 Indeed, when releasing a report in 1997 showing that British firms had reduced spending on innovation in 1996 – at a time when the lifespan of their established products was falling – the UK's Confederation of British Industry warned manufacturers that they would go to the wall unless they invested in developing new products (as reported in the *Guardian* of 9 June 1997). Interestingly from the point of view of the analysis of the current chapter, this report also indicated that the growth in collaboration between manufacturing companies and academics, universities and consultants had ended.

References

Allin, P. (1993), 'One hundred years of labour market indicators', *Employment Gazette*, December, Employment Department, pp. 553–560.

Anderman, S. (1997), 'Commercial cooperation, international competitiveness, and EC competition policy', in S. Deakin and J. Michie (eds), *Contracts, Cooperation, and Competition: Studies in Economics, Management, and Law*, Oxford: Oxford University Press.

Anderson, K. and Norheim, H. (1993), 'History, geography and regional economic integration', in K. Anderson and R. Blackhurst, *Regional Integration and the Global Trading System*, Hemel Hempstead: Harvester Wheatsheaf.

Archibugi, D. and Michie, J. (1995a), 'Technology and innovation: an introduction', *Cambridge Journal of Economics*, vol. 19, no. 1, February 1995, pp. 1–4.

Archibugi, D. and Michie, J. (1995b), 'The globalisation of technology: a new taxonomy', *Cambridge Journal of Economics*, vol. 19, no. 1, February 1995, pp. 121–140, reprinted in D. Archibugi and J. Michie (eds), *Technology, Globalisation and Economic Performance*, Cambridge: Cambridge University Press, 1997, pp. 172–197.

Archibugi, D. and Michie, J. (1997a), 'Technological globalisation and national systems of innovation', Chapter 1 of D. Archibugi and J. Michie (eds), *Technology, Globalisation and Economic Performance*, Cambridge: Cambridge University Press.

Archibugi, D. and Michie, J. (eds) (1997b), *Technology, Globalisation and Economic Performance*, Cambridge: Cambridge University Press.

Archibugi, D. and Michie, J. (eds) (1998), *Trade, Growth and Technical Change*, Cambridge: Cambridge University Press.

Archibugi, D., Howells, D. and Michie, J. (eds) (1999), *Innovation Systems in a Global Economy*, Cambridge: Cambridge University Press.

Arestis, P. and Sawyer, M. (1999), 'What role for the Tobin tax in world economic governance?', in J. Michie and J. Grieve Smith (eds), *Global Instability*, London: Routledge.

Armstrong, P., Glyn, A. and Harrison, J. (1991), *Capitalism Since 1945*, Oxford: Blackwell.

Arrighetti, A., Bachmann, R. and Deakin, S. (1997), 'Contract law, social norms and inter-firm cooperation', *Cambridge Journal of Economics*, vol. 21, no. 2 (March), pp. 171–195.

Atkinson, A. B. and Micklewright, J. (1991), 'Unemployment compensation and labor market transitions: a critical review', *The Journal of Economic Literature*, vol. XXIX, no. 4, December, pp. 1644–1727.

Bacon, R. and Eltis, W. (1976), *Britain's Economic Problem: Too Few Producers*, London: Macmillan.

Bairoch, P. (1976), *Commerce exterieur et développement économique de l'Europe au XIX siècle*, Ecoles des Hautes Etudes et Sciences Sociales.

Ball, M. and Wood, A. (1994), *How Many Jobs Does Construction Expenditure Generate?*, Discussion Paper in Economics 2/94, London: Birkbeck College.

Baumol, W. (1967), 'Macroeconomics of unbalanced growth', *American Economic Review*, vol. 57, pp. 415–426.

Baumol, W., Blackman, S. and Wolff, E. (1989), *Productivity and American Leadership: The Long View*, Cambridge MA: MIT Press.

Bayoumi, T. and Eichengreen, B. (1994), 'Monetary and exchange rate arrangements for NAFTA', *Journal of Development Economics*, 43/1.

Beale, N. and Nethercott, S. (1988), 'Job-loss and family morbidity: a study of factory closure', *Journal of the Royal College of General Practitioners*, vol. 35, pp. 510–514.

Beenstock, M., Capie, F. and Griffiths, B. (1984), 'Economic recovery in the United Kingdom in the 1930s', in Bank of England Panel Paper no. 23, April, *The UK Recovery in the 1930s*, pp. 29–56.

Benn, T. (1987), *Out of the Wilderness, Diaries 1963–67*, London: Hutchinson.

Berry, R., Kitson, M. and Michie, J. (1995), *Towards Full employment: The First Million Jobs*, London: Full Employment Forum.

Berry, R., Kitson, M. and Michie, J. (1996), 'Putting People First', *New Economy*, vol. 3, no. 3 (Autumn).

Bhagwati, J. (1993), 'Regionalism and multilateralism: an overview', in J. de Melo and A. Panagariya (eds), *New Dimensions in Regional Integration*, Cambridge: Cambridge University Press.

Bhagwati, J. and Irwin, D. (1987), 'The return of the Reciprocitarians: US trade policy today', *The World Economy*, vol. 10, no. 2, pp. 109–130.

Bishop, M. and Kay, J. A. (1988), *Does Privatization Work? Lessons from the UK*, London: London Business School.

Bloomfeld, A. (1968), *Patterns of Fluctuations in International Investment Before 1914*, Princeton: Princeton University Press.

Boardman, B. (1991), *Fuel Poverty: From Cold Homes to Affordable Warmth*, London: Belhaven Press.

Bolton (1971), *Small Firms: Report of the Committee of Inquiry on Small Firms*, London: HMSO.

Booth, A. (1987), 'Britain in the 1930s: a managed economy?', *Economic History Review*, vol. 40, December, pp. 499–522.

Bordo, M. D. (1992), 'Gold Standard theory', in P. Newman, M. Milgate and J. Eatwell (eds), *The New Palgrave Dictionary of Money and Finance*, vol. 2, London and Basingstoke: Macmillan.

Bordo, M. D. and Schwartz, A. J. (1984), *A Retrospective on the Bretton Woods System: Lessons for International Monetary Reform*, London: University of Chicago Press.

Borooah, V. (1988), 'Income distribution, consumption patterns and economic outcomes in the United Kingdom', *Contributions to Political Economy*, vol. 7, pp. 49–63.

Boyer, R. (1977), 'Commercial policy under alternative exchange rate regimes', *Cambridge Journal of Economics*, vol. 10, pp. 218–232.

Brander, J. A. and Spencer, B. J. (1984), 'Tariff protection and imperfect competition', in H. Kierzhkowski (ed.), *Monopolistic Competition in International Trade*, Oxford: Oxford University Press.

Broadberry, S. (1986), *The British Economy Between the Wars: a Macroeconomic Survey*, Oxford: Basil Blackwell.

Broadberry, S. (1993), 'Manufacturing and the convergence hypothesis: what the long-run data show', *Journal of Economic History*, vol. 53, December, pp. 772–795.

Broadberry, S. and Crafts, N. (1990a), 'The impact of the Depression of the 1930s on productive potential in the United Kingdom', *European Economic Review*, vol. 34, pp. 599–607.

Broadberry, S. and Crafts, N. (1990b), 'The implications of British macroeconomic policy in the 1930s for long-run growth performance', Centre for Economic Policy Research, Discussion Paper 386.

Brown, W. (1992), 'Collective rights', in J. Michie (ed.), *The Economic Legacy, 1979–1992*, London: Academic Press.

Buckley, P. and Michie, J. (1996), 'Introduction and overview', in P. Buckley and J. Michie (eds), *Firms, Organisations and Contracts: A Reader in Industrial Organisation*, Oxford: Oxford University Press, pp. 1–20.

Bullock, A., Duncan, J. and Wood, E. (1996) 'The survey method, sample attrition and the SME panel database', in A. Cosh and A. Hughes, *The Changing State of British Enterprise*, Cambridge: ESRC Centre for Business Research.

Burchell, B. (1992), 'Changes in the labour market and the psychological health of the nation', in J. Michie (ed.), *The Economic Legacy: 1979–1992*, London: Academic Press.

Burchell, B. and Wilkinson, F. (1997), 'Trust, business relationships and the contractual environment', *Cambridge Journal of Economics*, vol. 21, no. 2 (March), pp. 217–237.

Cambridge Economic Policy Group (CEPG) (1979), *Economic Policy Review*, Cambridge: Department of Applied Economics.

Cambridge Economic Policy Group (CEPG) (1992), 'Hands-off economics equals stagnation', *The Observer*, 19 April.

Capie, F. (1983), *Depression and Protectionism: Britain between the Wars*, London: George Allen & Unwin.

Capie, F. (1992), *Trade Wars: A Repetition of the Interwar Years?*, IEA Current Controversies, No. 2.

Carre, J. J., Dubois, P. and Malinvaud, E. (1976), *French Economic Growth*, Oxford: Oxford University Press.

Chan, K. (1978), 'The employment effects of tariffs under a free exchange rate regime', *Journal of International Economics*, vol. 8, pp. 415–424.

Church, K. (1992), 'Properties of the fundamental equilibrium exchange rate in models of the UK economy', *National Institute Economic Review*, no. 141, pp. 62–70.

Clark, J. M. (1961), *Competition as a Dynamic Process*, Washington DC: Brookings Institution.

Coakley, J. and Harris, L. (1992), 'Financial globalisation and deregulation', in J. Michie (ed.), *The Economic Legacy 1979–1992*, London: Academic Press.

Coates, D. (1994), *The Question of UK Decline: The Economy, State and Society*, Hemel Hempstead: Harvester Wheatsheaf.

Convery, P. (1996), 'The real cost of unemployment', *Working Brief*, Unemployment Unit, December 1995–January 1996, pp. 16–17.

Cooper R. N. (1992), 'Fettered to gold? Economic policy in the interwar period', *Journal of Economic Literature*, 30, pp. 2120–2128.

Cornwall, J. (1977), *Modern Capitalism, Its Growth and Transformation*, Oxford: Martin Robertson.

Cosh, A., Duncan, J. and Hughes, A. (1996), 'Size, age, survival and employment growth', in A. Cosh and A. Hughes (eds), *The Changing State of British Enterprise*, Cambridge: ESRC Centre for Business Research.

Cosh, A. and Hughes, A. (eds) (1996), *The Changing State of British Enterprise*, Cambridge: ESRC Centre for Business Research.

Cosh, A., Hughes, A. and Rowthorn, R. E. (1993), 'The competitive role of UK manufacturing industry: 1979–2003', chapter 2 of K. Hughes (ed.), *The Future of UK Competitiveness and the Role of Industrial Policy*, London: Policy Studies Institute.

Cosh, A., Hughes, A. and Rowthorn, R. E. (1994), The Competitive Role of UK Manufacturing Industry: 1950–2003 – A Case Analysis, mimeo, University of Cambridge.

Cosh, A., Hughes, A. and Wood, E. (1996), 'Innovation: scale, objectives, and constraints', in A. Cosh and A. Hughes (eds), *The Changing State of British Enterprise*, Cambridge: ESRC Centre for Business Research.

Costello, N., Michie, J. and Milne, S. (1989), *Beyond the Casino Economy: Planning for the 1990s*, London: Verso (2nd impression 1990).

Coutts, K. and Godley, W. (1992), 'Does Britain's balance of payments matter any more?', in J. Michie (ed.), *The Economic Legacy: 1979–1992*, London: Academic Press, pp. 60–67.

Coutts, K. and Rowthorn, R. (1995), *Employment in the United Kingdom: Trends and Prospects*, Cambridge: ESRC Centre for Business Research Working Paper No. 3 (February).

Coutts, K., Godley, W., Michie, J. and Rowthorn, B. (1992), 'Devaluation of sterling is no "quick fix"', *The Observer*, 3 May.

Crafts, N. (1988), 'The assessment: British economic growth over the long run', *Oxford Review of Economic Policy*, vol. 4, no. 1, pp. i–xxi.

Crafts, N. (1991), 'Reversing relative economic decline? The 1980s in historical perspective', *Oxford Review of Economic Policy*, vol. 7, no. 3, pp. 81–98.

Crafts, N. (1993), *Can Deindustrialisation Seriously Damage your Wealth?*, London: Institute of Economic Affairs.

Crafts, N. (1996), 'Deindustrialization and economic growth', *Economic Journal*, vol. 106, no. 434 (January), pp. 172–183.

Crafts, N.F.R. (1991), 'Economics and history', in D. Greenaway, M. Bleaney and I. Stewart (eds), *Companion to Contemporary Economic Thought*, London: Routledge, pp. 812–829.

Cripps, F. and Godley, W. (1978), 'Control of imports as a means to full employment and the expansion of world trade: the UK's case', *Cambridge Journal of Economics*, vol. 2, pp. 327–334.

CSO (1994), *Economic Trends: Annual Supplement*, London: HMSO.

CSO (1995), *Economic Trends: Annual Supplement*, London: HMSO.

Deakin, S. (1992), 'Labour law and industrial relations', in J. Michie (ed.), *The Economic Legacy: 1979–1992*, London: Academic Press.

Deakin, S. and Michie, J. (1997a), 'Contracts and competition: an introduction', *Cambridge Journal of Economics*, vol. 21, no. 2, March, pp. 121–125.

Deakin, S. and Michie, J. (1997b), 'The theory and practice of contracting', Chapter 1 of S. Deakin and J. Michie (eds), *Contracts, Co-operation, and Competition: Studies in Economics, Management and Law*, Oxford: Oxford University Press.

Deakin, S. and Wilkinson, F. (1997), 'Markets, cooperation, and economic progress', *New Economy*, vol. 4, no. 3 (Autumn).

Deakin, S., Goodwin, T. and Hughes, A. (1997), 'Cooperation and trust in inter-firm relations: beyond competition policy?', in S. Deakin and J. Michie (eds), *Contracts, Cooperation, and Competition: Studies in Economics, Management, and Law*, Oxford: Oxford University Press.

Deakin, S., Michie J. and Wilkinson F. (1992), *Inflation, Employment, Wage-Bargaining and the Law*, London: Institute of Employment Rights.

DeMartino, G. and Cullenberg, S. (1995), 'Economic integration in an uneven world: an internationalist perspective', *International Review of Applied Economics*, vol. 9, no. 1 (January), pp. 1–21.

Department of Employment (1991), Research Paper No. 87.

Department of Employment (1993a), *Employment Gazette*, October, London: HMSO.

Department of Employment (1993b), *New Earnings Survey*, London: HMSO.

Department of Employment (1994), *Employment Gazette*, February, London: HMSO.

Dickinson, D. (1995), 'Crime and unemployment', *New Economy*, vol. 2, pp. 115–120.

Dimsdale, N. H. (1981), 'British monetary policy and the exchange rate 1920–1938', in W. A. Eltis and P. J. N. Sinclair (eds), *The Money Supply and the Exchange Rate*, Oxford: Oxford University Press.

Dixit, A. (1984), 'International trade policy for oligopolistic industries', *Economic Journal*, vol. 94, Supplement, pp. 1–16.

Dixit, A. (1992), 'Investment and hysteresis', *Journal of Economic Perspectives*, vol. 6, no. 1 (Winter), pp. 107–132.

Dore, R. (1983), 'Goodwill and the spirit of market capitalism', *British Journal of Sociology*, vol. 34, no. 4, pp. 459–482; reprinted in P. Buckley and J. Michie (eds), *Firms, Organisations and Contracts: A Reader in Industrial Organisation*, Oxford: Oxford University Press, pp. 359–382.

Dore, R. (1998), 'Innovation and corporate stuctures: USA and Japan', in J. Michie and J. Grieve Smith (eds), *Globalization, Growth, and Governance: Creating an Innovative Economy*, Oxford: Oxford University Press.

Downie, J. (1958), *The Competitive Process*, London: Duckworth.

Eatwell, J. (1994), 'The coordination of macroeconomic policy in the European Community', in J. Michie and J. Grieve Smith (eds), *Unemployment in Europe*, London: Academic Press.

Eatwell, J. (1995), 'The international origins of unemployment', in J. Michie and J. Grieve Smith (eds), *Managing the Global Economy*, Oxford: Oxford University Press.

Economist (1994), 'A Bad Case of Arthritis', 26 February, pp. 92–93.

Eichengreen, B. J. (1979), 'Tariffs and flexible exchange rates', unpublished Ph.D. Dissertation, Yale University.

Eichengreen, B. J. (1981a), 'A dynamic model of tariffs, output and employment under flexible exchange rates', *Journal of International Economics*, vol. 11, pp. 341–359.

Eichengreen, B. J. (1981b), 'Sterling and the tariff, 1929–32', *Princeton Studies in International Finance*, 48.

Eichengreen, B. J. (1991), 'The interwar economy in a European mirror', Centre for Economic Performance, Discussion Paper 589, October.

Eichengreen, B. J. (1992), *Golden Fetters; the Gold Standard and the Great Depression, 1919–1939*, Oxford: Oxford University Press.

Eichengreen, B. J. (1994), '*Déjà vu* all over again: lessons from the Gold Standard for European Monetary Unification', Working Paper No. C94–032, Berkeley CA: Department of Economics, University of California.

Eichengreen, B. J. and Hatton, T. J. (eds) (1988), *Interwar Unemployment in International Perspective*, Dordrecht: Kluwer.

Eichengreen, B. J and Irwin, D. A. (1993), 'Trade blocs and the disintegration of world trade in the 1930s', National Bureau of Economic Policy Research, Working Paper no. 4445, Cambridge, MA: NBER.

Eichengreen, B. J., Tobin, J. and Wyplosz, C. (1995), 'Two cases for sand in the wheels of international finance', *Economic Journal*, vol. 105, no. 428 (January), pp. 162–172.

Elbaum, B. and Lazonick, W. (eds) (1986), *The Decline of the British Economy*, Oxford: Clarendon Press.

Eltis, W. (1996), 'How low profitability and weak innovativeness undermined UK industrial growth', *Economic Journal*, vol. 106, no. 434 (January), pp. 184–195.

Fearon, P. (1979), *The Origins and Nature of the Great Slump*, London: Macmillan.

Feinstein, C. H. (1972), *Statistical Tables of National Income and Expenditure and Output of the UK, 1855–1965*, Department of Applied Economics, Cambridge and Royal Economic Society.

Fisher, I. (1935), *The Clash of Progress and Security*, New York: Macmillan.

Ford, J. L. and Sen, S. (1985), *Protectionism, Exchange Rates and the Macroeconomy*, Oxford: Basil Blackwell.

Foster, S. with Burrows, L. (1991), *Urgent Need for Homes*, London: Shelter.

Frieden, J. A. (1994), 'Exchange rate politics: contemporary lessons from American history', *Review of International Political Economy*, 1/1, Spring, pp. 81–103.

Friedman M. (1980), 'Memorandum of evidence on monetary policy', *Memoranda on Monetary Policy*, House of Commons Treasury and Civil Service Committee, London: HMSO.

Friedman M. and Schwartz, A. (1963), *A Monetary History of the United States*, Chicago: University of Chicago Press.

Friedman, P. (1978), 'An econometric model of national income, commercial policy and the level of international trade: the open economies of Europe, 1924–1938', *Journal of Economic History*, 38, pp. 148–180.

Fuchs, V. (1968), *The Service Economy*, New York: Columbia University.

Galenson, W. and Zellner, A. (1957), 'International comparisons of unemployment rates', in National Bureau of Economic Research, *The Measurement and Behaviour of Unemployment*, Princeton, NJ: Princeton University Press.

Gershuny, J. (1978), *After Industrial Society*, London: Macmillan.

Gershuny, J. and Miles, I. (1983), *The New Service Economy*, London: Frances Pinter.

Glyn, A. (1992), 'The "productivity miracle", profits and investment', in J. Michie (ed.), *The Economic Legacy: 1979–1992*, London: Academic Press.

Glyn, A. (1995), 'Social democracy and full employment', *New Left Review*, May/June, pp. 33–55.

Glyn, A. (1997), 'Public spending, taxation and unemployment', in J. Michie and J. Grieve Smith (eds), *Employment and Economic Performance*, Oxford: Oxford University Press.

Glyn, A. and Rowthorn, B. (1994), 'European employment policies', in J. Michie and J. Grieve Smith (eds), *Unemployment in Europe*, London: Academic Press.

Glyn, A., Hughes, A., Lipietz, A. and Singh, A. (1990), 'The rise and fall of the Golden Age', in S. Marglin and J. Schor (eds), *The Golden Age of Capitalism: Reinterpreting the Postwar Experience*, Oxford: Clarendon Press.

Godley, W. (1986), 'Manufacturing and the future of the British economy'. Paper presented to 'Manufacturing or Services? A Conference on UK Industry and the Economy', Robinson College, Cambridge.

Gomes-Casseres, B. (1994), 'Group versus group: how alliance networks compete', *Harvard Business Review*, July–August, pp. 62–74.

Goodhart, C. (1975), *Money, Information and Uncertainty*, London: Macmillan.

Gregg P. and J. Wadsworth (1995), 'Making work pay', *New Economy*, vol. 2, no. 4 (Winter), pp. 210–213.

Grieve Smith, J. (1994), 'The Delors White Paper on unemployment', *International Review of Applied Economics*, vol. 8, no. 3 (September), pp. 341–347.

Hahn, F. and Matthews, R. (1994), 'Nicholas Kaldor (Lord Kaldor), 1908–1986', *Economic Journal*, vol. 104, no. 425 (July), pp. 901–902.

Halimi, S., Michie, J. and Milne, S. (1994), 'The Mitterrand experience', in J. Michie and J. Grieve Smith (eds), *Unemployment in Europe*, London: Academic Press.

Harcourt, G. C. (1994), 'A "modest" proposal for taming speculators and putting the world on course to prosperity', mimeo, University of Cambridge.

Harcourt, G. C and Kitson, M. (1993), 'Fifty Years of Economic Measurement: A Cambridge View', *Review of Income and Wealth*, pp. 435–447.

Harris, B. (1988), 'Unemployment, insurance and health in interwar Britain', in Eichengreen, B. and Hatton, T. J. (eds), *Interwar Unemployment in International Perspective*, Dordrecht: Kluwer, pp. 149–183.

Harris, L. (1995), 'International financial markets and national transmission mechanisms', in J. Michie and J. Grieve Smith (eds), *Managing the Global Economy*, Oxford: Oxford University Press.

Harrod, R. (1933), *International Economics*, Cambridge: Cambridge University Press.

Harvey, M. (1995), *Towards the Insecurity Society: the Growth of Mass Self-Employment and the Construction Industry*, London: Institute of Employment Rights.

Healey, N. M. (1993), 'The Conservative Government's "fight against inflation": ten years without cheers', in N. M. Healey (ed.), *Britain's Economic Miracle: Myth or Reality?*, London: Routledge.

Henderson, D. (1986), *Innocence and Design. The Influence of Economic Ideas on Policy* (The 1985 BBC Reith Lectures), Oxford: Basil Blackwell.

Hirst, P. and Thompson, G. (1992), 'The problem of globalization: international economic relations, national economic management, and the formation of trading blocs', *Economy and Society*, vol. 21, no. 4, pp. 357–396.

Hirst, P. and Thompson, G. (1996), *Globalisation in Question*, Cambridge: Polity Press.

HMSO (1993), *Households Below Average Income; A Statistical Analysis 1979–1990/1*, London: HMSO.

Holtham, G. and Mayhew, K. (1996), *Tackling Long-Term Unemployment*, London: IPPR.

House of Commons (1980), *Memoranda on Monetary Policy*, House of Commons Treasury and Civil Service Committee, London: HMSO.

House of Lords (1991), *Report from the Select Committee on Science and Technology*, London: HMSO.

Howells, J. and Michie, J. (eds) (1997), *Technology, Innovation and Competitiveness*, Cheltenham: Edward Elgar.

Howson, S. (1980), 'The management of sterling, 1932–39', *Journal of Economic History*, March.

Iammarino, S. and Michie, J. (1998), 'The scope of technological globalisation', *International Journal of the Economics of Business*, vol. 5, no. 3, pp. 335–353.

ILO (1940), *Year Book of Labour Statistics, 1940*, Geneva: International Labour Office.

IMF (1998), *World Economic Outlook: October 1998*, Washington DC: International Monetary Fund.

Itoh, M. (1994), 'Is the Japanese economy in crisis', *Review of International Political Economy*, 1/1, Spring, pp. 29–51.

Jacobs, M. (1994), *Green Jobs? The Employment Implications of Environmental Policy*. Report for the World Wildlife Fund.

Kaldor, N. (1951), 'Employment policies and the problem of international balance', *Review of Economic Studies*, vol. 19, pp. 42–49.

Kaldor, N. (1966), *Causes of the Slow Rate of Growth in the United Kingdom*, Cambridge: Cambridge University Press.

Kaldor, N. (1970), 'The case for Regional Policies', *Scottish Journal of Political Economy*, vol. 17, pp. 337–348.

Kaldor, N. (1971), 'Conflicts in national economic objectives', *Economic Journal*, vol. 81, pp. 1–16.

Kaldor, N. (1972), 'The irrelevance of equilibrium economics', *Economic Journal*, vol. 82, December.

Kaldor, N. (1978), 'The effect of devaluations on trade in manufactures', in *Further Essays in Applied Economics*, London: Duckworth.

Kaldor, N. (1980), 'Memorandum of evidence on monetary policy', *Memoranda on Monetary Policy*, House of Commons Treasury and Civil Service Committee, London: HMSO.

Kaldor, N. (1982), 'Limitations of the *General Theory*', *Proceedings of the British Academy*, 68.

Kaldor, N. (1985), *Economics Without Equilibrium*, New York: M. E. Sharpe.

Kaldor, N. and Kitson, M. (1986), 'The impact of import restrictions in the interwar period'. Report to the ESRC, Cambridge: Department of Applied Economics.

Kalecki, M. (1932), 'Is a capitalist overcoming of the crisis possible?', and 'On the Papen Plan', in J. Osiatynski (ed.), *Collected Works of Michael Kalecki*, Oxford: Oxford University Press, 1990.

Kalecki, M. (1943), 'Political aspects of full employment', in *Selected Essays on the Dynamics of the Capitalist Economy*, Cambridge: Cambridge University Press, 1971.

Kelly, R. (1994), 'A framework for European exchange rates in the 1990s', in J. Michie and J. Grieve Smith (eds), *Unemployment in Europe*, London: Academic Press.

Kelly, R. (1995), 'Derivatives: a growing threat to the international financial system', in J. Michie and J. Grieve Smith (eds), *Managing the Global Economy*, Oxford: Oxford University Press.

Kenen, P. B. (1992), 'Bretton Woods System', in P. Newman, M. Milgate and J. Eatwell (eds), *The New Palgrave Dictionary of Money and Finance*, vol. 1, London and Basingstoke: Macmillan.

Keynes, J. M. (1919), *The Economic Consequences of the Peace*, London: Macmillan.

Keynes, J. M. (1925), 'The economic consequences of Mr Churchill', *The Collected*

Writings of John Maynard Keynes, Vol. IX: *Essays in Persuasion*, pp. 207–230, published for the Royal Economic Society by Macmillan.

Keynes, J. M. (1936), *The General Theory of Employment, Interest and Money*, London: Macmillan.

Keynes, J. M. (1943), 'Speech before the House of Lords, 18th May 1943', in D. Moggridge (ed.), *The Collected Writings of John Maynard Keynes*, Vol. XXV, Chapter 1, London: Macmillan, 1980.

Kindleberger, C. P. (1973), *The World in Depression, 1929–1939*, Berkeley CA: University of California Press.

Kirkpatrick, C. (1995), 'Does trade liberalization assist third-world industrial development?', *International Review of Applied Economics*, vol. 8, no. 1 (January), pp. 22–41.

Kitson, M. (1992), 'The move to autarchy: the political economy of Nazi trade policy', Cambridge: Department of Applied Economics, Working Paper 9201.

Kitson, M. (1995), 'Seedcorn or chaff? Unemployment and small firm performance', ESRC Centre for Business Research, Working Paper No. 2.

Kitson, M. (1997a), *The Single Currency, Privatisation and the Private Finance Initiative: The Challenges Facing the Public Sector*, West Midlands: Unison.

Kitson, M. (1997b), 'The competitive weaknesses of the UK economy', in P. Arestis, G. Palma and M. Sawyer (eds), *Markets, Unemployment and Economic Policy: Essays in Honour of Geoff Harcourt*, London: Routledge.

Kitson, M. (1998), 'Investment', in B. Atkinson, F. Livesey and B. Milward (eds), *Applied Economics*, Basingstoke and London: Macmillan.

Kitson, M. (1999), 'Recession and economic revival in Britain: the role of policy in the 1930s and 1980s', *Contemporary European History*, vol. 8, no. 1, pp. 1–27.

Kitson, M. and Michie, J. (1994), 'Depression and recovery: lessons from the interwar period' in J. Michie and J. Grieve Smith (eds), *Unemployment in Europe*, London: Academic Press.

Kitson, M. and Michie, J. (1995), 'Trade and growth: a historical perspective' in J. Michie and J. Grieve Smith (eds) , *Managing the Global Economy*, Oxford: Oxford University Press.

Kitson, M. and Michie, J. (1996), 'Britain's industrial performance since 1960: underinvestment and relative decline', *Economic Journal*, January, vol. 106, pp. 196–212.

Kitson, M. and Michie, J. (1998a), 'Markets, competition, and innovation', ESRC Centre for Business Research Working Paper.

Kitson, M, and Michie, J. (1998b), 'Markets, competition, and innovation', in J. Michie and J. Grieve Smith (eds), *Globalisation, Growth, and Governance*, Oxford: Oxford University Press.

Kitson, M. and Solomou, S. (1990a), *Protectionism and Economic Revival: The British Interwar Economy*, Cambridge: Cambridge University Press.

Kitson, M. and Solomou, S. (1990b), 'The Interwar Trade Dataset: a guide to the statistics and sources', mimeo, Cambridge: Department of Applied Economics.

Kitson, M. and Solomou, S. (1991), 'Trade policy and the regionalization of imports in interwar Britain', *The Bulletin of Economic Research*, vol. 43, no. 2, pp. 151–168.

Kitson, M. and Solomou, S. (1995), 'Bilateralism in the interwar world economy', *Bulletin of Economic Research*, vol. 47, no. 3, pp. 197– 219.

Kitson, M. and Wilkinson, F. (1996), 'Markets and competition', in A. Cosh and A. Hughes (eds), *The Changing State of British Enterprise: Growth, Innovation and*

Competitive Advantage in Small and Medium Sized Firms 1986–95, Cambridge: ESRC Centre for Business Research.

Kitson, M. and Wilkinson, F. (1998a), 'Employment structure, recruitment, labour turnover, training and labour market flexibility', in A. Cosh and A. Hughes (eds) *Enterprise Britain*, Cambridge: ESRC Centre for Business Research.

Kitson, M. and Wilkinson, F. (1998b), 'Markets and competition', in A. Cosh and A. Hughes (eds), *Enterprise Britain*, Cambridge: ESRC Centre for Business Research.

Kitson, M., Michie, J. and Sutherland, H. (1997), 'The fiscal and distributional implications of job generation', *Cambridge Journal of Economics*, vol. 21, no. 1, January, pp. 103–120.

Kozul-Wright, R. (1995), 'Transnational corporations and the nation state', in J. Michie and J. Grieve Smith (eds), *Managing the Global Economy*, Oxford: Oxford University Press.

Krugman, P. (1982), 'The macroeconomics of protection with a floating exchange rate', *Carnegie-Rochester Conference Series on Public Policy*, Vol. 16, pp. 141–182, Amsterdam: North-Holland.

Krugman, P. (1994a), 'Competitiveness: a dangerous obsession', *Foreign Affairs*, Vol. 73, no. 2 (March/April), pp. 28–44.

Krugman, P. (1994b), *Rethinking International Trade*, Cambridge MA: MIT Press (first published, 1990).

Krugman, P. (1994c), *Peddling Prosperity; Economic Sense and Nonsense in the Age of Diminished Expectations*, London: W.W. Norton.

Kuznets, S. (1966), *Modern Economic Growth: Rate, Structure and Spread*, New Haven CT: Yale University Press.

Lane, C. (1997), 'The social regulation of inter-firm relations in Britain and Germany: market rules, legal norms and technical standards', *Cambridge Journal of Economics*, vol. 21, no. 2 (March), pp. 197–215.

Lang, T. and Hines, C. (1993), *The New Protectionism: Protecting the Future Against Free Trade*, London: Earthscan Publications.

Laursen, S. and Metzler, L. (1950), 'Flexible exchange rates and the theory of employment', *Review of Economics and Statistics*, vol. 32, pp. 281–299.

Lawson, N. (1992), *The View from no. 11*, London: Bantam Press.

Layard, R., Nickell, S. and Jackman, R. (1991), *Unemployment: Macroeconomic Performance and the Labour Market*, Oxford: Oxford University Press.

Lazonick, W. (1986), 'The Cotton Industry', in B. Elbaum and W. Lazonick (eds), *The Decline of the British Economy*, Oxford: Clarendon Press.

Lazonick, W. (1991), *Business Organisation and the Myth of the Market Economy*, Cambridge: Cambridge University Press.

League of Nations (1939), *Review of World Trade 1938*, Geneva: League of Nations.

League of Nations (1944), *International Currency Experience*, Geneva: League of Nations.

Lebergott, S. (1964), *Manpower in Economic Growth*, New York: McGraw Hill.

Lewis, A. (1981), 'The rates of growth of world trade, 1830–1973', in S. Grassman and E. Lundberg (eds), *The World Economic Order: Past and Prospects*, London and Basingstoke: Macmillan.

Lewis, W. A. (1949), *Economic Survey, 1919–1939*, London: George Allen & Unwin.

Lewis, W. A. (1954), 'Economic development with unlimited supplies of labour', *The Manchester School of Economic and Social Studies*, pp. 139–191.

Lloyd, P. J. (1992), 'Regionalisation and world trade', *OECD Economic Studies*, vol. 1, Spring, pp. 7–44.

Lucas, R. (1988), 'On the mechanisms of economic development', *Journal of Monetary Economics*, No. 22 (July).

Macaulay, S. (1962), 'Non-contractual relations in business: a preliminary study', paper read at the annual meeting of the American Sociological Association, August 1962; revised version reprinted in P. Buckley and J. Michie (eds) (1996), *Firms, Organisations and Contracts: A Reader in Industrial Organisation*, Oxford: Oxford University Press, pp. 339–358.

McCombie, J. and Thirlwall, T. (1992), 'The re-emergence of the balance of payments constraint', in J. Michie (ed.), *The Economic Legacy: 1979–1992*, London: Academic Press, pp. 68–74.

Maddison, A. (1962), 'Growth and fluctuations in the world economy, 1870–1960', *Banca Nazionale del Lavoro Quarterly Review*, vol. XV, no. 61 (June), pp. 127–195.

Maddison, A. (1982), *Phases of Capitalist Development*, Oxford: Oxford University Press.

Maddison, A. (1991), *Dynamic Forces in Capitalist Development*, Oxford: Oxford University Press.

Mariti, P. and Smiley, R. H. (1983), 'Co-operative agreements and the organization of industry', *Journal of Industrial Economics*, vol. 31, pp. 437–451; reprinted in P. Buckley and J. Michie (eds), *Firms, Organisations and Contracts: A Reader in Industrial Organisation*, Oxford: Oxford University Press, pp. 276–292.

Marquand, J. (1979), 'The service sector and regional policy in the United Kingdom', London: Centre for Environmental Studies.

Marsden, D. and Ryan, P. (1991), 'Initial training, Labour market structure and public policy: intermediate skills in British and German industry', in P. Ryan (ed.), *International Comparisons of Vocational Training for Intermediate Skills*, Lewes: Falmer Press.

Martin, R. (1994), 'Stateless monies, global financial integration and national economic autonomy: the end of geography?', in S. Corbridge, R. Martin and N. Thrift (eds), *Money, Power and Space*, Oxford: Blackwell.

Marx, K. (1867–94), *Capital*, London: Lawrence & Wishart, 1970–72.

Matthews, K. and Benjamin, D. (1992), *US and UK Unemployment Between the Wars: A Doleful Story*, London: Institute of Economic Affairs.

Matthews, K. P. G. and Minford, P. (1987), 'Mrs Thatcher's economic policies, 1979–1987', *Economic Policy*, October.

Metcalf, D. (1989), 'Water notes dry up: the impact of the Donovan Reform proposal and Thatcherism at work on labour productivity in British manufacturing productivity', *British Journal of Industrial Relations*, vol. 27, pp. 1–31.

Michie, J. (1987), *Wages in the Business Cycle: An Empirical and Methodological Analysis*, London: Frances Pinter Publishers.

Michie, J. (1993), *Maastricht: Implications for Public Services*, Manchester: UNISON.

Michie, J. (1995), 'Introduction' to J. Michie and J. Grieve Smith (eds), *Managing the Global Economy*, Oxford: Oxford University Press.

Michie, J. (1997), 'Cooperate or compete?', *New Economy*, vol. 4, no. 3 (Autumn).

Michie, J. and Grieve Smith, J. (eds) (1994), *Unemployment in Europe*, London: Academic Press.

Michie, J. and Grieve Smith, J. (eds) (1995), *Managing the Global Economy*, Oxford: Oxford University Press.

Michie, J. and Grieve Smith, J. (eds) (1996), *Creating Industrial Capacity: Towards Full Employment*, Oxford: Oxford University Press.

Michie, J. and Grieve Smith, J. (eds) (1999), *Global Instability*, London: Routledge.

Michie, J. and Prendergast, R. (1997), 'Innovation and competitive advantage', in J. Howells and J. Michie, (eds), *Technology, Innovation and Competitiveness*, Cheltenham: Edward Elgar.

Michie, J. and Sheehan, M. (1999), 'HRM practices, R&D expenditure and innovative investment: evidence from the 1990 Workplace Industrial Relations Survey (WIRS)', *Industrial and Corporate Change*, vol. 8, no. 2, pp. 211–233.

Michie, J. and Wilkinson, F. (1992), 'Inflation policy and the restructuring of the labour market', in J. Michie (ed.), *The Economic Legacy: 1979–1992*, London: Academic Press.

Michie, J. and Wilkinson, F. (1993), *Unemployment and Workers' Rights*, London: Institute of Employment Rights.

Michie, J. and Wilkinson, F. (1994), 'The growth of unemployment in the 1980s', in J. Michie and J. Grieve Smith (eds), *Unemployment in Europe*, London: Academic Press.

Michie, J. and Wilkinson, F. (1995), 'Wages, government policy and unemployment', *Review of Political Economy*, vol. 7, no. 2, pp. 133–149.

Middleton, R. (1981), 'The constant employment budget balance and British budgetary policy, 1929–39', *Economic History Review*, vol. 34, May, pp. 266–286.

Milne, S. (1997), *Making Markets Work: Contracts, Competition and Co-operation*, London: Birkbeck College (available free of charge from j.michie@bbk.ac.uk).

Mitchell, B. R. (1975), *European Historical Statistics, 1750–1970*, London: Macmillan.

Mitchell, B. R. (1983), *International Historical Statistics: The Americas and Australasia*, London: Macmillan.

Moggridge, D. E. (1972), *British Monetary Policy 1924–31: The Norman Conquest of $4.86*, Cambridge: Cambridge University Press.

Moss Kanter, R. (1994), 'Collaborative advantage: the art of alliances', *Harvard Business Review*, July–August, pp. 96–108.

Moss, B.N and Michie, J. (1998), *The Single Currency in National Perspective. A Currency in Crisis*, London: Macmillan.

Mundell, R. A. (1961), 'Flexible exchange rates and employment policy', *Canadian Journal of Economics*, vol. 27, pp. 509–517.

Myrdal, G. (1957), *Economic Theory and Underdeveloped Regions*, London: Duckworth.

Newell, A. and Symons, J. S. V. (1988), 'The macroeconomics of the interwar years: international comparisons', in B. Eichengreen and T. J. Hatton (eds), *Interwar Unemployment in International Perspective*, Dordrecht: Kluwer.

Nolan, P. (1989), 'Walking on water? Performance and industrial relations under Thatcher', *Industrial Relations Journal*, vol. 20, no. 2, pp. 81–92.

Nolan, P. and Marginson, P. (1990), 'Skating on thin ice? David Metcalf on trade unions and productivity', *British Journal of Industrial Relations*, vol. 28, no. 2, pp. 227–247.

Nolan, P. and O'Donnell, K. (1995), 'The political economy of productivity: Britain 1945–1994', mimeo.

Nolan, P., Saundry, R. and Sawyer, M. (1997), 'Choppy waves on air and sea', *New Economy*, vol. 4, no. 3 (Autumn), pp. 167–172.

O'Mahony, M. (1993), 'International measure of fixed capital stocks: a five-country study', National Institute of Economic and Social Research, Discussion Paper no. 51, September.

OECD (1994), *The OECD Jobs Study: Evidence and Explanations* (Part I and Part II), Paris: OECD.

Ohmae, K. (1990), *The Borderless World: Management Lessons in the New Logic of the Global Market Place*, London: Collins.

Ohmae, K. (1993), 'The rise of the region state', *Foreign Affairs*, Spring, pp. 78–87.

Ohmae, K. (1995), 'Putting global logic first', *Harvard Business Review*, January/February, pp. 119–125.

Oliver, N. and Blakeborough, M. (1998), 'Innovation networks: the view from the inside', in J. Michie and J. Grieve Smith (eds), *Globalization, Growth, and Governance: Creating an Innovative Economy*, Oxford: Oxford University Press.

Oswald, A. (1997), 'Happiness and economic performance', *Economic Journal*, November.

Oughton, C. and Whittam, G. (1996), 'Competitiveness, EU industrial strategy and subsidiarity', in P. Devine, Y. Katsoulacos and R. Sugden (eds), *Competitiveness, Subsidiarity and Industrial Policy*, London: Routledge, pp. 58–103.

Oulton, N. and O'Mahony, M. (1994), *Productivity and Growth: A Disaggregated Study of British Industry, 1954–86*, Cambridge: Cambridge University Press.

Panić, M. (1990), 'Economic development and trade policy', DAE Working Paper, No. 9006, Department of Applied Economics, University of Cambridge.

Panić, M. (1992), *European Monetary Union: Lessons from the Classical Gold Standard*, London: Macmillan.

Panić, M. (1995), 'The Bretton Woods System: concept and practice', in J. Michie and J. Grieve Smith (eds), *Managing the Global Economy*, Oxford: Oxford University Press.

Parker, D. (1993), 'Privatisation ten years on', in N. M. Healey (ed.), *Britain's Economic Miracle: Myth or Reality?*, London: Routledge.

Patel, P. (1995), 'Localised production of technology for global markets', *Cambridge Journal of Economics*, vol. 19, no. 1 (February), pp. 141–154; reprinted in D. Archibugi and J. Michie (eds) (1997), *Technology, Globalisation and Economic Performance*, Cambridge: Cambridge University Press.

Petit, P. (1986), *Slow Growth and the Service Economy*, London: Frances Pinter.

Philpott, J. (1994), 'Unemployment, inequality and inefficiency', in A. Glyn and D. Milliband (eds), *Paying for Inequality*, London: IPPR/River Oram Press.

Piachaud, D. (1994), 'A price worth paying? The cost of mass unemployment', *Economic Report*, Employment Policy Institute, vol. 8, no. 6, September.

Pilat, D. (1996), 'Labour productivity levels in OECD countries: estimates for manufacturing and selected service sectors', OECD, Economics Department Working Papers, No. 169.

Pivetti, M. (1993), 'Bretton Woods through the lens of state-of-the-art macrotheory and the European Monetary System', *Contributions to Political Economy*, vol. 12, pp. 99–110.

Pomfret, R. (1988), *Unequal Trade: the Economics of Discretionary International Trade Policies*, Oxford: Basil Blackwell.

Porter, M. E. (1994), 'The role of location in competition', *Journal of the Economics of Business*, vol. 1, no. 1 (February), pp. 35–39.

Raphael, A. (1992), 'Beware the siren devaluers who lure us to ruin', *The Observer*, 26 April.

Redmond, G. and Sutherland, H. (1995), *How has tax and social security policy changed since 1978?: a distributional analysis*, Microsimulation Unit Discussion Paper No. 9508, DAE, University of Cambridge.

Redmond, G., Sutherland, H. and Wilson, M. (1995), *POLIMOD: An Outline*, Microsimulation Research Note No. 5, DAE, University of Cambridge.

Redmond, J. (1980), 'An indicator of the effective rate of the pound in the 1930s', *Economic History Review*, vol. 33, pp. 83–91.

Richardson, G. B. (1972), 'The organisation of industry', *Economic Journal*, pp. 883–896; reprinted in P. Buckley and J. Michie (eds) (1996), *Firms, Organisations and Contracts: A Reader in Industrial Organisation*, Oxford: Oxford University Press, pp. 59–74.

Richardson, H. W. (1967), *Economic Recovery in Britain, 1932–9*, London: Weidenfeld and Nicolson.

Robinson College Working Group (1999), *Agenda for a New Bretton Woods*, International Papers in Political Economy, vol. 6, no. 1, London: University of East London and the University of Leeds.

Robinson, J. (1966), *The New Mercantilism, An Inaugural Lecture*, Cambridge: Cambridge University Press; reprinted in *Collected Economic Papers*, Vol. 4, Oxford: Blackwell, 1973.

Robson, P. (1984), *The Economics of International Integration*, London: George Allen & Unwin.

Romer, C. (1990), 'The Great Crash and the onset of the Great Depression', *Quarterly Journal of Economics*, 105, pp. 597–624.

Romer, P. (1986), 'Increasing returns and long-run growth', *Journal of Political Economy*, vol. 94 (October), pp. 1002–1037.

Romer, P. (1990), 'Endogenous technical change', *Journal of Political Economy*, vol. 98 (October), pp. S71–S102.

Romer, P. (1994), 'New goods, old theory and the welfare costs of trade restrictions', *Journal of Development Economics*.

Rostas, L. (1948), *Comparative Productivity in British and American Industry*, Cambridge: Cambridge University Press.

Rostow, W. W. (1960), *The Stages of Economic Growth*, Cambridge: Cambridge University Press.

Rowlatt, P. (1994), 'Inflation down – but will it last?', *New Economy*, pp. 130–134.

Rowthorn, B. (1992), 'Government spending and taxation in the Thatcher era', in J. Michie (ed.), *The Economic Legacy: 1979–1992*, London: Academic Press.

Rowthorn, R. (1977), 'Conflict, inflation and money', *Cambridge Journal of Economics*, September, pp. 215–239.

Rowthorn, R. E. (1995), 'Capital formation and unemployment', *Oxford Review of Economic Policy*, vol. 11, no. 1, pp. 26–39.

Rowthorn, R. E. and Wells, J. (1987), *Deindustrialisation and Foreign Trade*, Cambridge: Cambridge University Press.

Sawyer, M. (1995), 'Obstacles to full employment in capitalist economies', in P. Arestis and M. Marshall (eds), *The Political Economy of Full Employment: Conservatism, Corporatism and Institutional Change*, Aldershot: Edward Elgar.

Saxenhouse, G. (1985). 'Services in the Japanese economy', in R. E. Inman (ed.), *Managing the Service Economy: Prospects and Problems*, Cambridge: Cambridge University Press.

Schefold, B. (1980), 'The general theory for a totalitarian state? A note on Keynes's preface to the German edition of 1936', *Cambridge Journal of Economics*, vol. 4, no. 2, June, pp. 175–176.

Schor, J. (1992), 'Introduction', to T. Banuri and J. Schor (eds), *Financial Openness and National Autonomy*, Oxford: Clarendon Press.

Schumpeter, J. A. (1942), *Capitalism, Socialism and Democracy*, London: George Allen & Unwin.

Schumpeter, J. A. (1947), *Capitalism, Socialism and Democracy*, 2nd ed., London: George Allen & Unwin.

Schumpeter, J. A. (1961), *The Theory of Economic Development*, trans. R. Opie, Oxford: Oxford University Press.

Schwartz, A. J. (1986), 'Alternative monetary regimes: the Gold Standard', in C. D. Campbell and W. R. Dougan (eds), *Alternative Monetary Regimes*, Baltimore: Johns Hopkins University Press.

Scott, M. F. G. (1989), *A New View of Economic Growth*, Oxford: Clarendon Press.

Scott, M. F. G. (1992), 'Policy implications of "A New View of Economic Growth"', *Economic Journal*, vol. 102, pp. 622–632.

Sengenberger, W. and Wilkinson, F. (1995), 'Globalization and labour standards', in J. Michie and J. Grieve Smith (eds), *Managing the Global Economy*, Oxford: Oxford University Press.

Singh, A. (1977), 'UK industry and the world economy: a case of de-industrialisation?', *Cambridge Journal of Economics*, vol. 1, no. 2 (June).

Singh, A. (1987), 'Deindustrialisation', in J. Eatwell, M. Milgate and P. Newman (eds), *The New Palgrave Dictionary of Economics*, London: Macmillan.

Singh, A. (1992), 'The political economy of growth', in J. Michie (ed.), *The Economic Legacy: 1979–1992*, London: Academic Press.

Singh, A. (1999), 'Asian capitalism and the financial crises', in J. Michie and J. Grieve Smith (eds), *Global Instability*, London: Routledge.

Singh, A. and Zammit, A. (1995), 'Employment and unemployment: north and south', in J. Michie and J. Grieve Smith (eds), *Managing the Global Economy*, Oxford: Oxford University Press.

Small Business Research Centre (SBRC) (1992), *The State of British Enterprise: Growth, Innovation and Competitive Advantage in Small and Medium-Sized Enterprises*, Cambridge: Small Business Research Centre, University of Cambridge.

Solomou, S. (1988), *Phases of Economic Growth, 1850–1973: Kondratieff Waves and Kuznets Swings*, Cambridge: Cambridge University Press.

Solow, R. M. (1970), *Growth Theory: An Exposition*, Oxford: Oxford University Press.

Standing Committee on Public Health (1994), *Housing, Homelessness and Health*, London: The Nuffield Provincial Hospital Trust.

Stanners, W. (1993), 'Is low inflation an important condition for high growth?', *Cambridge Journal of Economics*, vol. 17, pp. 79–107.

Stoneman, P. and Francis, N. (1992), 'Double deflation and the measurement of output and productivity in UK manufacturing 1979–1989', Warwick Business School Discussion Paper.

Storey, D. (1994), *Understanding the Small Business Sector*, London: Routledge.

Summers, R. (1985), 'Services in the international economy', in R. E. Inman (ed.), *Managing the Service Economy: Prospects and Problems*, Cambridge: Cambridge University Press.

Sutherland, H. (1995), 'Minimum wage benefits', *New Economy*, vol. 2, no. 4 (Winter), pp. 214–219.

Sutton, J. (1994), 'History matters. So what?', *Journal of the Economics of Business*, vol. 1, no. 1 (February), pp. 41–44.

Tarling, R. W. and Wilkinson, F. (1997), 'Economic functioning, self sufficiency, and full employment', in J. Michie and J. Grieve Smith (eds), *Employment and Economic Performance*, Oxford: Oxford University Press.

Temin, P. (1989), *Lessons from the Great Depression*, Cambridge MA: MIT Press.

Thirlwall, A. P. (1979), 'The balance of payments constraint as an explanation of international growth rate differences', *Banca Nazionale del Lavoro Quarterly Review*, March.

Thirlwall, A. P. (1994), 'Cumulative causation', in P. Arestis and M. Sawyer (eds), *The Elgar Companion to Radical Political Economy*, Aldershot: Edward Elgar.

Tiratsoo, N. and Tomlinson, J. (1994), 'Restrictive practices on the shopfloor in Britain, 1945–60: myth and reality', *Business History*, vol. 36, no. 2 (April), pp. 65–82.

Tobin, J. (1978), 'A proposal for international monetary reform', *The Eastern Economic Journal*, July–October, reprinted in J. Tobin, *Essays in Economics: Theory and Policy*, Cambridge MA: MIT Press, 1982.

Triffin, R. (1960), *Gold and the Dollar Crisis*, New Haven CT: Yale University Press.

Ullah, P. (1990), 'The association between income, financial strain and psychological well-being among unemployed youths', *Journal of Occupational Psychology*, vol. 63, pp. 317–330.

van der Ploeg, F. (ed.) (1994), *The Handbook of International Macroeconomics*, Oxford: Basil Blackwell.

Walters, A. A. (1986), *Britain's Economic Renaissance*, Oxford: Oxford University Press.

Weinstein, M. W. (2000), 'Students seek some reality amid the math of economics', *Items and Issues*, New York: Social Research Council, Winter.

Wells, J. (1993a), 'Factors making for increasing international economic integration', unpublished manuscript, University of Cambridge.

Wells, J. (1993b), 'The trouble with Thatcher', *New Economy*, Autumn, pp. 52–56.

Wells, J. (1994), 'Unemployment in the UK: the missing million', *European Labour Forum*, No. 13.

Wells, J. (1995), 'Crime and unemployment', *Employment Policy Institute Economic Report*, vol. 9, no. 1, February, London: Employment Policy Institute.

Wilkinson, F. (1992), *Why Britain Needs a Minimum Wage*, London: Institute for Public Policy Research.

Wood, A. (1994), *North–South Trade, Employment and Inequality: Changing Fortunes in a Skill-Driven World*, Oxford: Clarendon Press.

Wood, E. (1998), 'The determinants of innovation in small and medium-sized enterprises', in J. Michie and J. Grieve Smith (eds), *Globalization, Growth, and Governance: Creating an Innovative Economy*, Oxford: Oxford University Press.

World Bank (1999), *Global Economic Prospects and the Developing Countries 1998/9: Beyond Financial Crisis*, Washington DC: World Bank.

Worswick, G. D. N. (1984), 'The recovery in Britain in the 1930s', in Bank of England Panel , Paper no. 23, April, *The UK Recovery in the 1930s*, pp. 5–28.

Young, A. (1928), 'Increasing returns and economic progress', *Economic Journal*, December.

Index